A Sensory Approach to STEAM Teaching and Learning

Did you know you have the power and the materials at your fingertips to facilitate the actual brain growth of students?

This book is a practical resource to engage K–6 students with STEAM content through their five senses: seeing, listening, touch/movement, smell, and taste. It combines historical research, practical suggestions, and current practices on the stages of cognitive development and the brain's physical response to emotion and novelty; to help you learn ways to transform ordinary lesson plans into novel and exciting opportunities for students to learn through instruction, exploration, inquiry, and discovery.

In addition to providing examples of sensory-rich unit plans, the authors take you through the step-by-step process on how to plan a thematic unit and break it down into daily seamless lesson plans that integrate science, technology, engineering, arts, and mathematics.

With 25 themed STEAM unit plans and activities based on national standards, up-to-date research on brain science, and real classroom experience, this book shows multiple ways to develop and deliver active multisensory activities and wow your students with sights and sounds as soon as they come through the door of your classroom.

Kerry P. Holmes is a professor emerita of elementary education at the University of Mississippi, USA.

Jerilou J. Moore is a professor emerita in the School of Education at the University of Mississippi, USA.

Stacy V. Holmes is an associate professor emeritus of electrical engineering at the University of Mississippi, USA.

Also Available from Routledge Eye On Education
www.routledge.com/k-12

The A in STEAM
Lesson Plans and Activities for Integrating Art, Ages 0–8
By Jerilou J. Moore and Kerry P. Holmes

Hands-On STEAM Explorations for Young Learners
Problem-Based Investigations for Preschool to Second Grade
By Allison Bemiss

Getting Started with STEAM
Practical Strategies for the K-8 Classroom
By Billy Krakower and Meredith Martin

Sparking Curiosity through Project-Based Learning in the Early Childhood Classroom
Strategies and Tools to Unlock Student Potential
By Elizabeth Hoyle Konecni

A Sensory Approach to STEAM Teaching and Learning

Materials-Based Units for Students K-6

Kerry P. Holmes, Jerilou J. Moore, and Stacy V. Holmes

NEW YORK AND LONDON

Designed cover image: Kerry P. Holmes, Jerilou J. Moore, and Stacy V. Holmes

First published 2023
by Routledge
605 Third Avenue, New York, NY 10158

and by Routledge
4 Park Square, Milton Park, Abingdon, Oxon, OX14 4RN

Routledge is an imprint of the Taylor & Francis Group, an informa business

© 2023 Kerry P. Holmes, Jerilou J. Moore, and Stacy V. Holmes

The right of Kerry P. Holmes, Jerilou J. Moore, and Stacy V. Holmes to be identified as authors of this work has been asserted in accordance with sections 77 and 78 of the Copyright, Designs and Patents Act 1988.

All rights reserved. No part of this book may be reprinted or reproduced or utilised in any form or by any electronic, mechanical, or other means, now known or hereafter invented, including photocopying and recording, or in any information storage or retrieval system, without permission in writing from the publishers.

Trademark notice: Product or corporate names may be trademarks or registered trademarks, and are used only for identification and explanation without intent to infringe.

Library of Congress Cataloging-in-Publication Data
Names: Holmes, Kerry P., author. | Moore, Jerilou J., author. | Holmes, Stacy V., author.
Title: A sensory approach to STEAM teaching and learning : materials-based units for students K-6 / Kerry P. Holmes, Jerilou J. Moore, Stacy V. Holmes.
Description: New York, NY : Routledge, 2023. | Includes bibliographical references and index.
Identifiers: LCCN 2022052472 (print) | LCCN 2022052473 (ebook) | ISBN 9781032269993 (hardback) | ISBN 9781032269979 (paperback) | ISBN 9781003290889 (ebook)
Subjects: LCSH: Science--Study and teaching (Elementary) | Technology--Study and teaching (Elementary) | Engineering--Study and teaching (Elementary) | Arts--Study and teaching (Elementary) | Mathematics--Study and teaching (Elementary) | Interdisciplinary approach in education. | Sensory stimulation.
Classification: LCC LB1585 .H634 2023 (print) | LCC LB1585 (ebook) | DDC 372.35--dc23/eng/20230118
LC record available at https://lccn.loc.gov/2022052472
LC ebook record available at https://lccn.loc.gov/2022052473

ISBN: 978-1-032-26999-3 (hbk)
ISBN: 978-1-032-26997-9 (pbk)
ISBN: 978-1-003-29088-9 (ebk)

DOI: 10.4324/9781003290889

Typeset in Galliard
by MPS Limited, Dehradun

Access the Support Material: www.routledge.com/9781032269979

We dedicate this book to the wonderful teachers in Mississippi who opened our eyes to multisensory teaching through their own examples, the amazing work we observed in their classrooms, and the ideas they freely and enthusiastically shared to excite students to the world of learning.

Contents

List of Figures x
Acknowledgments xvi
Author Biographies xvii

Introduction 1

PART I
The Role of the Senses in Teaching and Learning 5

1 The Brain and Sensory Learning 7
Introduction 7
Rat and Human Brains 7
How Sensory Experiences Affect the Brain 8
Inside a Child's Head 9
Putting It All Together 11
Information Processed Through Each of the Five Senses 12
Schema Theory 12
Ways to Maximize Sensory Input 13
Conclusion 19
References 19

2 Emotion and Serial Position Effects on Learning: Multisensory Sets
and Closures 22
Introduction 22
The Wow Effect! 22
Early Research on the Serial Effect on Learning 23
Examples of Sets 24
Examples of Closures 26
Ways to Collect Materials 27
Ways to Store Materials 28

Conclusion 28
References 28
Children's Books 30

3 The Role of the Five Senses in Vocabulary Building   31
Introduction 31
Essential Information About Vocabulary Instruction 31
Preparation for Vocabulary Instruction 32
Ways to Teach Vocabulary Through the Five Senses 33
Visual Experiences 33
Auditory Experiences 34
Tactile-Kinesthetic Experiences 35
Smell Experiences 37
Taste Experiences 38
Conclusion 38
References 39

4 Thematic Planning for Teaching and Learning through the Senses   41
Introduction 41
The Importance of Sensory Materials on Cognitive Development: An Historical Overview 42
National and State Standards 44
Nine-Step Thematic Unit Plans for STEAM Learning 50
Conclusion 55
References 56

PART II
Planning Sensory-Rich STEAM Unit Plans   61

5 Rabbits and Hares   63
Introduction 63
Science Unit Plan > Biology and Physics 63
Technology Unit Plan > Keywords, Searches, Graphs, and Spreadsheets 73
Engineering Unit Plan > Mechanical Engineering 80
Art Unit Plan > Visual, Music, and Drama 87
Mathematics Unit Plan > Measurement, Data, and Statistics 94

6 The Water Cycle   102
Introduction 102
Science Unit Plan > Chemistry and Physics 102
Technology Unit Plan > Computer Operations, Searches, QR codes, and Game Templates 111

Engineering Unit Plan > Civil Engineering 118
Art Unit Plan > Visual Art and Drama 125
Mathematics Unit Plan > Measurement, Data, and Statistics 134

7 Nutrition and Health   141
Introduction 141
Science Unit Plan > Biology and Chemistry 141
Technology Unit Plan > Search, Keywords, Avatar 147
Engineering Unit Plan > Chemical Engineering 154
Art Unit Plan > The Visual Arts 160
Mathematics Unit Plan > Fractions, Percent, and Decimals 169

8 Continental and Oceanic Landforms   176
Introduction 176
Science Unit Plan > Geology 176
Technology Unit Plan > Search, Keywords, PowerPoint, Book, and Puzzle Making 186
Engineering Unit Plan > Civil Engineering 193
Art Unit Plan > Visual Arts 200
Mathematics Unit Plan > Geometry 209

9 Astronomy and Seasons   216
Introduction 216
Science Unit Plan > Physics 216
Technology Unit Plan > Keywords, Word Documents, and Digital Pictures 224
Engineering Unit Plan > Electrical Engineering 231
Art Unit Plan > Music and Dance/Movement 237
Mathematics Unit Plan > Rates 247

10 Problems and Pitfalls Planning Multisensory STEAM Unit Plans   252
Introduction 252
First Steps 252
Online Reference 256

Index   257

Figures

1.1	Cerebral Cortex	9
1.2	The Human Brain	10
1.3	Individual Brain Cell	11
1.4	Axon and Dendrite Transmitters	11
1.5	Neural Forest Connections	12
1.6	Link Ness Monster Graphic Organizer	15
1.7	QR Code: How the brain compensates for sensory loss and points to its early evolutionary roots	19
1.8	QR Code: The story behind "Lunch atop a skyscraper: The photo that inspired Great Depression era America"	20
1.9	QR Code: Neurotechnology and brain stimulation in pediatric psychiatric and neurodevelopmental disorders	20
1.10	QR code: Paper Clips Project	20
1.11	QR code: Paper Clips Project	21
1.12	QR code: Sensorial education and the brain	21
1.13	QR code: The basics of brain development	21
2.1	Serial Position Effects on Attention	23
2.2	QR Code: Sound Bible: Heartbeat Sounds	25
2.3	QR Code: The memory effects and the stories behind them	29
2.4	QR Code: Serial position effect	29
2.5	QR Code: Primacy/Recency Effect: Retention during a learning episode	29
3.1	QR code: Dictionary.com	39
3.2	QR code: National Reading Panel	39
3.3	QR code: Hirsch: Making education great again?	40
3.4	QR code: Which of the following helps photosynthesis?	40
3.5	QR code: Census Bureau reports at least 350 languages spoken in U.S. homes	40
4.1	QR code: NGSS, Next Generation Science and Engineering Standards	44
4.2	QR code: The Next Generation Science Newsletter	45
4.3	QR code: NGSS, Next Generation Science Standards	45
4.4	QR code: NGSS, Next Generation Science Standards: Engineering Design	46
4.5	QR code: NSTA, National Science Teaching Association. Science and Engineering Practices	46
4.6	QR code: NSTA, National Science Teaching Association Position Statements	46
4.7	QR code: Mississippi Department of Education Instructional Planning Guides for Science K-8	47
4.8	QR code: International Society for Technology in Education	47
4.9	QR code: National Coalition for Core Arts Standards	48

4.10	QR code: Mississippi Department of Education College-and-Career Readiness Arts Learning Standards	48
4.11	QR code: NCTM, National Council of Teachers of Mathematics	49
4.12	QR code: Common Core State Standards for Mathematics Practice and Content	49
4.13	QR code: Mississippi Department of Education Instructional Planning Guides for Mathematics K-12	50
4.14	QR code: Mississippi Department of Education Mathematics Scaffolding	50
4.15	QR code: Effects of a statewide pre-kindergarten program on children's achievement and behavior through sixth grade	56
4.16	QR code: Early academic training produces long-term harm: Research reveals potential risks of academic preschools and kindergartens	56
4.17	QR code: National Council of Teachers of Mathematics (NCTM, n.d.). Executive summary	58
5.1	Rabbit Profile	65
5.2	Hare Profile	66
5.3	Newton's First Law of Motion Applied to Kicking a Soccer Ball	67
5.4	Potential and Kinetic Energy in a Pendulum	68
5.5	Potential and Kinetic Energy	69
5.6	Force to Produce Kinetic Energy	69
5.7	QR code: What is a Force?	70
5.8	QR code: Forces and Motion	71
5.9	QR code: Dozens upon Dozens of Pictures of Rabbits and Hares	71
5.10	QR code: These Are 10 Most Fascinating Facts about Rabbits	71
5.11	QR code: Arctic Hares	71
5.12	QR code: Rabbits Body Language	72
5.13	QR code: Wild Hare Sprinting and Hopping	72
5.14	QR code: Cute Rabbits Eating	72
5.15	QR code: Force, Mass, and Acceleration	72
5.16	Rabbit Profile	76
5.17	Hare Profile	76
5.18	4 × 4 Graph with Two-Inch Squares	77
5.19	QR code: Pictures of skeletons of rabbits and hares	79
5.20	QR code:	79
5.21	Rabbit Skeleton	82
5.22	Hare Skeleton	83
5.23	QR code: Images of Skeletons of Rabbits and Hares	85
5.24	QR code: Habits and physical characteristics of rabbits and hares	86
5.25	QR code: Rabbit Body Systems	86
5.26	QR code: Rabbit Anatomy: Understand Bunnies from Ear to Tail	86
5.27	Rabbit Profile	89
5.28	Hare Profile	89
5.29	Cartoon Drawing	91
5.30	QR code: Wild Hare Sprinting and Hopping	93
5.31	QR code: Rabbit Body Language: Meaning Behind 15 Strangest Rabbit Behaviors/Rabbit Jaw Dropping Facts	93
5.32	QR code: Still Picture of Rabbits and Hares	93
5.33	QR code: Lyrics to the story of Peter and the Wolf Op. 67, Sergei Prokofiev	94
5.34	QR code: ASTOR, Hopping through culture: the rabbit in art	94

5.35	Hare Skeleton	97
5.36	Rabbit Skeleton	99
5.37	QR code: Images of rabbit skeletons	100
5.38	QR code: Images of hare skeletons	101
5.39	QR code: YouTube Multiple Images of Rabbits and Hares Jumping	101
5.40	QR code: YouTube Multiple Images of Wild Hare Sprinting and Hopping	101
6.1	Decayed Dinosaur	105
6.2	Water Cycle	106
6.3	Molecular Structure of Three States of Water	106
6.4	Water Molecule Gumdrop Model	107
6.5	QR code: Tonga Hunga-Hunga Ha'api volcano	109
6.6	QR code: What is the Water Cycle and Can the Water Cycle Be Disrupted?	109
6.7	QR code: Disruptions to the Water Cycle: The Dust Bowl	110
6.8	QR code: Diagram of Water Cycle	110
6.9	QR code: The Water Cycle	110
6.10	QR code: Dinosaur Stock Photos: Fossil Dinosaur Fight, Tyrannosaurus and Triceratops	110
6.11	Sample QR Code	113
6.12	QR code: The Water Cycle for Schools and Students	116
6.13	QR code: Water Cycle	116
6.14	QR code: 8 Fast Free Water Cycle Resources and Activities	116
6.15	QR code: Discover Water: The Role of Water in Our Lives	116
6.16	QR code: Examples of Color Words	117
6.17	QR code: Using QR Codes in the Classroom	117
6.18	QR code: QR Code Activities	117
6.19	QR code: Water Cycle	117
6.20	QR code: Internet 4 Classrooms: Tutorial for Microsoft Office	118
6.21	QR code: Fun QR code activities	118
6.22	TinkerToy Turbine	121
6.23	Dam	122
6.24	QR code: An Overview of the 1889 Tragedy	124
6.25	QR code: Reclamation/Projects & Facilities/Dams	124
6.26	QR code: 10 Largest Dams in the World	124
6.27	QR code: Hydroelectric Power: How it Works	125
6.28	QR code: Saturday Science: Build a Dam	125
6.29	Water Cycle	128
6.30	Different Types of Puppets	130
6.31	Example of a Simple and Articulated Water Drop Puppet	130
6.32	QR code: Bracelet activity for the water cycle	132
6.33	QR code: Easy Water Cycle Drawing	132
6.34	QR code: H_2O – The Mystery, Art, and Science of Water	132
6.35	QR code: Teaching the Water Cycle: Activities, Resources, and a Freebie	133
6.36	QR code: BrainPop Jr. Water Cycle	133
6.37	QR code: Teacher Planet: Water Cycle	133
6.38	QR code: Exploring the Water Cycle Through Music!	133
6.39	QR code: Water Cycle Song: Sing Along GoNoodle	134
6.40	Bodies of Water: Collection	137
6.41	QR code: Climate Kids: What is the Water Cycle?	139
6.42	QR code: National Oceanic and Atmospheric Administration: Water Cycle	139

6.43	QR code: Water Cycle	139
6.44	QR code: NASA Precipitation Education	140
7.1	Nutritional Facts	144
7.2	QR code: USDA My Plate: Protein Foods	146
7.3	QR code: Vegetables and Fruits High in Sodium	146
7.4	QR code: Everyday Health: 11 Best and Worst Oils for Your Health	147
7.5	QR code: Nutrition and healthy eating. Carbohydrates	147
7.6	QR code: Computer-Generated Avatar	152
7.7	QR code: My Plate from the United States Department of Agriculture	152
7.8	QR code: United States Department of Agriculture	153
7.9	QR code: USDA My Plate	153
7.10	QR code: 5 Online Resources for Great Nutrition Lessons	153
7.11	QR code: What is Heat?	159
7.12	Bottles of Cold and Hot Water with Balloons	157
7.13	QR code: How does sunscreen work?	159
7.14	QR code: Hot and Cold Science Experiments for Kids	159
7.15	Jett Pointing to Upcycled Food Group Sculpture	163
7.16	Food Container Made into Fish	164
7.17	QR code: Analysis of Artwork	167
7.18	Imitation of Cézanne's Pastel Chalk Still Life	165
7.19	QR code: Famous Fruit and Vegetable Paintings	167
7.20	QR code: Famous Fruit and Vegetable Paintings	167
7.21	QR code: Cezanne's Still Life Art Work	168
7.22	QR code: Sculpture Project Ideas for Preschool and Kindergarten Kids	168
7.23	QR code: 3D Art & Sculpture	168
7.24	QR code: Eric Carle Museum: Painting with Found Materials	168
7.25	Pie Chart: Nutrition Percentages	172
7.26	QR code: 3rd Grade: Understand fractions	174
7.27	QR code: 3rd and 4th Grade: Get Reading for Fractions	175
7.28	QR code: 4th Grade: Add and Subtract Fractions	175
7.29	QR code: 5th Grade: Multiply fractions, Divide fractions, Multiply decimals	175
7.30	QR code: 6th Grade: Ratios, Rational Numbers and Rates	175
8.1	Four Layers of the Earth	180
8.2	Worldwide Tectonic Plates	181
8.3	QR code: Layers of the Earth	183
8.4	QR code: Images for World map of Tectonic Plates and Fault Lines	183
8.5	QR code: Plate Tectonics Map - Plate Boundary Map	183
8.6	QR code: 7 Major Tectonic Plates: The World's Largest Plate Tectonics	183
8.7	QR code: How Many Tectonic Plates are There?	184
8.8	QR code: Earth Science for Kids: Plate Tectonics	184
8.9	QR code: Images of Rock Folding	184
8.10	QR code: Images for Pacific Ring of fire in Japan	184
8.11	QR code: Earthquakes and Tsunamis for Kids	185
8.12	QR code: Earthquakes for Kids/ Classroom Learning Videos	185
8.13	QR code: Earthquakes 101 National Geographic	185
8.14	QR code: Earthquake Destruction	185
8.15	Continental and Oceanic Landforms	188
8.16	QR code: Puzzle Ideas	190
8.17	QR code: Example of a PowerPoint Presentation on Landforms	191

8.18	QR code: Free Projects	192
8.19	QR code: Three Links to "Books to Make."	192
8.20	QR code: Hidden Picture Games	192
8.21	QR code: Make Your Own Crossword Puzzle Here	192
8.22	QR code: Puzzlemaker: Create Your Own Puzzles	193
8.23	Beam Bridge	196
8.24	Arch Bridge	196
8.25	Truss Bridge	196
8.26	Truss Bridge Made of Playing Cards	197
8.27	QR code: Bridges	199
8.28	QR code: Let's Make Bridges	199
8.29	QR code: How Are Bridges Built? A Visual Guide	199
8.30	QR code: Why Did the Bridge Collapse?	199
8.31	QR code: Why the Tacoma Narrows Bridge Collapsed	200
8.32	QR code: The Tacoma Narrows Bridge Collapse	200
8.33	Doodles and Zentangles	203
8.34	Landform Sculpture with Natural Materials	205
8.35	QR code: How to Draw an Easy Landscape	206
8.36	QR code: 80 Easy, Simple & Cool Patterns to Draw for Beginners	207
8.37	QR code: Doodle Art 1	207
8.38	QR code: Inspired By Zentangle: Patterns and Starter Pages	207
8.39	QR code: Romero Britto for Kids	207
8.40	QR code: Deep Space Sparkle: How to Teach Line and Pattern	208
8.41	QR code: Beverly Taylor Sorenson Arts Learning Program	208
8.42	QR code: Easy How to Draw Mountains Tutorial by Kathy Barbro	208
8.43	QR code: Mapping Landforms	208
8.44	Quadrilaterals	212
8.45	Triangles vice Quadrilaterals	212
8.46	QR code: Geometry of the Earth	214
8.47	QR code: Identification of the Earth's Features from Maps	214
8.48	QR code: 4th Grade Science: Patterns of the Earth's features	215
8.49	QR code: Geometry - Definition with Examples	215
8.50	QR code: Features That Make Up The Earth – Landforms	215
8.51	QR code: Earth's land features	215
9.1	QR code: Hap Palmer, Spinning on the Same Ball	222
9.2	QR code: Here Comes the Sun	222
9.3	Earth's Hemispheres	220
9.4	Solstices and Equinoxes of the Earth	221
9.5	QR code: Images for Picture of the Earth with an Imaginary Axis	223
9.6	QR code: Map of the World with Equator and Hemispheres	223
9.7	QR code: Illustrations of Earth's Seasons	223
9.8	QR code: Images of Newton's First Law of Motion	223
9.9	QR code: Images of Newton's 2nd Law of Motion	224
9.10	Model of the Earth's Revolution Around the Sun	227
9.11	QR code: NASA Logo	229
9.12	QR code: Online Tutorials for Trifold Brochures	230
9.13	QR code: Online Tutorials for Trifold Brochures	230
9.14	QR code: Online Tutorials for Trifold Brochures	230
9.15	QR code: CRAAP Test to Evaluate Sources	230

9.16	Solar System	234
9.17	QR code: Solar System Educational Teaching Poster Chart	236
9.18	QR code: NASA Space Place: Solar System	236
9.19	QR code: 26 Solar System Project Ideas for Kids that Are Out of this World	237
9.20	QR code: 26 Solar System Project Ideas for Kids that Are Out of this World	237
9.21	Dramatization of the Earth's Movement Around the Sun	241
9.22	QR code: Boom Chick a Boom Summer Songs	244
9.23	QR code: Autumn Leaves by Roger Williams	244
9.24	QR code: Rustle of Spring by Christian Sinding, piano by Amaral Vieira	244
9.25	Upcycled Props for Dance and Movement	242
9.26	QR code: Vivaldi's The Four Seasons	245
9.27	QR code: Vivaldi's The Four Seasons, Violin Concerto No. 4 in F Minor, (Christian Li, child violinist)	245
9.28	QR code: Vivaldi's The Four Seasons Translated to Another Medium	245
9.29	QR code: Colorful Creative Pictures and Music of Autumn	246
9.30	QR code: Classics for Kids: Rhythm, Moving; Listening; Describing; Creating	246
9.31	QR code: Richard Clayderman Piano Instrumental Music: Autumn Leaves	246
9.32	QR code: The Physics Factbook. An Encyclopedia of Scientific Essays	251
9.33	QR code: The Latest News on the Solar System and the Universe	251
9.34	QR code: StarChild: A Learning Center for Young Astronomers	251
10.1	QR code: Instructional Design: Bloom's Taxonomy	256

Acknowledgments

Debbie Meyers for using her talents as an artist to draw figures that help clarify the text in the book.

Felicia Pollard for the photos she took for many of the figures.

Author Biographies

Kerry P. Holmes, Ed.D., is a professor emerita of elementary education at the University of Mississippi. Her research and publications are on the use of multisensory materials in content area lessons, vocabulary, and early reading. She was awarded The School of Education Outstanding Researcher and Outstanding Faculty Researcher. She taught kindergarten and 1st grade for five years in California, was a substitute teacher in special needs and K–12 classes in Virginia, and taught 1st grade in a critical needs school in Mississippi. She is co-author of *The A in STEAM: Lesson Plans and Activities for Integrating Art, Ages 0–8* (2021) published by Routledge, and the author of *Engaging Reluctant Readers through Foreign Films* (2005).

Jerilou J. Moore, Ph.D., professor emerita at the University of Mississippi School of Education, has taught art and technology classes for teachers. She enjoys judging district- and state-level art contests for children ages 5 to 19. This gives her an opportunity to see the development of their creative talents and how they learn and grow through creative thinking and problem solving. She developed ideas for children's art and technology over the years during the time she was an elementary principal, administrator, teacher, art judge, and university professor. She was twice awarded Teacher of the Year by students and faculty at the University of Mississippi School of Education. Her publications, presentations, and grants focus on reading, technology, and the arts. She is author of *The A in STEAM: Lesson Plans and Activities for Integrating Art, Ages 0–8* published by Routledge (2021).

Stacy V. Holmes, Ph.D., is an assistant dean emeritus, School of Engineering, at the University of Mississippi. He spent 27 years in the Navy, and retired as a captain, USN. He began his academic career at the University of Mississippi where he taught electrical engineering and mathematics courses as well as graduate education courses in statistics.

Introduction

A lesson on the parts of a plant taught by one of Holmes's 3rd-grade student teachers brought home the importance of the potential richness of sensory learning. Her student teacher spent hours creating a poster with colorful cutouts of the parts of a plant. As he taught, he named the parts and their functions. She was impressed by his hard work, but unimpressed by the level of learning that was going on during the lesson. Throughout his lesson, she thought, "What if you brought the class outside to pull weeds that grew between the cracks and gaps in the pavement near the classroom?" Demonstrating how to locate weeds and how to pull them up without breaking the plant would have enabled students to have individual specimens of weeds that contained all the parts on the chart. With their specimens, students could not only look at the parts of their plants, but they could feel and smell the parts as they dissected their plant. They could run their fingers down the long tap root and see how dirt sticks to it and closely inspect leaves and any blooms and seeds. The poster would have been useful as a reference or an opportunity for review.

The purpose of this book is to show how teachers can plan lessons that enable students to use their five senses: visual, auditory, tactile/kinesthetic, smell, and taste during learning through unit plans. The unit plans are centered around five themes: Rabbits and Hares, The Water Cycle, Health and Nutrition, Landforms, and Astronomy and the Seasons. Each theme can be taught through each of the STEAM content areas: Science, Technology, Engineering, Art, and Mathematics. This book is divided into two parts.

Part I. The Role of the Senses in Teaching and Learning

Chapters 1–4 include information about the brain and how sensory information is processed, how serial position (the sequence of a lesson) affects attention, 28 ways to teach vocabulary, and how to plan each step of a thematic unit plan. Teachers are introduced to the importance of the five senses: visual, auditory, tactile/kinesthetic, smell, and taste and the way they have been used for learning since prehistoric time.

Chapter 1: The Brain and Sensory Learning

It seems fitting to begin this book with the role of the brain in learning and how information is stored and communicated through its different parts. Research, first conducted on rats, and continued on the brains of deceased orphans, has shown overwhelming that sensory experiences are responsible for brain growth and development. Teachers will find multiple suggestions on ways they can increase their students' brain growth through sensory experiences.

Chapter 2: Emotion and Serial Position Effect on Learning: Multisensory Sets and Closures

Did you know there are two critical times when teachers have students' attention and that both times are frequently underutilized? Hopefully, after you read this chapter, you will be convinced to plan ways to take advantage of these two times. This chapter arms you with over 30 ways to make the best use of the critical times students are most attentive.

Chapter 3: The Role of the Five Senses in Vocabulary Building

How can students understand what they read and hear if they do not understand the meaning of the words? It is never too early to teach students words related to academic content. Young students will encounter the vocabulary learned in kindergarten throughout the grades into high school. In this chapter, teachers will find information about how many words students learn in a year and how many words teachers should teach in a day. Chapter 3 provides over 30 ways to teach vocabulary before, during, and after a lesson through the five senses.

Chapter 4: Thematic Planning for Teaching and Learning through the Senses

By now, we hope teachers are convinced that through the lessons they plan, they help their students' brains physically grow larger. In this chapter, teachers will learn how to select and use materials with students beginning in kindergarten and continuing through grade six. This chapter provides a brief background on Piaget's stages of cognitive development and Bruner's discovery learning to understand the progression of students' physical and cognitive development. The HELP Hierarchy of Effective Lesson Planning outlines possible materials teachers can use in their lessons that begin with the most authentic ones, Real World, and end with orally and aurally delivered information.

Part II. Planning Sensory-Rich STEAM Unit Plans

Chapters 5–9 contain 25 sensory unit plans centered around five themes: Rabbits and Hares, Water Cycle, Health and Nutrition, Landforms, and Astronomy and Seasons. Each theme is addressed through the STEAM content areas: Science, Technology, Engineering, Art, and Mathematics. Sensory information inherent in the unit plans affords students multiple pathways for learning. Students build on this learning through a themed approach where they connect information across the curriculum. For example, content about rabbits and hares introduced in science, continues throughout technology, engineering, art, and mathematics lessons. These themed unit plans enable students to learn academic content from various viewpoints through their involvement with multisensory materials. Teachers can use the thematic unit plans for their lessons, or as models for writing their own.

Chapter 5: Rabbits and Hares

Students will learn about rabbits and hares, gravitational and applied forces that affect hopping, potential and kinetic energy, and Newton's 1st law of motion.

Chapter 6: The Water Cycle

Includes unit plans on the properties, sources, and cycles of water through multiple experiments, visuals, and connections to real-world needs and experiences.

Chapter 7: Nutrition and Health

Leads students through the need for healthy eating and for ways to identify healthy and unhealthy foods. An emphasis is on reading and calculating nutrition values on food labels.

Chapter 8: Continental and Oceanic Landforms

This chapter focuses on the layers of the Earth with an emphasis on the crust and the mantle. Students will learn how the movement of tectonic plates, under the crust they walk on, are responsible for many of the landforms such as mountains and volcanoes formed on land and under the oceans. Landforms are also created by factors related to the water cycle such as precipitation rates, erosion, wind, and temperature.

Chapter 9: Astronomy and Seasons

We included numerous activities throughout the STEAM plans to help students understand how the Earth's axial tilt as it revolves around the Sun causes seasonal differences around the world. Students' can use their real-world experiences with day and night to learn how the rotation of the Earth on its axis causes both daytime and darkness during a 24-hour period.

Chapter 10: Problems and Pitfalls Planning Multisensory STEAM Unit Plans

One of the things that makes this book unique is our chapter on problems and pitfalls. Teachers will read about the steps we took to write sensory unit plans and the problems and pitfalls we encountered. This chapter is meant to share mistakes and blind alleys so that teachers will not be surprised or discouraged when faced with similar situations. It contains a treasure trove of useful information that presents an insightful and honest approach to unit planning. It is our fervent hope that teachers will learn from our experiences and plan big, bold thematic unit plans loaded with sensory experiences for their students.

Part I

The Role of the Senses in Teaching and Learning

Chapters 1–4
Brain Growth in Students K-6 through Multisensory Experiences for STEAM Learning

Part 1

The Role of the Senses in
Teaching and Learning

Chapter 1

The Brain and Sensory Learning

Introduction

How does the environment affect brain development? You will learn about the effects of the environment on brain growth and the disturbing findings from two sets of studies conducted years apart by Marian Diamond and neuroscientists from the Bucharest Early Intervention Project. The way individual senses support each other and even compensate for ones that are missing are illustrated through the lives of Helen Keller, who lost her visual and auditory senses at an early age. It also includes information on Daniel Kish, a blind cyclist mountain guide, and Temple Grandin, a person with autism who remembers events of the world and solves problems through picture and pattern thinking.

This chapter provides an overview of the brain and how the five senses input information from classroom experiences to students' brains that help their brains grow and develop. It includes early research by Bartlett (1967) on learning and schema theory and hierarchies of concrete and abstract materials developed by Dale (1969) and Piaget (1950). Dr. Martha Pierson of the Baylor College of Medicine (2021, p. 1) exquisitely summed up the importance of multisensory learning when she said sensory experiences should be "a feast for the mind, a banquet of sensory information." (Pierson, 2021)

In their work with preservice teachers, the authors found that too many did not include multisensory materials in their STEAM lessons: Science, Technology, Engineering, Art, and Mathematics. Data from 363 lesson plans showed that 61% of the lessons were to be taught by visual and auditory methods without the support of the less used, but vitally important, senses of touch/movement, smell, and taste. Furthermore, results showed that when they planned to engage their class with multisensory materials, it was the teacher, not the students, who handled the materials. Students only engaged in hands-on experiences with multisensory materials 18% of the time (Holmes, Holmes, & Watts, 2012).

This chapter ends with a description of each of the five senses: visual, auditory, tactile-kinesthetic, smell, and taste and multiple examples of ways teachers can include them in their lessons. QR codes accompany the online references at the end of this chapter.

Rat and Human Brains

Research from two separate sets of studies clearly document the necessity for teachers, parents, and caregivers to create Pierson's "banquet of sensory information" for their children beginning at birth and extending through the stages of learning.

Rosenzweig, Bennett, and Diamond (1972), found that brain development is directly influenced by sensory experiences. They compared the brains of hundreds of rats raised in environments with toys and companions to those raised without toys or companions. They found that rats raised in enriched environments had significantly larger brains, as measured by the weight of the cerebral cortex, than rats raised with minimal sensory input.

Having heard from a volunteer who had worked in orphanages in Romania and was struck by the lack of attention infants received, Diamond extended her research to human brains. She compared the weight of the cerebral cortex of deceased orphans who lived in a sensory-emotionally deprived environment to those who were raised in an enriched sensory and nurturing environment. She found a physical link between sensory experiences and brain growth. Ultimately, the results of her studies on animals and humans improved the conditions in many orphanages and zoos (Diamond & Hopson, 1998).

Since the initial Rosenzweig, Bennet, and Diamond studies, subsequent studies have been conducted on the influx of Romanian infants and children raised in orphanages after the 1989 fall of Nicolae Ceausescu, a communist dictator. During his reign, Ceausescu encouraged poverty-stricken parents to turn their children over to state-run orphanages. Studies focused on the health, social-emotional functioning, and cognition of young children raised in orphanages and compared data to those that were sent to foster homes. There is moderate evidence to show that children who were removed from an orphanage and sent to foster homes increased their health, social emotional functioning, and cognition (Kondo & Hannan, 2019).

The big question today is whether this increase in social-emotional functioning and cognitive development, after months and years of deprivation, can diminish over time. Research on the plasticity of the brain, its ability to be molded by new experiences, has shown that the underdeveloped cerebral cortex of a child who had missed critical periods of development began to grow neural networks that sustain and even perpetuate learning (Kondo & Hannan, 2019). It is up to teachers, parents, and caregivers to continue growth and development by providing positive socio-emotional experiences through laughter, eye contact, physical contact, and patience in addition to enriching the learning environment. There is definitely hope for these children!

How Sensory Experiences Affect the Brain

When students experience learning through multiple senses, each sense imparts information to different parts of their brains. Each part of the brain is specialized for visual, auditory, movement, touch, smell, and taste. The senses work together to support survival and enrich learning. If people are deprived of one sense, the other senses become dominant forces for learning information about their immediate surroundings (Rosenblum, 2010; Delgoshen, 2016).

Through a childhood illness at 18 months, Helen Keller became blind and deaf. She relied on touch, movement, smell, and taste to learn and understand the world around her. Her experiences clearly show how the remaining senses supported each other and compensated for the two sensory channels that did not work. Keller, who lived to be 87 years old, spent her first years learning to speak, read, and write. She learned to read through touch, by first feeling letters traced on her hand, raised letters, and later by Braille. She learned to speak by feeling facial movements, lip positions, and vibrations of speakers' vocal cords. Later, she learned English, French, German, and Latin; read classic literature; and studied history, science, and mathematics. Social involvement coupled with sensory experiences throughout Keller's life were the key factors for her success in learning and leading a full life (Keller, 1996).

Rosenblum (2010) interviewed people who are blind and described how they used hearing as a substitute for sight through echolocation. Daniel Kish, a totally blind guide, took cyclists safely through difficult mountain trails and passages by making clicking sounds every 1–2 seconds so he could hear the sounds as they bounced off nearby obstacles including trees and rocks. Echolocation, a compound word "echo" and "location," means that people who have difficulty seeing in the dark can learn to rely on reflected sound to navigate safely around nearby objects.

This simple experiment devised by Rosenblum (2010, p. 9) will help you understand echolocation and how it benefits people with poor or no eyesight.

> Hold your hand up about one foot or 0.3048 meters in front of your face with your palm facing your mouth. Now put your front teeth together, open your lips, and make a continuous *shhhhhh* sound. As you make this sound, slowly bring your hand toward your mouth. You will hear the *shhhh* change as you bring your hand closer. To really hear the sound change, repeatedly move your hand back and forth, closer and farther from your mouth. You will hear a *whooshing* sound that changes with your hand position.

Inside a Child's Head

If only teachers could see what is going on in the brains of the students they teach! They could understand what catches students' interest, what causes them to drift away from instructional moments by staring into space, playing with their pencils, and even tugging at loose threads on their socks. Why do these moments of inattention occur, and what can teachers do about them? One way to address this question is for teachers to understand the basic principles of the inner workings of their students' brains and the way they develop.

The mature human brain weighs approximately three pounds and is protected by a hard, bony skull. The brain has two hemispheres divided by a fissure called the corpus collosum that enables communication between the two hemispheres. The cerebral cortex, also called gray matter, is the covering of the brain with a thickness of 2–4 mm, 1/8th of an inch, roughly the thickness of the rind of a cantaloupe. See Figure 1.1.

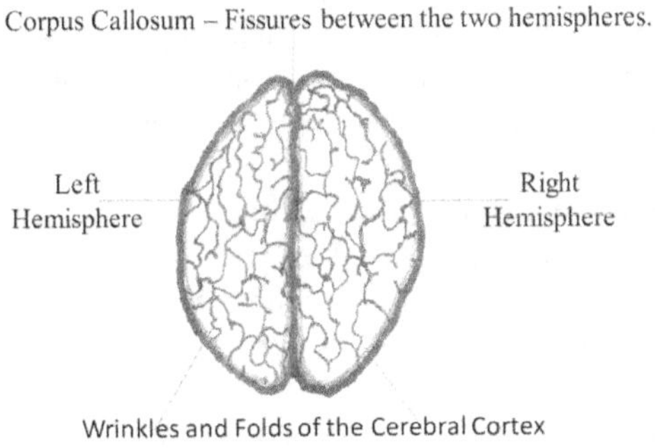

Corpus Callosum – Fissures between the two hemispheres.

Left Hemisphere

Right Hemisphere

Wrinkles and Folds of the Cerebral Cortex

Figure 1.1 Cerebral Cortex.

Approximately half of the weight of our brain mass is created and contained in the cerebral cortex and contains an aggregate of nerve cells called neurons (Newquist, 2004). Because of the limited space within the skull, the cerebral cortex is stuffed inside the human skull, causing it to be heavily wrinkled with folds, grooves, and valleys. Unfolded, the cortex is about the size of a regular pillow case and would require an extra-large head!

Within the cerebral cortex, specialized neurons receive sensory information through sight, hearing, movement, touch, smell, and taste and communicate this information to other neurons. This communication involves billions of neurons capable of trillions of connections that make possible the higher intellectual functions of humans. This is what separates us from animals with less developed brains.

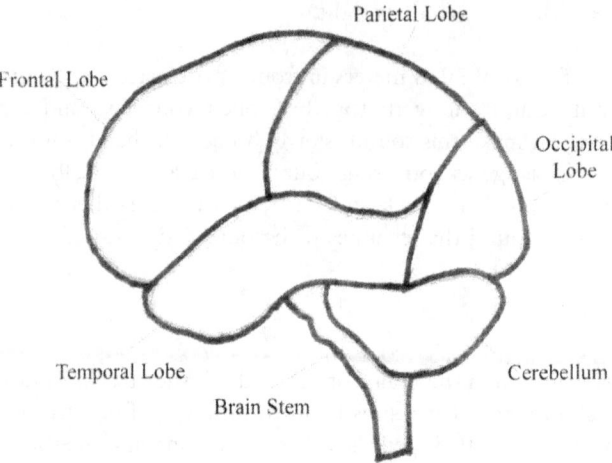

Figure 1.2 The Human Brain.

Figure 1.2 shows the primary parts of the brain: the cerebral cortex, four lobes, (occipital, frontal, temporal, and parietal), fissure between the two halves of the brain, cerebellum, and the brain stem. Look closely and you will see the 1/8th inch band of gray matter that covers the cerebral cortex and contains specialized neural cells.

As you read the descriptions of the of the lobes of the brain and the cerebellum, keep in mind that each has several specialized functions that serve multiple purposes as they receive and processes incoming information from the sensory organs (eyes, ears, nose, mouth, and skin).

Frontal Lobe: Comprises the largest part of the brain. This lobe enables powers of consciousness, reasoning, problem solving, planning, decision making, and speech in addition to attention and memory. These higher-level mental processes are dependent on information from the five senses.

Parietal Lobe: Sensory information from the five senses: viewing, hearing, touching/moving, smelling, and tasting, are stored and released from this lobe. Think of your parietal lobe as a processing center for the incoming senses. This helps to make sense of the multitude of sensory experiences that bombard your brain. These sensory experiences overlap with information processed through the other lobes of the brain.

Temporal Lobe: Located in the mid-brain, distributes sensory information related to hearing, taste, and smell. Most people are able to smell over 1,000 scents. These scents enter our consciousness through the olfactory bulbs located in the roof of the nasal passages and trigger memories of events. The temporal lobe also helps process complex visual information that aids in differentiating multiple colors, patterns, and moving images.

Occipital Lobe: Located in the back of the brain, processes visual information related to depth, distance, location, color, and object identity. This lobe is also linked with recognition, recall, and memory. Visual memories are stored in this part of the brain.

The cerebellum, called the "little brain," aids voluntary movements such as coordination, balance, and spatial navigation. The information the cerebellum receives from the four lobes is processed to aid kinesthetic activities such as sports, driving, drama, dancing, running, and walking that require motor control, coordinated movement, and spatial navigation. The cerebellum assists the eye movement of students when reading, the fine motor control when writing, and the movement of mouth, lips, and vocal cords when speaking.

In the last trimester of pregnancy, the fetus's brain develops the cerebral cortex that enables him or her to engage in voluntary actions such as kicking and thumb sucking. At birth, the infant's brain has millions of neural cells within the cortex that transmit information to each other. The human brain increases in size nearly four times from birth to preschool age. By age six, the child's brain is about 90% of the size of an adult brain. The brain continues to grow and change throughout life through mental and physical experiences. Mature human brains have roughly a hundred billion neurons (Stiles & Jernigan, 2010).

Each neuron has a cell body that is equipped to transmit and receive messages from other neurons. Communication is enabled by electrical and chemical transmissions from the axons to the dendrites. See Figures 1.3 and 1.4.

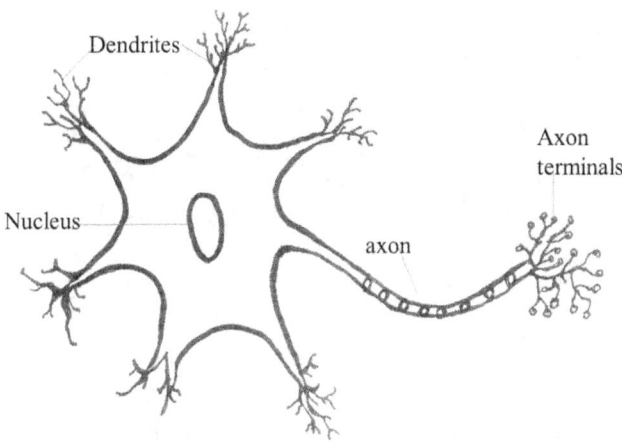

Figure 1.3 Individual Brain Cell.

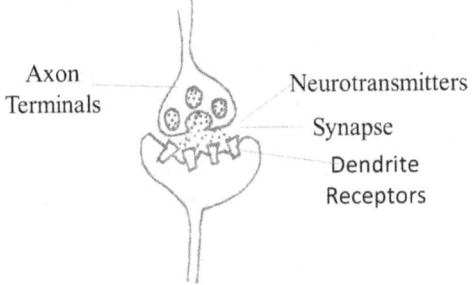

Figure 1.4 Axon and Dendrite Transmitters.

Putting It All Together

It is helpful to remember that axons transmit and dendrites receive information. This communication occurs across small gaps called synapses. All of this is going on in your students' heads as they gather information from their senses.

Your goal as a teacher is to have students engage in as many multisensory experiences as possible to help them make numerous neural connections within their brains. You are

12 The Role of the Senses in Teaching and Learning

helping your students' brains grow heavier as the density of neural connections increase! So, how does information that is perceived by one part of the brain travel to other relevant parts of the brain that further enriches incoming information? The 100 billion neurons when stimulated make trillions of connections. This plethora of connections has such a strong resemblance to clusters of tree branches, they are often referred to as neural forests. See Figure 1.5.

Figure 1.5 Neural Forest Connections.

In spite of their close proximity, the nerve cells never touch. Instead, they transmit information across an electrochemical synaptic gap.

Information Processed Through Each of the Five Senses

Of the five senses, the visual sense is unquestionably dominant. Normally sighted students are all visual learners. People's attention is attracted to movement. They can identify animals and objects by looking at just a small part such as the end of an animal's tail or a part of a cup handle. The other four senses contribute to survival and learning in varying degrees. The auditory sense enables people to detect approaching animals or cars and is assisted by visual facial features and mouth formation as they listen to speech. Even though smell, touch, and taste have been found to contribute less information, their additional input to the total learning experience is important. Lessons that depend solely on seeing and hearing alone miss out on valuable information afforded by the other three senses. These senses play a vital role in learning by clarifying and enriching what students see and hear.

Schema Theory

For at least 100 years, cognitive psychologists have studied schema theory to determine the ways isolated bits of information are learned, organized, and stored in memory. Schema relates to the way we connect new knowledge to stored knowledge. Through students' sensory actions on materials, they will learn critical basic facts to support and promote abstract thinking that is supported by prior knowledge. Deep thinking requires judgments of reasonableness that require logic, curiosity, inquiry, and the ability to make inferences through thoughtful actions. Piaget (1971, p. 28) said, "All knowledge is linked to action and that the evolution of actions presupposes coordination." Students' coordination, their mental organization of sensory materials, is necessary to perform actions that transform and reconstruct their ideas.

Students' background knowledge, stored in schematic mental folders, is critically important for new learning. The more senses involved in learning over time, the more ways information can be stored in memory. Fun stories abound with everyday examples of schema building. Children who have a schema for the parts of a dog have a mental picture of an animal with four legs, two ears, and a tail. Initially, they are likely to call a horse, an animal with features that fit their schema, "a doggie." As children see and interact with more animals, they add their different features to their schema and become more adept at distinguishing finer differences among animals.

Sir Fredrick Bartlett is credited for first publicizing his hierarchy on schema theory in 1932. He theorized that learned information from multiple senses is added to existing mental folders, or in the case of new experiences, new mental folders. Through his studies on memory using a Native American legend, *War of the Ghosts*, Bartlett found it was more difficult for participants who were not familiar with the cultural names and terms expressed in the legend to make sense of the story. Their accuracy in recalling facts and the sequence of events was not nearly as great as the participants familiar with the culture related to the legend (Bartlett, 1967, p. 124). Bartlett's study on cultural differences points out the importance of planning to aid students who are unfamiliar with the terminology and experiences within the lesson (Table 1.1).

Table 1.1 Terms Used Retelling a Ghost Story by People From Two Different Cultures

Native American Memory	British Memory
Egulac and Kalama territories	Omitted names from retelling story
Seal hunting	Fishing
Canoe	Boat
Paddles	Oars
Recounted events in 330 words	Recounted events in 180 words

Ways to Maximize Sensory Input

Emotion and novelty are powerful forces that serve as catalysts for learning. The closer the materials used in lessons resemble the real world, the more likely they will evoke emotional responses based on the students' prior experiences and knowledge. Novel materials, or materials placed in unexpected places, are ways to promote students' curiosity. Expect noises of surprise and interest as students enter a darkened classroom with a loud rocket-launch sound effect, see a live rabbit in a large cage, or are greeted by a hanging model of a skeleton.

Rarely are the senses isolated during learning. As you read each of the descriptions of the senses and suggestions on ways to include them in your lessons, look for other ways you can use or modify these ideas in your teaching.

Visual Learning

Temple Grandin, a woman with autism, vividly describes the ways that viewing animals, objects, pictures, and patterns helped her learn, saying that she converted her visual experiences into full color movies that she played in her head (Grandin, 2013). Transferring Grandin's ability to think in pictures to children with and without autism provides teachers ways to help their students clarify and organize their thinking based on their visual experiences.

Thinking in pictures is the way most normally sighted people remember their world because they process concrete images at a faster rate than abstract words. Teachers can use pictures and objects as tools to aid oral and written communication by having students slow down and focus on specific details including colors, patterns, and the relationships of the parts to one another. This "taking-time-to smell-the-roses" approach to teaching is easily applied to "taking-time-to-view-the-world."

Students pick up on visual cues important to survival and learning. They can tell when others are excited, happy, sad, or angry. To build on these emotional cues, teachers can add gestures and model ways to work on an assignment or project augmented by changes in speech tone and volume. The more energetic, and even goofy the movements, the more they will attract attention. Excellent teachers move around the classroom, varying the speed and tempo of their movements and speech. They all used facial expressions, hand gestures, and eye contact.

Other visual cues include color. Road signs and signals such as stop lights are prime examples of the effects colors have on our attention, behavior, and emotions. Students are familiar with road signs. If they have not paid attention to them, or forgot their colors, take them outside to see nearby road signs, or show them pictures.

Visual images that aid learning are still and moving pictures, photographs, timelines, graphic organizers maps, charts, and icons. Students respond to novelty such as high interest pictures found in comic book–style graphic novels. Novel visuospatial relationships such as the picture of a group of men sitting on a steel beam at the top of a skyscraper in the 1932 photo, *Lunch Atop a Skyscraper* described and shown by Ishak (2020) (Materials and Resources), attracts attention and evokes emotional responses that remain in memory. Visual perceptions such as a picture of a large baby chick standing by a farmer (Moore & Holmes, 2021, p. 20) or a vanishing road (Moore & Holmes, 2021, p. 33) stimulate thinking and conversations that promote learning about the effects size and distance have on our vision.

Make a Monster Theme Graphic Organizer

Demonstrate ways for students to create a monster as they read and learn about rabbits and hares or information from other themes. Have students write the name of the theme and one or more experiences they have had related to the theme at the top of the page of a large sheet of paper. In the middle of the paper, have students draw a large oval, leaving space to add legs, head, neck, and any other parts they want for their monster. Each time students have a question and learn an important fact that answers the question, they can draw two parts to their monster, one that includes their question and one for their answer to the question. Make sure they draw the parts large enough to write a brief sentence inside the part. Students can add as many parts as they want, but each one has to contain a science question and important fact that answers the question. Holmes used this idea with a fifth-grade science class that was reading information on volcanoes from their textbook. The students did not want to stop reading! When the teacher wanted to move on from the lesson, they said, "I want to add more information to my monster!" Figure 1.6 shows a completed monster.

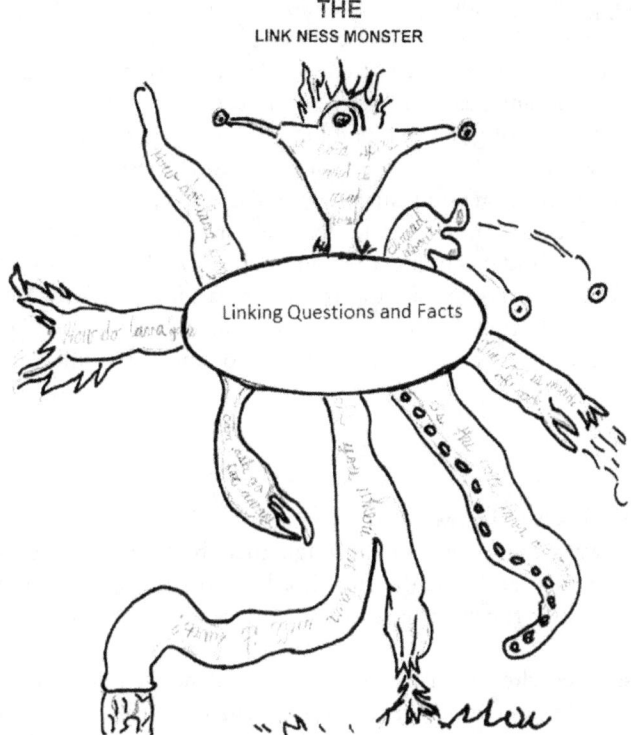

Figure 1.6 Link Ness Monster Graphic Organizer.

The text of the monster reads:

Head of the Monster
I can read and spell the words in my book.

Questions	Answers
How does lava form?	Lava is melted rock.
How does lava move?	It moves down a mountain.
When you were in lava does it hurt?	It would hurt because it is very hot.
Where is lava?	

Auditory Learning

Hearing is another important survival sense that leads to learning. We can often hear sounds before we see their sources. The snapping of a twig or the crunch of leaves alerts us to an approaching person or animal. The sound of thunder indicates a storm with potentially dangerous lightning. Sound is aided by other senses. We may smell the leaves, feel the hot humid air before an approaching storm, and see falling leaves or the approaching dark clouds.

All topics presented by the teacher orally and discussed by the students offer valuable information. Class discussions enable the students to express what they know and think, and hear other viewpoints from their classmates. With auditory learning accounting for roughly 11% of what is learned, it is best to support the auditory presentation of information with visuals, movement and touch, smell, and taste. Good speakers use a variety of auditory techniques to capture the interest of the students and maintain their attention. Techniques include changing the volume, speed, rhythm, mood, and emphasis on speech sounds.

It is a good idea to practice techniques of good speaking before reading a book to the class, giving directions, and lecturing on a topic. One teacher said she wrote questions and other helpful ways to involve students on sticky notes and stuck them on selected pages of the books she read to the class. This same technique can be used for lecture notes or a textbook.

Audio books can be used to involve students in literature and nonfiction. Songs, music, and recordings of animal sounds are excellent sources of information for learning STEAM content. Try playing YouTube videos of goats bleating if you want your students to have a good laugh. Of course, unless you are studying goats, use other animal noises to amuse and inform your students.

Tactile/Kinesthetic Learning

Tactile/kinesthetic includes direct touch and movement. These senses, often combined, capture students' attention through the ways things feel and through their body movements. The development of the senses of movement and touch begins shortly before birth and continues throughout life. Here are a few ideas for touch and movement activities you can do with your students.

Show your class the trailer, selected clips, or the entire film of an American documentary, *Paper Clips Project*, that engaged middle school students in mathematics, writing, and social studies in Whitwell, Tennessee. Students wrote letters to people around the world asking for donations of paper clips for their project on the Holocaust. They strove to collect 6,000,000 paper clips to represent the 6,000,000 Jewish people killed by Nazis during World War II. As the paper clips poured in from donors, students were engaged in counting them, watching large numbers of paper clips grow into piles, and sifting through the piles of paper clips to gain a better understanding of what the numbers actually represent (Paper Clips Project, 1998).

When teaching vocabulary, use painters' tape to put up two words, one on each wall. Say a definition and have students lean toward the word they think is correct. For mathematics, have students relate positive and negative numbers to something they can picture, such as above and below sea level. Label one wall "above sea level" and the other wall, "below sea level." Hold up positive and negative numerals and have students lean toward the wall with the correct label. For science, use pairs of words such as "vertebrates" and "invertebrates" or "interphase" (cell growth) and "mitosis" (cell division). Call out the name of an animal or the phases of the cell cycle and have students lean toward, move to, or point to the wall with the correct word (Wormeli, 2001).

Make up, or have students help to make up, fingerplays or movements using words from the lesson. Though finger plays and movements are used for very young children, some never lose their appeal for older students. Fingerplays such as *Five Green Speckled Frogs* involve basic mathematics. Science songs such as *Dry Bones*, "The toe bone connected to the foot bone, the foot bone connected to the heel bone ... ," serve to teach connected information. Repetitive song movements such as, *Head, Shoulders, Knees, and Toes* actively involve the students as they touch, move, recite, or sing the words. Hap Palmer (1998), has recorded many songs that include movement while teaching content such as *Take Me Out to the Ball Game* and *Action Fractions* that can be used for active learning.

Touch

When shopping, how often do you feel an overwhelming urge to touch the produce or a piece of clothing that interests you? Your students are the same way. When introducing them to a lesson with physical props and manipulatives, give them time to touch and manipulate them. They will anyway, so make this a part of your lesson!

The following examples show how to use touch as a primary emphasis for learning. Present students with textured letters made from sandpaper, felt, or other materials they can feel and trace with their fingers when teaching letter recognition, vowels, consonants, blends, digraphs, and spelling. Have students feel physical differences in shape, hardness, weight, volume, force, temperature, and texture of objects. If the lesson is on constructing a bridge, an engineering feat, the material's weight, volume, texture, and shape can be gained through touch. If the lesson is on air pressure, knowledge of volume and force is aided through touch when blowing up a balloon to the maximum extent without popping it. Musical keyboards, drums (homemade or store bought), brass, and wind instruments aid the development of touch through force, lip movement, mouth position, and eye-hand coordination.

Movement

Holmes's first-grade students were distracted from their lessons if an ant crawled nearby or if a fly buzzed around the classroom. No matter how good her carefully planned lesson was, it could always be disrupted by a mere ant or fly. Movement indicates a change in our surroundings, and that change can be neutral, pleasurable, or dangerous.

If your students have been sitting a long time, or begin to lose interest, plan ways to let them move during your lesson. Movement is not only a fresh change-of-pace, it rejuvenates students by increasing the oxygen flow to the brain and other parts of the body. Look for ways to combine movement with learning.

In comedy movies we all laugh at someone who cannot walk into a room without bumping into walls and knocking over trays of food and drink. It is obvious that this bumbling person does not have a good sense of spatial orientation. Spatial orientation related to students' proximity to each other, to objects, and even to walls is developed through sporting events, dance, and drama. As students move, they develop spatial orientation and are able to adjust their behaviors.

Through music, students can use fractions required for musical timing as they sing and dance to a wide variety of educational songs found online for children. When selecting songs, make sure they have a strong rhythm that encourages the use of vigorous movements to accented beats. Through drama, students can reenact situations such as the movement of planetary objects in our solar system and natural cycles such as the water cycle.

Stories in children's books can be acted out. Books should have rich vocabulary for students to dramatize based on the concepts you are teaching. Here is an example of an old African folk story, *Anansi The Trickster Spider,* that can be dramatized to teach about animals that live in the mountains, plateaus, plains, deserts, and forests of Africa.

In this story, a clever little spider falls under the spell of a moss-covered rock. The spider immediately recognizes that when he encounters the rock and says, "Isn't this a strange hmm, hmmmmm, hmm" he becomes weak and falls to the ground. The mischievous spider quickly recognizes he can trick other animals into repeating the phrase "Isn't this a strange hmm, hmmmmm, hmm" and they too will become weak and fall to the ground at which time he can steal their food. A little deer outwits Anansi and the story has a happy ending (Garner, 2018).

Smell

From earliest times, smell was essential for survival. Types of smells include fruity, floral, spicy, burnt, resin-adhesives, and putrid. Even today, differences in smells could mean the difference between life, sickness, and death. The smell of food is essential to our health for detecting edible foods from ones that are poisonous or rotten, the smell of fire alerts us to a home or nearby forest fire, and the smell of gas alerts us to the danger of toxic fumes.

Due to pollen and weather changes, we can smell the air we breathe. Before asking students to smell flowers, pine needles, and leaves, check with the parents or guardians to make sure one or more of your students is not allergic to specific scents. Make sure pungent smells and smells from chemical compounds are used in well-ventilated spaces or outdoors.

Pleasant and unpleasant smells have a very strong impact on our memories. Most likely you remember the smell of a skunk. On a more pleasant note, you likely have strong memories of freshly mown grass, flowers, and simmering stews. Cooking smells, long remembered, can even make our mouths water! These memories, triggered by smells, usually come to mind unbidden without conscious effort and create pictures in our minds of nostalgic and current times.

Taste

Tastes range from sweet, sour, salty, and salty bitter. We have preferences for different types of taste and different tolerances to spicy foods, nuts, and dairy products. Check with parents and guardians to learn about children's food allergies before integrating the sense of taste into your lessons.

Each culture is known for its cuisine based on available food sources. In all cultures, food is an important part of celebrations. Including the sense of taste in content area lessons stimulates interest and helps students make connections between what they know and new learning on such topics as health, culture, plant and animal resources, farming, production, and distribution.

Multisensory Experiences

To give students first-hand sensory experiences, take them on listening or discovery walks designed to support learning for specific themes. Walks can be outside the school to listen or look for sounds of nature, weather conditions, and vehicles. Field trips to nearby streams and ponds, a local farm, or a local sporting event provide many different sensory experiences.

Before each walk or field trip, elicit background knowledge and teach content about what students will likely see and hear. For example, before a fifth-grade teacher in a critical-needs school in Los Angles, California, Rafe Esquith, took his students to a local baseball game, he spent days helping them learn the history and rules of baseball, how to score the game, and how to act in public places. He integrated movement by having his students practice playing baseball using the terminology for the names of each position and for scoring. Once at the game, the students were interested in following the game because they knew about the history, the players and their positions, and how to score the game. His students yelled and cheered, but the difference between random yelling and cheering by most students, and yelling and cheering to celebrate a good play was due to their knowledge of baseball (Esquith, 2003).

Conclusion

Multiple studies on the importance of sensory engagement show that there is a vast history of the positive effects the senses have on learning. Students' engagement with sensory materials and movement should be an integral part of lessons. Teachers should allow time for spontaneous exploration along with planned systematic exploration of multisensory materials and movements.

Though we divided the senses into individual categories, it is essential to remember that the senses work together in connected learning experiences. When students use touch and fine motor movements to construct a model of a robot, they should first see and read about examples of robots, view the materials they have for construction, and listen to stories about robots before they begin to explore and manipulate materials to use for their robot. Touch adds important information to construction as students feel the weight, texture, and plasticity of materials. Through movement, they can apply this information to trial-and-error attempts to build a robot that responds to their commands.

As teachers, you have opportunities to help your students make billions and trillions of neural connections that originate through the sensory organs: eyes, ears, nose, mouth, and skin. These connections add weight to the cerebral cortex. You have physically made your students' brains grow! It is easy to see why the connections made between the axon terminals and the dendrite receivers begin to look like a forest of networks. Next time you view trees, especially deciduous trees that have lost their leaves, notice the similarity in appearance between the tangle of branches of the trees, and the all-important connections between the axons and dendrites in your students' heads. It is striking!

References

Bartlett, F. (1967). *Remembering: A study in experimental and social psychology.* England: Cambridge University Press.

Dale, E. (1969). *Audiovisual methods in teaching (3rd ed.).* New York: Dryden Press.

Delgoshen, A. (2016). *How the brain compensates for sensory loss and points to its early evolutionary roots.* Hebrew University of Jerusalem. Accessed from https://medicalxpress.com/news/2016-01-brain-compensates-sensory-loss-early.html See Figure 1.7 for QR code.

Diamond, M. & Hopson, J. (1998). *Magic trees of the mind: How to nurture your child's intelligence, creativity, and healthy emotions from birth through adolescence.* New York: Penguin Putman, Inc.

Esquith, R. (2003). *There are no shortcuts.* New York: Anchor Books.

Garner, L. (2018). *Anansi the trickster spider (2nd ed.).* England: Mad Movement Media.

Grandin, T. (2013). *The autistic brain: Helping different kinds of minds succeed.* New York: Mariner Books.

Holmes, K., Holmes, S.V., & Watts, K. (2012). A descriptive study on the use of materials in vocabulary lessons. *Journal of Research in Childhood Education, 26* (2), 237–248.

Ishak, N. (2020). *The story behind "Lunch atop a skyscraper: The photo that inspired Great Depression era America."* https://allthatsinteresting.com/lunch-atop-a-skyscraper See Figure 1.8 for QR code.

Keller, H. (1996). *Helen Keller: The story of my life.* USA: Dancing Unicorn Books.

Kondo, M.A. & Hannan, A.J. (2019). Neurotechnology and brain stimulation in pediatric psychiatric and neurodevelopmental disorders. *Environmental stimulation modulating the pathophysiology of neurodevelopmental disorders* (pp. 31–54). Cambridge: Academic Press. Accessed from https://www.sciencedirect.com/science/article/pii/B9780128127773000039 See Figure 1.9 for QR code.

Moore, J.J. & Holmes, K.P. (2021). *The A in STEAM: Lesson plans and activities for integrating art.* New York and London: Routledge.

Newquist, H.P. (2004). *The great brain book: An inside look at the inside of your head.* New York: Scholastic Inc.

Palmer, H. (1998). Take me out to the ballgame and action fraction. From *Can a Jumbo Jet Sing the Alphabet?* Recorded by Hap Palmer on Hap-Paul Music CD.

Paper Clips Project (1998). Accessed from https://oneclipatatime.org/paper-clips-project/paper-clips-film/ See Figure 1.10 for QR code.

https://oneclipatatime.org/paper-clips-project/ See Figure 1.11 for QR code.

Piaget, J. (1950). *The psychology of intelligence.* In M. Piercy & D.E. Berlyne (Trans.). London and New York: Routledge.

Piaget, J. (1971). *Biology and knowledge: An essay on the relations between organic regulations and cognitive processes.* Chicago and London: The University of Chicago Press and Edinburgh University Press.

Pierson, M. (2021). Re: Sensorial education and the brain. Accessed from https://ageofmontessori.org/education-and-the-brain/ See Figure 1.12 for QR code.

Rosenblum, L.D. (2010). *See what I'm saying: The extraordinary powers of our five senses.* London: W.W. Norton & Company, Inc.

Rosenzweig, M.R., Bennett, E., & Diamond, M.C. (1972). Brain changes in response to experience. *Scientific American, 226,* 22–30.

Stiles, J. & Jernigan, T.L. (2010). The basics of brain development. *Springer Neuropsychology Review, 20* (4), 327–348. Accessed from https://www.ncbi.nlm.nih.gov/pmc/articles/PMC2989000/. See Figure 1.13 for QR code.

Wormeli, R. (2001). *Meet me in the middle: Becoming an accomplished middle-level teacher.* Portland: Stenhouse.

Chapter 2

Emotion and Serial Position Effects on Learning: Multisensory Sets and Closures

Introduction

What does a pile of leaves, a ticking alarm clock, and a skeleton have to do with this chapter? We will give you a hint: they all serve to capture students' attention at the beginning of a lesson. This is critically important because without attention, there can be no learning. As teachers, we are duty-bound to get and keep students' attention. We are in competition with just about every living thing that crosses our students' field of view in addition to multiple distractions that come from the home and within the classroom. To get students' attention, we remember saying things like, "Everyone's eyes on me." "I want you to listen!" You could go so far as to quote Shakespeare and say, "Friends, Romans Countrymen, lend me your ears." Or simply, "Pay attention!!!" If you want to know more about getting students' attention, you came to the right place! You are reading the right chapter if you want to learn how to capture attention by peaking students' interests at the start of the lesson and rekindling it at the end of your lesson.

In this chapter, you will read about the research that has spanned over 100 years on the topic of attention, interest, and memory. Most notably, you will read about Hermann Ebbinghaus's 1885 research on the serial effect on the presentation of information which he coined, the "Primacy-Recency Effect." You will also learn about von Restorff's research on the "isolation effect" that added novelty to the study of serial position.

Information from this chapter will help you get your lesson off to a strong start and close with a bang. This chapter focuses on sets and closures. You will find 20 teacher-tested activities to start your lesson and 10 activities to end it using methods and props that add drama and novelty that fit with your daily objectives. Of course, once you have students' attention, you have to do something to sustain it. A carefully planned lesson with multisensory materials suggested in Chapter 1 and ideas for sets and closures in this chapter provide many ways to involve students and keep their attention, once you have gotten it. Online references at the end of this chapter include QR codes.

The Wow Effect!

Neuroscientists and education psychologists, Immordino-Yang and Faeth (2010), studied the effects of emotions on learning and found that emotions, relevant to objectives, are an important part of learning and must be planned into academic lessons. They described the connection of emotions to learning as "a rudder that guides a ship" (p. 73).

Failure generates negative emotions; success generates positive emotions. Think back to times when you experienced both types of emotions and how they affected your attitude toward learning. To reduce inattention and negative feelings, Immordino-Yang and Faeth advise teachers to connect lessons to students' interests, prior experiences, and prior knowledge. Sets and closures can provide numerous opportunities for students to make connections between what they know and the new incoming information. Students are much more comfortable when they have something of their own to connect to new information. Novelty through multisensory sights and sounds can elicit emotions of curiosity and excitement. The opening and closing of lessons should have elements of novelty that lead to open-ended thinking and questioning about the upcoming lesson and recent learning.

Sousa (2003) divides the lesson time into "prime time" and "down time." These times are easy to picture on a slightly distorted uppercase letter U (Figure 2.1).

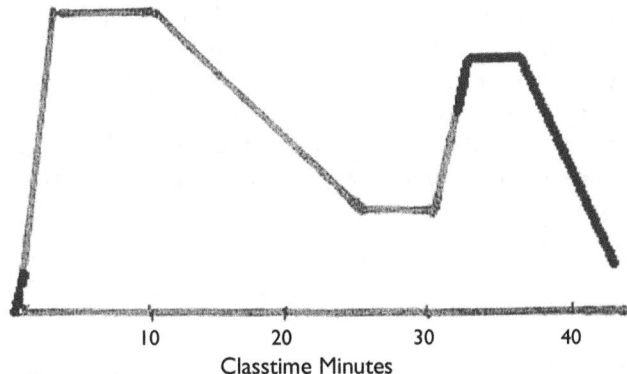

Figure 2.1 Serial Position Effects on Attention.

Students' attention and memory is greatest at the beginning of a lesson where they are at the top of the U, primed to learn. This prime time is the time to dig in and begin teaching. Delay collecting milk money and even taking attendance, as students' attention and learning begin to decline into "down time." Around the middle of the lesson, when attention and retention are sitting at the bottom of the U, take steps to increase interest through a well-planned closure. Though not as great as the initial prime time for learning, this upward sweep toward the top of the U is another prime time you don't want to miss!

Early Research on the Serial Effect on Learning

The inclusion of sets and closures in lessons is backed by a solid research base on attention and memory that dates back nearly 100 years ago from von Restorff (1933), Glanzer and Cunitz (1966), MacLeod (2008), and MacLeod (2020) built on Ebbinghaus's earlier 1885 work on students' memory of a list of words (Ebbinghaus, 1913). Researchers used lists of syllables and words to test whether the serial position, the way information was ordered in a list, had an effect on memory. Students were presented with a list of syllables or written words and asked to recall the ones they had read. They were able to remember more of the first and the last words on the list than the words in the middle.

However, Ebbinghaus and von Restorff found that not only is the placement of the content important for recall, but novel words at *any* place within the presentation of information attract attention and are most likely to be remembered. They found that a colored word, oddball word, and shocking word in any order on the list, stood out enough to be remembered. Words related to gross, scary things, and acceptable current vernacular can have shock value. Find the oddball word in this list of fruits: banana, apple, melon, blueberry, giraffe, grape, strawberry, cherry, pineapple.

Find the shocking word in this list of unrelated random words: ball, tree, cup, car, dog, puke, flower, dish, book, pencil, water, rock. Which ones do you remember?

Examples of Sets

Sets are brief, planned experiences designed to excite the students about the upcoming lesson. Within a set, teachers review prior learning and connect it to new learning as spelled out in the daily objectives. Use novelty to attract attention and involve students' emotions to foster learning and memory through an environment of unexpected pictures, displays, props, movement, music, and sound effects. Though sets are always used to begin a lesson, you can use these ideas to plan mini-sets when an interruption to your lesson occurs, or when you start a new topic within the lesson. Change the pace when students' attention begins to wane.

The following ideas are based on ones we gathered from Rick Wormeli, a middle school teacher and author (2001); Sammie Thorell, an elementary school librarian; K–6 preservice teachers; and elementary teachers we met in the classroom and at international, national, and local conferences. Many of these ideas set the stage for learning before the students even enter the classroom. Hopefully, these examples will inspire you to come up with your own way to use materials for sets.

The Classroom Environment

Greet students at the door wearing a funny hat, such as one that looks like a bat or the solar system, or a costume. Wear a colorful hat to signal read-aloud times. Hats and costumes can be purchased after the holidays at a discounted price, or made and decorated from bits and pieces of materials found in your own home.

Before a lesson on plants' life cycles and seasonal behaviors of deciduous trees, dump a pile of leaves in the doorway of your classroom, deep enough so students have to walk through them. Be sure to bring a garbage bag, broom, and large dustpan for cleanup.

Before having students build something, place a large display of different-sized pieces of wood in the doorway for them to step over as they enter the classroom.

Hang colored crepe paper streamers over the door to the classroom to create a water or rain forest effect.

Put a piece of yellow crime tape across the entrance to the classroom. Tell students to enter quietly so no one knows they are there. Relate the crime to your lesson.

Boxes and Bags

You can do a lot with boxes and bags to get students' attention. Be sure to put them in a prominent place. Ideas for boxes can be adapted for any content area theme. Many of the ideas for the use of boxes and bags came from Rick Wormeli (2005, 2001) and Sammie Thorell (2016).

Place a box with air holes on your desk with a small animal such as a frog or a turtle in it. Have the students listen for sounds from the box and make predictions about what is inside. Be sure to have a safe place to keep or release the animal once students have guessed what the subject of the lesson will be.

Place a picture, artifact, model, or toy that goes with the theme of the lesson in a large box or bag labeled "Warning! Open with extreme caution!" To build suspense, nestle the object in lots of wadded up newspaper or packing paper to make it difficult to find. Call on one student to open the box or bag and another student to reach in to find the item. You could make the sounds of a drum roll, or have the class do it until the student finds and holds up the mystery item.

To build suspense, display a large closed box with a ticking clock with the alarm set to go off at a specified time. Have students answer one or two questions related to the previous day's lessons before the clock goes off!

Carry a box filled with vocabulary words and matching definitions from your lesson. Have each word and definition written on separate index cards. Walk around the classroom saying, "I bet you don't know what I have in this box!" Pretend to trip and drop the box so the contents fall and scatter. Let students dash to pick up the contents before beginning your lesson. Have them work together to match the words with their definitions. You can also use non-breakable items that go with your unit, such as plastic dinosaurs. Have students separate them into herbivores and carnivores or match them to the time periods each one lived.

Fill a small box with non-breakable content related to the lesson, such as a stuffed animal and various types of rabbit food. Give the students a few hints about what is in the box to get them thinking. Have several students shake the box and guess what they will be learning that day.

Nest three pillow cases, one inside another. Put an object related to your theme in the bottom pillow case. Ask three students to find the object and solve the mystery of the subject of the day's lesson. The first two students will pull out empty pillow cases; the last student will find the object and show it to the class.

Sounds

Place dog toys that squeak at each student's place or in the middle of a table for students to squeak when they have a question or agree with what you are saying during the lesson. Let students get the "squeaks" out of their system before laying down the law on when and how to use them.

Have sounds of the ocean, birds chirping, or goats bleating (This one is fun!) as students enter the room. You can also use sounds of train whistles, thunder, cars honking, or bouncing balls. The sky's the limit. Just be sure to match the sounds to the unit or lesson.

Before an anatomy lesson on the heart, build suspense by reading from Edgar Allan Poe's *The Tell-Tale Heart*, 2015. Darken the room and play a recording of a loud heartbeat from Sound Bible, https://soundbible.com/tags-heartbeat.html, or have someone stand out of sight and make a steady beat on a drum to mimic a heart beating. See Figure 2.2 for a QR code.

Music

Have music about rabbits or other themes playing at a medium to high volume. For a rabbit theme, play songs such as *Little Bunny Foo Foo* or *Little Peter Rabbit* as students enter the room.

To combine fractions with music, have students march into the room to John Philip Sousa's marches using quarter notes and eighth notes to time their steps.

Have students enter the classroom or transition to your lesson to the pace of the music they hear in "Hungarian Rhapsody Number 2" by Franz Liszt. Music from this rhapsody has a variety of melodies and tempos heard in animated cartoons. Use this dramatic music to have students move like animals, clouds, and other lesson themes.

Play *What a Wonderful World*, sung by Louis Armstrong, as students enter the classroom before teaching about trees, flowers, skies, clouds, and rainbows.

Have George Gershwin's *Rhapsody in Blue* playing as students enter the room. The beautiful soaring jazz-like music can help students conjure up images of flying through clouds or over mountain ranges.

Examples of Closures

Closures are typically shorter than sets. They refocus students' attention on the skills and concepts taught during the lesson. This is the time to rekindle students' interests and help them make relevant emotional connections to what they learned. Closures must be carefully planned to meet these exalted goals in a short period of time.

From our own teaching experiences and observing student teachers, we found that it is very, very difficult to leave time for this important part of the lesson. Too often, we had to rush through the closure because we were running out of time. Trying to "wing it" by simply re-stating some high points of the lesson was not enough to attract and keep students' attention. Furthermore, we saw that older students learned that when the closure begins, they are about to leave, and get fidgety and lose interest in our final parting words and activities.

Here is what the students miss when the closure is rushed or skipped altogether. Students do not have the opportunity to organize or make sense of the information from the lesson and may leave with areas of confusion. Students do not have the opportunity to show you what they learned, what interested them, and parts they did not understand. This information is vital to help you prepare for the next day's lesson. So, our advice is to grit your teeth and leave at least five minutes before the lesson ends to engage your students in planned closing activities that would reinforce their learning and provide vital feedback for you.

The following activities are closure examples that can be adapted for your grade level and objectives. We hope they will inspire you to come up with even more.

In School

Have students share thoughts through speaking or writing in a journal about the most interesting or important thing they learned in the lesson. If you are in a self-contained classroom, have students leave their journals open so you can read what they thought was most interesting or most important.

Provide white boards and markers for students to write vocabulary or short answers to questions to hold up in class for the teacher to see. Our student teachers provided their students with individual white boards cut for them along with a drilled hole at the top from a local lumber store. They attached a sock with a dry-erase marker to the hole, giving their students the tools for writing and erasing their answers.

Use an exit slip for students to write the most important thing they learned or something they did not understand on a slip of paper shaped like a fish and drop it into a fishbowl on the way out of class. Or, have students write information on a sticky note and leave it on the door as they leave.

Similar to an exit slip, have a box labeled "Stump the Chump" or some other catchy title for students to write one question that they think will be difficult for their teacher to answer.

The teacher draws out as many as possible before the end of the class and tries to answer the questions.

To get an insight about what your students know, list three or more "I Can Statements" from your lesson, and have students write a checkmark next to the ones they know. Here is an example, "I can create a nutritious diet for a rabbit that contains at least three foods."

Give students a sticky note and have them write one key concept they learned from the lesson. Have them work in small groups to discuss and sequence their concepts in the order of importance and stick them on the wall. Ask students to walk around and read the sticky note sequences or, in the interest of time, call on a few volunteers to read what they posted. After the students leave, read the sticky notes to learn about the concepts they thought were most important and the way they sequenced them.

Give older students a paper with one or two words or key concepts you have written from the lesson, the more complex the better. Tell them they are to write a simple definition of the word or description of the content that a first grader can understand.

Give students a copy of a few key words or concepts from the lesson and ask them to draw or doodle pictures that represent them.

Out of School

Direct students to look for examples of the lesson's content as they walk or ride home. Examples could include information about plants, animals, weather, clouds, shadows, landforms, natural and structural designs, shapes, and patterns. Tell students they can share information about what they saw at the start of the next day's lesson.

Ask students to think of one thing from their lesson to share with their family or friends and share this information with the class the next day.

Ways to Collect Materials

Sammie Thorell (2016) spent her teaching career collecting artifacts to use as props related to the books she read to her students. She bought costumes and props after the holidays when they were on sale online and from large party and novelty stores. She has an extensive collection of hats, accessories, and props to go along with the theme of a book. For example, she wore a frog hat when reading *The Wide Mouth Frog* by Keith Faulkner and Jonathan Lambert (1996). She wore a cow costume, which began simply as a pair of boots and a scarf made from a piece of fabric with the colors and markings of a cow. She added to her cow costume over the years and wore it when she read the book, *Two Cool Cows* by Toby Speed and Berry Root (1997). She made many themed hats by attaching pictures, flowers, plants, and other decorations to an old hat. She was after, and achieved, the "wow effect" from her students.

Collecting materials for lessons easily can become a fun hobby. You can find free and inexpensive materials for your lessons from a number of sources. We contacted friends and asked whether they had any materials we could use in our classrooms. They sent a random assortment including a large box of animal pictures, children's books, and children's science magazines such as *Ranger Rick* that students could read or cut up to create a collage or illustrate their writing. Garage sales are a rich source of inexpensive materials for the classroom. The fun is in the hunt! You never know what you will find! Some antique shops sell collections of arrow heads and fossils, and the Internet has a variety of reasonably priced star and planet projectors, rock and mineral collections, and fossils. Local museums may have materials to loan teachers. Public libraries offer more than books, many have puppets and games that can be checked out. Moore put an easel with a wish list outside the door to her classroom and received many wonderful materials from parents, grandparents, and other family members as well as school staff including custodians, librarians, and cafeteria workers.

Ways to Store Materials

We observed ways K–6 teachers organized and stored materials they gathered for their lessons. One teacher stored sets of materials in suitcases with wheels. This was very handy for moving heavy loads, especially from classroom to classroom. Teachers stored materials for students in areas they could safely reach such as unused cubby holes, low shelves, and boxes on the floor or countertops, each labeled with the names of the materials. The most popular way we saw to store materials, when not in use, was to use stackable plastic storage containers labeled for each unit of study and stored on a top shelf.

Conclusion

All students enter the classroom with a host of good and bad emotions, yet they are expected to shed them once the lesson begins. Educators have said that disengaged students are one of their biggest challenges (Hunt & Holmes, 2018). We know without attention a well-planned lesson will fall flat on its face. Once students become interested and curious about learning, they will work harder to conquer the goals of the lessons you plan. Thanks to researchers such as Ebbinghaus and von Restorff that date back to the 1800s and early 1900s and current researchers who continued their work on attention, retention, and novelty, we now know that the peak times students are most engaged in learning are at the beginning and end of a lesson. From their studies, we know why we should start lessons with a flourish and how to end lessons with a review of key information and encouragement for students to look for evidence of what they learned outside the classroom.

First and foremost, the suggestions for sets and closures are meant to be connected to the daily objectives. Valuable classroom time taken up with a fun activity that does not prime or inform students on information from the lesson is time wasted.

The use of materials, sounds, and movements at any time during the lesson gives students opportunities to learn through multiple sensory pathways. Multisensory materials give students a variety of ways to explore, discover, and represent what they are learning before, during, and after a lesson.

We seek to understand our world through personal concrete experiences and materials afforded to us through our culture. One must look only to the plethora of metaphors that occur in everyday language to understand people's dependence on linking concrete objects to abstract ideas. For example, teachers must *bridge* the difference between the students' prior knowledge and new learning.

References

Ebbinghaus, H. (1913). *Memory: A contribution to experimental psychology.* New York: Teachers College, Columbia University.
Glanzer, M. & Cunitz, A.R. (1966). Two storage mechanisms in free recall. *Journal of Verbal Learning and Verbal Behavior, 5* (*4*), 351–360.
Hunt, A.B. & Holmes, K.P. (2018). Innovative sets and closures: Evidence-based ways to engage students. *Kappa Delta Pi Record, 54* (*3*), 116–121.

Immordino-Yang, M.H. & Faeth, M. (2010). The role of emotion and skilled intuition in learning. In D. A. Sousa (Ed.), *Mind, brain, and education: Neuroscience implications for the classroom* (pp. 66–81). Blooming: Solution Tree Press.

MacLeod, C.M. (2020). Zeigarnik and von Restorff: The memory effects and the stories behind them. *Memory and Cognition, 48,* 1073–1088. Accessed from 10.3758/s13421-020-01033-5 See Figure 2.3 for QR code.

MacLeod, S. (2008). Serial position effect. *Simply Psychology.* Accessed from https://www.simplypsychology.org/primacy-recency.html See Figure 2.4 for QR code.

Sound Bible: Heartbeat Sounds. Accessed from https://soundbible.com/tags-heartbeat.html See Figure 2.2 for QR code.

Sousa, D. (2003). Primacy/Recency Effect: Retention during a learning episode. Accessed from https://www.lancsngfl.ac.uk/secondary/math/download/file/How%20the%20Brain%20Learns%20by%20David%20Sousa.pdf See Figure 2.5 for QR code.

Thorell, S. (2016). Engaging students through excitement. Presented at the University of Mississippi, Oxford, MS.

von Restorff, H. (1933). Uber die wirtung von bereichsbildungen im spurenfeld. *Psychologische Forschung, 18(1)*, 299–342.

Wormeli, R. (2001). *Meet me in the middle: Becoming an accomplished middle-level teacher*. Portland: Stenhouse.

Wormeli, R. (2005). *Summarization in any subject: 50 techniques to improve student learning*. Portland: Stenhouse Publishers.

Children's Books

Faulkner, K. & Lambert, J. (1996). *The wide mouth frog*. USA: Dial Books

Poe, E.A. (2015). *The tell-tale heart (includes a beating heart)*. Philadelphia: Running Press.

Speed, T. & Root, B. (1997). *Two cool cows*. USA: Puffin.

Chapter 3

The Role of the Five Senses in Vocabulary Building

Introduction

Many teachers teach about photosynthesis and respiration. Read this passage and describe the process of photosynthesis to yourself based on the definition from Testbook.com (2018):

> ... a process that exclusively takes place in the chloroplasts through photosynthetic pigments such as chlorophyll a, chlorophyll b, carotene and xanthophyll. All green plants and a few other autotrophic organisms utilize photosynthesis to synthesize nutrients by using carbon dioxide, water and sunlight.

For most of us, the definition contains too many unknown words to read and understand, no matter how many times we read it. Think about your attitude as you were plowing through the definition of photosynthesis. To make sense of the passage, you would have had to look up and learn the terms that got in the way of comprehension before you could understand it well enough to describe to another person. We deliberately selected a passage we found difficult to understand to drive home the point that students who are asked to read about topics must first be taught the vocabulary.

Students in the 21st century need to "think like scientists" and "think like historians." (Hirsch, cited by Stroud, 2020). We have extended this list of thinkers to include technology, engineering, the arts, and mathematics. Students need to think like professionals in each of the STEAM subjects. Before students can think about a subject, they must be able to understand the words they hear and read.

Through this chapter, teachers will find a variety of ways to teach vocabulary through explicit instruction, informal instruction, and incidental encounters with words. We included commonly used activities with Latin and Greek prefixes, suffixes, and root words because they comprise over 60% of the words used in science and technology (Dictionary.com., 2015).

There are a total of 28 activities on ways to teach academic vocabulary for STEAM: Science, Technology, Engineering, Art, and Mathematics through each of the five senses of visual, auditory, tactile/kinesthetic, smell, and taste.

Essential Information About Vocabulary Instruction

Students learn about 3,000 new words each year. Of these 3,000 words, teachers should teach explicitly about 290–460 words per year, 9–12 words per week (Stahl & Nagy, 2006). Students learn the rest of the words through informal instruction and incidentally through print and speech. To promote independent word learning, students must learn to value words and their meanings.

DOI: 10.4324/9781003290889-5

The three levels of instruction for word learning serve important roles (National Reading Panel, 2000).

Formal: Selected words taught explicitly to students.
Informal: Embedded instruction by the teacher through emphasis as words occur in text and accompanied frequently by student engagement (e.g., repeating words)
Incidental: No planned instruction. Students learn through exposure to sophisticated words that occur most often through print and talk.

The teachers' goal is to flood students with specialized content-area words through well-planned sensory tasks. The words selected by the teacher and taught explicitly with modeling and guided practice are like big memorable waves. Words that are taught informally by the teacher are like the smaller waves that swirl around students. The hundreds and thousands of other words students learn in casual encounters throughout the lesson are like little waves lapping at their feet and are learned incidentally at some level through exposure.

Do not be afraid to include sophisticated words related to your lessons to students at any age. At a faculty meeting when Holmes was teaching 1st grade in a critical needs school, she asked for a copy of the vocabulary words given to the 5th grade teachers and promptly ran off a copy for each student in her class. Before she passed them out to the students, she explained that these were supposed to be for 5th-grade students only. Her students put them into their special folder, one they used after they completed their work. They were excited to study these sheets and learned words far beyond Holmes's expectations. The idea they were learning words that older students learned was a huge motivating and uplifting feeling for them.

Students must know definitions of words so well, they can recall them easily when reading, listening and speaking. Because students only learn a small number of words through formal instruction, they must learn how to use cues independently to help them determine the meaning of a word they see or hear. In addition to using context to help understand the meaning of words, students can be greatly aided by learning Greek and Latin prefixes, suffixes, and root words. This is time well spent because of their frequent use in science and technology.

Students in the United States do not speak with one voice; they come from homes where at least 1 of 350 languages are spoken (United States Census Bureau, 2015). Cognates are sets of words from two different languages that share similar meanings, spellings, and pronunciation. A large number of cognates in the English language share a common origin with Latin and the Romance languages of French, Spanish, and Italian. Many English and Spanish words are easy to identify by their root words such as correcto, distancia, básico. Learning cognates will help students who speak a language other than English assimilate into the classroom. Teachers can find lists of cognates for any language online and in a vast number of print sources.

Preparation for Vocabulary Instruction

Do not overload your students with too many unknown or little-known words in your first lesson. Instead, select two to three targeted words to teach through formal instruction. Start with what students know about a topic and use words they already know to teach academic words that deepen and extend their knowledge. Teach the definition of a root word so students can build on this definition when adding suffixes and prefixes. Even if you know the meaning of the words you plan to teach, look up their definitions. To understand why, try this experiment: Choose a vocabulary word you know from your lesson. Without looking it up, write a definition. Set your definition aside and look up the same word in a dictionary. After reading the definition from the dictionary, without peeking, rewrite the definition you wrote, and compare the two. In most instances, the definition you wrote after looking up the word up is more organized and thorough. Make sure you know the words deeply enough to create accurate and clear student-friendly definitions. Write your student-friendly definitions ahead of time. Tell, not read, them to the students.

Once new words are introduced to students, they should have multiple and varied exposures to them over time. The strategies that follow are far more effective than having students write the words and definitions five to ten times each.

Ways to Teach Vocabulary Through the Five Senses

We organized activities by the senses students would use with the full recognition that the five senses have a synergistic relationship with one another. When combined, each contributes to and enriches the meaning of vocabulary words.

Visual Experiences

Limitations on learning exist when students rely on text or oral instruction alone to infer the meaning of a word. However, when text is combined with visual materials that include pictures, maps, timelines, and concrete materials, students can put the information they are learning about a word into a larger more meaningful context.

Look It Up

Show students how to use age-appropriate glossaries and dictionaries to look up and review definitions to extend their knowledge of content area words. Look for ways students can use visuals such as charts, graphs, maps, concrete objects, and gestures to support word meaning.

View the Real World

Use real-world experiences inside and outside the classroom and gather real-world artifacts for students to examine and describe. Have students view and analyze the properties of their artifact such as color, size, patterns, and parts and describe them using newly learned vocabulary.

Make a Prediction

Show a picture related to the lesson and have students write words they think will apply to the lesson.

Break the Code

Have students examine printed words to identify letters, blends, and digraphs to help them unlock the meaning of words. Breaking the written code is an essential skill for reading and the pronunciation of words.

Build a Word

Teach the way a root word's meaning can be changed with the addition of prefixes and suffixes. Make cards with root words, prefixes, and suffixes large enough for students to see from the back of the classroom. Call for a volunteer to hold the card with the root word such as "meter." Pass out cards with prefixes /milli/, /kilo/, micro/, /peri/, and suffixes /ing/, /ed/, /s/, and /'s/.

One by one, have students stand next to the root word and hold up their card to change its meaning or part of speech.

Make Two Words Into One

Similar to the Build a Word Activity, students combine two words into one word and show its meaning through the use of real objects, fluids, or dramatic actions. For example, "cup" and "cake" when combined, can be shown with a real "cupcake." The words "water" and "fall," when combined into waterfall, can be shown by pouring water. Extend by having students create vocabulary cards and come up with the materials or dramatic actions they can use to show meaning.

Make a Book of Compound Words

Have students fold a piece of construction paper in half horizontally and make a cut down the top half and draw a Sun on the left flap and glasses on the other half. Have them write the compound word sunglasses on the uncut half of the paper, so when they lift each of the top flaps, they see both words combined into a single word. Repeat this activity using different compound words and have students join several compound words together with yarn to make a book.

Create a Table Display

Create a table display using concrete objects that represent a specific category. For example, use a ruler, yard stick, empty liter bottle, scale, and clock for the category of measurement. Have students name the category they think the words belong to. Once students are familiar with common characteristics related to measurement (length, volume, and weight) have them create their own categories and seek objects that fit them.

Auditory Experiences

Sound can be used through oral instruction and discussion for initial and deep learning. The auditory sense provides pleasurable, even captivating, input through a variety of sounds that includes speech tones and music. Sounds can be playful when used in rhymes and songs and instructive when alerting students to changes in the environment. Students benefit from listening to their own voice when reading aloud or rehearsing facts.

Listen for the Word

Break up long passages from books or other written material to read to children. Select two to three words to teach before reading the passages. Emphasize the words while reading and review them after reading. Have students raise their hands when they hear the word during the lesson.

Identify an Onomatopoeia

Have students listen for words that sounds like their meaning such as "bang," "slurp," and "choo-choo" when reading or describing passages related to the lesson. Animal sounds such as "meow," "cluck- cluck- cluck," and "hee-haw" are common examples of onomatopoeia in the popular children's song, *Old McDonald*.

Enjoy the Drama

Use prosody: pitch, stress, speed, and rhythm of speech when instructing or reading passages from a book. Information read aloud is greatly enhanced when the reader uses highly expressive speech while reading and emphasizing vocabulary. Have students use prosody when using vocabulary from the lesson.

Wake Up the Daydreamers

Find words that can be used as sound effects, such as the "pitter-patter" of rain," the sonic "boom" of an airplane flying faster than the speed of sound, or the "growl" of a wild animal. When reading or speaking, be DRAMATIC! You are bound to attract the attention of any daydreamers! Find and practice using sounds, including onomatopoeia, when telling or reading information to your students. Have students think of related words and create sound effects for them.

Listen to the Sound

For a lesson on identifying smaller sounds from things with mechanical parts such as switches, dials, push buttons, keys on a computer, and a handheld or an electric pencil sharpener, have students label the object and use their vocabulary to describe the sounds they hear when moved or hit. Sounds from various musical instruments or opening and closing doors and drawers all help students to listen critically to sounds.

Share Your Words

Pair students who are English language learners with students who are English speakers. Have them find objects related to the lesson with similar root words (cognates) such as the English "big" and the Spanish "grande" and the English "plant" and the Spanish "planta." Have pairs of students share the objects they found that are pronounced or mean almost the same in both languages.

Make Your Own Tongue Twisters

Using words in tongue twisters is a way to provide a unique review of words students learned. First read and have students say a couple of easy tongue twisters and then have them create their own using two or more words from the lesson. Say some of the examples from Fry, Kress, and Fountoukidis (2000, p. 405) to get started:

- A regal rural ruler
- Six sharp smart sharks
- A noisy noise annoys an oyster

Tactile-Kinesthetic Experiences

Touch and movement give students a different way to learn and use words about the physical attributes of concepts, objects, and animals. Students can show their learning through descriptive vocabulary, gestures, hand, arm, and body movements.

Explore by Touch

Connect vocabulary to concrete objects and living things to provide additional information to specific words related to a theme. Ask students to describe the way an animal feels, such as a rabbit's fur. Have students explore an object through touch by feeling its weight, texture, size, and moveable parts.

Act Like a Rabbit

Have students pretend they are hopping like a rabbit, mimicking the way rabbits chew by moving their jaws up to 150 times a minute. Movement adds yet another layer of meaning to words students can use to explain their movements. Students can also describe the force it takes for animals to move.

Chase Your Shadow

Have students chase their shadows and use their vocabulary to describe why their shadows change as they move.

Name That Artifact

Bring in real-world artifacts and have students touch and explore their characteristics without looking and try to name what it is. Remind them to use related vocabulary when talking to others.

Act Out!

Choose a word from the lesson and prepare questions to ask students to act out the meaning of the word. For the word "vicious" say, "Show what you would do if you encountered something vicious." Have them use synonyms such as "cruel" and "merciless" for vicious when they describe their actions. Repeat by having students act out an antonym for vicious, such as "benevolent" and "giving."

Describe the Attributes

For words that can be represented by real materials or their representations, bring in a set of materials for groups of four students. For example, if the targeted word is "plastic," bring in a set of different types of plastic items for students to explore, analyze, and describe their attributes.

Play Word Basketball

Display the two targeted words so everyone can see them. Give each student two sheets of paper and have them write one word on each sheet. Then have them wad up the paper into a ball. Place a laundry basket, box, or trashcan in the middle of the room and have the students "shoot the ball" into the "basket" and say the name of the word. Balls that miss the basket will be "rebounded" by the students. They first have to read the word and gave a definition before shooting the ball toward the basket. After each ball is thrown, repeat the word and its meaning. Continue rebounding until you run out of time or the students' interest wanes (adapted from Guillaume (2012)).

Toss the Ball at the Word Wall

Create a word wall of words from a STEAM content area you are teaching. Except for proper nouns, write all words in lower case letters. Have the students throw the ball at a word on the word wall and define the word they hit. A variation is to tape the names of the words on a ball. Toss the ball to the students and have them read a word that is under one of their thumbs. After reading, they toss the ball to another student, who must come up with a definition or sentence using the word.

Smell Experiences

Be sure to check for allergies before choosing aromas to use in your classroom.

Because learning is dependent on memory, use smell, whenever possible, to accompany your lessons. Smells, good and bad, can trigger a flood of memories that help students remember facts about past experiences.

Identify the Cotton Ball Smell

Have students use their vocabulary to describe smells as metallic, chemical, pungent, earthy, fruity, sour, nasty, and pleasant. Saturate cotton balls with different types of smells for students to test.

Connect Two Smells (Adapted From Graves (2009))

Write words that describe scents in two columns. Have students determine a relationship between the two words and use them in a sentence. Do this orally, though students can write their sentences before sharing them.

Column 1	Column 2
pungent	earthy
metallic	chemical
fruity	citrus
nasty	pleasant

Go on a Smell Walk

Take your students for a smell scavenger walk inside or outside the school. When inside, make sure you go past the cafeteria. A good time to detect smells outside is before a storm or when plants are in bloom. Areas with a lot of pine trees give off a pleasant aroma. Alert students to use the vocabulary they learned or are learning in their descriptions of what they smelled.

Describe That Smell

Make a chart for each student, or a small group of students, labeled with eight types of smells: metallic, chemical, pungent, earthy, fruity, sour, nasty, and pleasant. Have students list the things they smelled on their walk or from the cotton ball activity and identify each type of smell. Have them write as many adjectives as they can to describe each of the types of smell.

Smell the Food You Eat

Arrange some common foods and have students do a smell blind-test of each one to identify the types of smells they detect for each of the foods.

Taste Experiences

Be sure to check for allergies before asking students to taste foods.

Students all have specific likes and dislikes when it comes to food. The following activities will help them go beyond the typical vocabulary they use, such as "yucky" and "icky," and use the vocabulary you want to emphasize in your lessons.

Use Your Words

Ask students to explore the taste of a food such as an orange and a piece of candy. They can describe the tastes of foods and liquids as bitter, sour, sweet, salty, savory, or pleasant. Have them use their vocabulary to explain why they chose certain words to describe the foods they tasted.

Use Your Tongue

Give each student, or a small group of students, a bag with grapes, lemon slices, pretzels, and candy. Also give them a stiff sheet of paper labeled with each type of taste (bitter, sour, sweet, and salty). Have students taste each food and match the food to a specific taste. Students can also categorize food types as putrid and savory. The goal is to have them experience taste differences and use vocabulary in their oral, and written descriptions. If your lesson is on anatomy, have students identify the sense organ (tongue) and the placement of the taste receptors on the different parts of the tongue.

Taste the Food You Should Eat

You probably thought of this, but we have to say it anyway. Do not use the foods from your smelling activity. Provide fresh, un-sniffed food for students' taste test! Relate the tasting activities to nutrition and make sure students use vocabulary from the lesson as they discuss what they liked and what they did not like. Make sure they explain their preferences.

Act It Out

Vocabulary charades (Marzano & Pickering, 2005, p. 57) is an excellent way to engage students through discussion and movement while learning and reviewing critical words. Plan words related to taste that can be accompanied by actions and have students act out their meanings. One student is the actor and the only one who knows the word. The rest of the class tries to guess the word by watching the actor's actions. Another approach is to organize students into teams. One person at a time is the actor and chooses a word from a bag. The team must guess the meaning.

Conclusion

Without attention, there is no learning. Without knowledge of words, there is no comprehension. Attention to word meaning, enriched by the knowledge of Greek and Latin root words, is essential to learning. Arming students with the knowledge of important words before they engage in a learning experience is not only necessary, but it will make it possible for them to make important discoveries and engage in meaningful explorations of concepts and ideas. Without the frustration of dealing with incomprehensible words, students are free to learn and develop their curiosity about what they are learning. Curiosity is a strong driving force that sustains students' attention and propels them toward deeper learning.

There are a large number of cognates in the English language that share a common origin with Latin and the romance languages of French, Spanish, and Italian. The use of cognates helps students learning another language begin with familiar words. Cognates also give these students an opportunity to teach their language to their classmates and their teacher.

References

Dictionary.com (2015). Accessed from https://duckduckgo.com/?q=Dictionary.com&t=chromentp&ia=web See Figure 3.1 for QR code.

Fry, E.B., Kress. J.E., & Fountoukidis, D.L. (2000). *The reading teacher's book of lists.* Paramus: Prentice Hall.
Graves, M.F. (2009). *Teaching individual words: One size does not fit all.* New York: Teachers College Press.
Guillaume, A.M. (2012). *K-12 classroom teaching: A primer for new professionals.* Boston, MA: Pierson.
Marzano, R.J. & Pickering, D.J. (2005). *Building academic vocabulary: Teacher's manual.* Alexandria: ASCD.
National Reading Panel (U.S.) & National Institute of Child Health and Human Development (U.S.). (2000). *Report of the National Reading Panel: Teaching children to read: An evidence-based assessment of the scientific research literature on reading and its implications for reading instruction.* U.S. Department of Health and Human Services, Public Health Service, National Institutes of Health, National Institute of Child Health and Human Development. Accessed from https://www.nichd.nih.gov/publications/product/247. See Figure 3.2 for QR code.

Stahl, S.A. & Nagy, W.E. (2006). *Teaching word meanings*. Mahwah: Lawrence Erlbaum Associates.
Stroud, G.L. (2020). Hirsch: Making education great again? Accessed from https://kentuckyschooltalk.org/2020/09/hirsch-making-education-great-again. See Figure 3.3 for QR code.

Testbook.com (2018). *Which of the following helps photosynthesis?* Accessed from https://testbook.com/question-answer/which-of-the-following-helps-in-photosynthesis–6172df7a64aee7ef6ccd8f39. See Figure 3.4 for QR code.

United States Census Bureau (2015). *Census Bureau reports at least 350 languages spoken in U.S. homes.* Accessed from https://www.census.gov/newsroom/archives/2015-pr/cb15-185.html. See Figure 3.5 for QR code.

Chapter 4

Thematic Planning for Teaching and Learning through the Senses

Introduction

The thematic units plans in Part II of this book integrate each of the five STEAM content areas, Science, Technology, Engineering, Art, and Mathematics with a common theme. Themes used in Chapters 5–9 come from ones popular in K–6 classrooms we observed: Rabbits and Hares, Water Cycle, Nutrition and Health, Landforms, and Astronomy and Seasons. You will find nine steps for writing unit plans along with descriptions and explanations of their purpose with an emphasis on sensory materials-based learning. You may be surprised to learn that writing objectives is not the first step in writing a unit plan that leads to rigorous, rather than surface level learning. First, you must become an expert on the content you plan to teach. The Online References at the end of each unit plan in Chapters 5–9 contain a collection of national and state standards as well as visual and written information to use as you write your plans. Online references are accompanied by a QR code for easier access.

Together, teachers can select a theme and choose and share the content and standards their students should meet. This helps to write cohesive plans that tie together the concepts, facts, and skills for each content area involved. Through a themed plan, teachers can teach students basic skills and concepts within each theme and help them understand how they fit together into a larger more meaningful context. Students who dislike learning in one content area, may learn to like it when combined with content areas more interesting to them. The song, "A Spoonful of Sugar Helps the Medicine Go Down," from the *Sound of Music* is a good message for combining students' least favorite content areas with ones they like.

The broad themes we chose for our unit plans can be taught using different multisensory approaches to teach related concepts within each theme. For example, for "Astronomy and Seasons," we selected the Earth's tilted axis and its effect on the seasons. Teachers can engage students in movement and drama by having them walk around a center point (the Sun) while tilting their bodies about 23° and maintaining their heads to point in the same direction to demonstrate the effect on seasons in both hemispheres. Teachers can also have students feel the current seasonal weather and illustrate the position of the Earth's tilt on the hemisphere where they live.

The following example of thematic planning for a life-science biology theme on "Cows," comes from two teachers in Batesville, Mississippi, where they combined direct instruction and authentic learning experiences. One teacher taught language arts and one taught science in a school that backed up to a fenced field where cows grazed. This provided a real-world opportunity for an integrated learning experience between science and language arts.

The science teacher prepared to take her class outside to view the cows. She explained that the students were to observe the cows, write notes on what they observed, and give their notes to students in the language arts class to use to write an essay on cows. The students brainstormed

DOI: 10.4324/9781003290889-6

important facts they could gather about cows such as size, appearance, anatomy, movement, and eating habits. They were encouraged to draw illustrations to go along with their notes.

The students in the English class were to write an informational essay on cows using the information provided by the science students. The more information they received from the science students, the more detailed they could be when writing their essay. The English teacher based the writing assignment on the content and standards he wanted his students to learn.

The Importance of Sensory Materials on Cognitive Development: An Historical Overview

The use of sensory materials and their effect on cognitive development and learning is not new. Tables 4.1 and 4.2 show how two highly respected developmental psychologists, Jean Piaget (1896–1980) and Jerome Bruner (1915–2016), organized the stages of cognitive development around children's interactions with concrete materials. These stages inform and remind parents and teachers of the universal process children go through on their way to independent thinking. It is critically important to understand that the stages of development are not always age-dependent and varies among children.

Piaget observed children's cognitive trajectories and organized them by age, actions, and levels of thinking. Piaget's statement, "It is not possible to arrive at "concrete" operations without undergoing some sensorimotor preparation." (1971, p. 18) emphasizes the importance of providing sensorimotor opportunities at the more advanced levels of cognitive development.

Table 4.1 Piaget's 1971 Four Stages of Cognitive Development

Stage	Age	Reflexes, Actions, and Thinking
Sensorimotor	Birth–24 months	Rapid development through random reflexive and groping movements progress to sensory induced deliberate movements leading to goal setting and schema formation.
Pre-operative	2–7 years	Continued development through symbolic and pretend play. Learn and use oral speech sounds and words and identify written letters and words. Engage in pre-logical thinking that leads to intuitive thought, questioning, and reasoning through sensory experiences.
Concrete-Operations	7–11 years	Beginnings of logical thought and questioning based on direct sensory interactions such as the ability to understand that area and volume stay the same when formed into different shapes. These are the times that perceptual and motor schema growth accelerate through language, imagery, and actions with objects that include manipulation, organization, classification, comparison, deconstruction, and reconstruction.
Propositional Formal Operations	11 and up	Advanced, sophisticated, and hypothetical thought independent of concrete referents. Understands abstract terms such as obligation, freedom, morality, and love. High interest facilitates abstract thinking. Students and adults are on a trajectory to engage in operations involving multiple parts, reasoning, engaging in substantive discussions, and forming hypotheses.

Bruner's Discovery Learning Model categorized materials and tasks according to children's levels of sensory learning. Bruner found that students of all ages benefit by going through each of the three stages as they build learning from their previous experiences. These experiences ultimately lead to their ability to test hypotheses, engage in critical observations, make predictions, make judgments, and form conclusions.

Table 4.2 Bruner's 1966 Three Modes of Knowledge Representation

Enactive (actions)	Iconic (images)	Symbolic (words/symbols)
Ages 0–1	Ages 1–6	Ages 7 and up
Learning occurs through action and motor tasks that include tactile and visual hands-on exploration and manipulation as well as hearing, smell, and touch.	Learning is introduced and remembered through the observation of visual images. Begins to learn and remember symbolic symbols for mathematics and language.	The learning and use of oral and written symbols: numerals, letters, words necessary for language and continued knowledge formation

Holmes's (2011) HELP Hierarchy, inspired by the work of Piaget and Bruner, lists the types of materials that enable sensory learning that are available to today's teachers. HELP is intended to help teachers imagine and incorporate as many senses as possible into the lessons they plan. Rather than being organized by age-related development, this hierarchy lists six levels of materials that can be used in lessons beginning with the most authentic materials. The more authentic the materials, the more insights students gain about the topic being studied. Real-world materials, real-world artifacts, and their representations can boost students' recall of meaningful experiences and prior knowledge from their lives that teachers can connect to new skills and concepts. See Table 4.3.

Table 4.3 HELP: Hierarchy for Effective Lesson Planning

Real-World Experiences	Found inside and outside the classroom: patterns, shapes, structures, landforms, living things, weight, touch, smell, taste, weather, night sky, gravitational and applied forces
Real World Artifacts	Items removed from their natural environment and brought into the classroom: rocks, soil, plants, and classroom pets
Representations	Synthetic representations of artifacts found in the real world: three-dimensional figures, models, and toys
Visuals	Two-dimensional images of the real-world: photos, paintings, drawings, video clips, and smartboards
Written	Communication and reception of information from print and digital sources: books, handouts, posters, magazines, spreadsheets, graphs, presentation software, and social media
Oral and Aural	Auditory communication and reception: read aloud books, digital sources, eBooks, audio books, lectures, discussion questions, songs, music, nature, and animal sounds

To use the HELP hierarchy to determine possible materials to use in a lesson, look first to real-world materials, and, if not feasible, then look to representations of the real world, and move down the hierarchy for the best possible fit for the objective. Students can be involved in learning through multiple senses in a single lesson. The visual and auditory senses activated in most lessons pair well with one or more of the other senses of tactile/kinesthetic, smell, and taste. Digital sources that involve sight and sound expand learning beyond the classroom. Use the hierarchy to choose the highest level of materials for your lesson that involves students in as many relevant multisensory experiences as possible.

Engaging students with real-world learning does not have to take an inordinate amount of time. A walk outside to feel the effects of weather, view clouds, and experiment with shadows are just a few examples of the potential learning experiences that await your students just steps outside the classroom. Opportunities for learning can occur inside the school and the classroom. Take your students on a trip down the hall to walk along parallel lines on floor tiles or push toy cars along the parallel lines to see whether they will ever collide. These experiences serve to focus students' attention at any age on the critical attributes of materials that lead to more abstract concept formation and learning through exploration, inquiry, experimentation, and discovery.

National and State Standards

It is important to consult national and state standards for each STEAM content area to guide you as you write your unit plans. They are the road map that shows what students should learn and be able to do at each grade level. The following is a description of the standards on STEAM subjects and their websites that we found inordinately helpful.

Science

The Next Generation Science Standards (NGSS) address science and engineering topics of life, forces, energy, Earth and space, weather, and structural properties of matter. These standards are based on the NGSS Cross Cutting core ideas and practices that can be taught in kindergarten and built upon through grade 12. Cross Cutting concepts include Structure and Function, Patterns, Similarity and Diversity, Cause and Effect, Systems and System Models, Stability and Change, Scale, Proportion and Quantity, and Energy and Matter. They facilitate connections among the branches of science and provide a common vocabulary for teachers and students to understand and use.

NGSS, https://www.nextgenscience.org/ See Figure 4.1 for QR code.

The Next Generation Science Newsletter (2022) is an exciting find! Through the newsletter, you can download monthly newsletters and find information and links to current peer-reviewed information on science teaching.

NGSS, https://www.nextgenscience.org/news/january-2022-ngss-now-newsletter See Figure 4.2 for QR code.

Science and Engineering Practices

NGSS-Next Generation Science Standards, NSTA-National Science Teaching Association, and the MDE-Mississippi Department of Education recognize the close relationship of science and engineering. The branches of engineering addressed in the unit plans in this book are Mechanical, Chemical, Electrical, Civil, and Geological. Each branch has specialized information that can be introduced to young students and developed throughout higher grades. NSTA includes cross-cutting concepts such as Planning and Carrying Out Investigations and Performance Expectations that require students to use a systematic approach as they work.

The Mississippi Department of Education Instructional Planning Guides for science provide a variety of research and standards-based units. Links to guides are for kindergarten through grade 8 and biology and chemistry. The guides have sections on themed units of study based on the Mississippi College-and-Career Readiness Standards. Unit plans include conceptual connections, real-world connections and phenomena, embedded science and engineering practice, cross-cutting concepts, and core vocabulary.

All three organizations clearly outline content and procedures for grades K–12 and emphasize beginning the instruction of basic skills for science, mathematics, and engineering in kindergarten. As students advance, they engage in engineering practices such as planning, sketching, or drawing preliminary ideas for design, and comparing two or more designs for similarities, differences, strengths, and weaknesses. At this level, students should carry out investigations and be able to analyze and interpret data using their knowledge of science and mathematics to explain the problems and strengths of their design.

NGSS, Next Generation Science Standards
https://ngss.nsta.org/CrosscuttingConceptsFull.aspx See Figure 4.3 for QR code.

NGSS, Next Generation Science and Engineering Standards, (2017) https://www.nextgenscience.org/ See Figure 4.1 for QR code.

NGSS, Next Generation Science Standards: Engineering Design (2003–2022) https://study.com/academy/lesson/engineering-education-national-state-standards.html See Figure 4.4 for QR code.

NSTA, National Science Teaching Association. Science and Engineering Practices (2014) https://ngss.nsta.org/PracticesFull.aspx See Figure 4.5 for QR code.

NSTA, National Science Teaching Association Position Statements (2022) https://www.nsta.org/nstas-official-positions See Figure 4.6 for QR code.

Thematic Planning for Teaching and Learning through the Senses   47

MDE, Mississippi Department of Education Instructional Planning Guides for Science K–8
https://www.mdek12.org/secondaryeducation/science/Instructional-Planning-Guides-for-Science-K-12 See Figure 4.7 for QR code.

Technology

The ISTE standards focus on ways to involve students with access to technology to seek knowledge and communicate their ideas. Goals are written for educators, students, and education leaders. These standards, directed at different audiences, yet important to all, focus on competencies to help students be successful in a digital world. The competencies listed for all three audiences are directed at helping students set and meet learning and communication goals through self-motivated trial and error. In today's digital world, learning about just any topic is at the students' fingertips. With a world increasingly wired for communication, the standards focus on the use of digital tools in a purposeful, meaningful, ethical, and safe way. Communication through imagery, animation, sounds, and oral and written language enables students to go beyond reading a written report to the class. With the help of the ISTE Standards, teachers can plan ways to open up a whole new world for students to communicate knowledge and ideas effectively through multiple venues.

ISTE, The International Society for Technology in Education (2017)
https://www.iste.org/standards/iste-standards-for-students See Figure 4.8 for QR code.

Art

From Archimedes and Gutenberg to Mozart: science, technology, engineering, and mathematics, all share dispositions, skills, and knowledge used in the arts. Prevalent in every culture, the arts, including dance and movement, media, theater and drama, and visual arts, heighten learning through the dispositions of hard work, practice, experimentation, creativity, and an awareness and appreciation of aesthetics and beauty. Artistic literacy focuses on the knowledge of concepts and skills students need to play an instrument, sing, dance, act, draw, paint, perform, and use technology to augment traditional art forms. The National Core Art Standards (NCAS) has four Anchor Standards: Creating, Performing, Responding, and Connecting. Through these standards students begin to develop ideas for their work, organize their ideas, and analyze the meaning they want to convey before they complete their work. Before presenting their work, students should further analyze and make more refinements with a focus on the message they want to convey. Before students present their work, they would benefit by comparing it to similar works where artists used the same techniques to carry the same or similar message. This gives them an opportunity to emphasize events that contributed to their work such as prior experiences, history, or culture.

NCAS, National Core Art Standards (2015)
https://www.nationalartsstandards.org/ See Figure 4.9 for QR code.

The MDE, Mississippi Department of Education College-and-Career Readiness Arts Learning Standards focus on the five arts, dance, media arts, music, theater, and visual arts. The standards are based on the NCAS conceptual framework of Creating, Performing, Responding, and Connecting. The primary focus of the Mississippi arts curriculum is to provide a universal way for all students to communicate.

MDE, https://mdek12.org/ESE/Arts See Figure 4.10 for QR code.

Mathematics

A synthesis of the National Council of Teachers of Mathematics (NCTM) and the Common Core State Standards for Mathematics (CCSS) shows a focus on rigorous learning goals for students in grades K–6. Though they emphasize slightly different learning outcomes, the, Content Standards for the CCSS and NCTM share common goals.

CCSS Content Standards	NCTM Content Standards
Counting and Cardinality	Number and Operations
Operations and Algebraic Thinking	Algebra
Number Operations in Base Ten	Geometry
Measurement and Data	Measurement
Geometry	Data Analysis and Probability

The Process Standards list what students should know and be able to do as they advance through the grades. The emphasis given to each of these standards varies across grade levels. The CCSS Standards, though more detailed, overlap to a degree with the NCTM Standards.

CCSS Process Standards	NCTM Process Standards
Make sense of problems and persevere in solving them.	Problem Solving
Reason abstractly and quantitatively.	Reasoning and Proof
Construct viable arguments and critique the reasoning of others.	Communications
Model with mathematics.	Connections
Use appropriate tools strategically.	Representations
Attend to precision.	
Look for and make use of structure.	
Look for and express regularity in repeated reasoning.	

NCTM, National Council of Teachers of Mathematics
https://www.nctm.org/standards/ See Figure 4.11 for QR code.

CCSS, Common Core State Standards for Mathematics
http://www.corestandards.org/wp-content/uploads/Math_Standards1.pdf See Figure 4.12 for QR code.

The Mississippi Instructional Planning Guides provide numerous resources and clear guidelines based on national standards for K–12 mathematics. They include recommendations for high-quality instructional materials, instruction and planning, and assessment in addition to standards-based professional development resources for each grade level. The Planning guides include the use of technology for mathematics learning such as Applets, Demos, Interactives, Virtual Manipulatives, Real World Application, and Vocabulary.

MDE, Mississippi Department of Education Instructional Planning Guides for Mathematics K–12 https://www.mdek12.org/secondaryeducation/mathematics/Instructional-Planning-Guides-for-Mathematics-K-12. See Figure 4.13 for QR code.

The Mississippi Scaffolding Documents for English Language Arts and Mathematics, are organized into three strands to aid teacher planning for student mastery of the standards. They include what students should know, levels of conceptual understanding, and what students should be able to learn based on informal and formal assessment.

MDE, Mississippi Department of Education Mathematics Scaffolding Document https://www.mdek12.org/sites/default/files/Offices/Secondary%20Ed/ELA/ccr/Math/04.Grade-4-Math-Scaffolding-Doc.pdf. See Figure 4.14 for QR code.

Nine-Step Thematic Unit Plans for STEAM Learning

Sensory experiences within the plans afford students multiple pathways for concept learning and vocabulary development related to STEAM.

Become an Expert

Thoroughly know the content you plan to teach. Just as you seek top experts for medical or financial advice, you must strive to be the expert on the content of the lessons you plan and teach to your students. Your students deserve a top expert teacher! Consult multiple print and online sources for information on your theme. The deep knowledge you acquire about the subjects you teach will have a serious impact on the way you plan, teach, diagnose and predict problems, and assess learning.

Essential Questions

Now that you are an expert on content, you know a tremendous number of concepts and facts you want your students to learn. You are faced with too many facts and too little time. What is an expert to do? At this point in your planning, consult the standards and choose the concepts and skills you think are most important to teach within or across the STEAM subjects. From your wealth of knowledge, determine the essential questions you want students to consider, grapple with, and even stew about, as they use information from the lesson to form their answers. Essential questions are big open-ended questions that should form the framework of your unit and used in daily lessons. They cause your students to think deeply about what they have learned and investigate further to seek information for their answers. Be sure to have students justify or explain their answers.

An example of an essential question for teachers is, "How does becoming an expert on content impact lesson planning?" When carefully written, essential questions should inspire curiosity that leads to a purpose for learning. When fully engaged, students will come up with high- and low-level questions of their own that lead to further investigation and learning (Wiggins & McTighe (2013)). Display essential questions along with your list of objectives to jump-start students' thinking. They may even stop students from asking the age-old question, "Why do we have to learn this?"

Objectives

Objectives spell out what you want students to learn and be able to do. Think of objectives as destinations. Some objectives can take days or even weeks for students to get to their destination. Select objectives that will help students answer the essential questions you have posed to them. Categorize the objectives and then choose two or three to teach each day.

It is just a matter of months that separate young students in pre-K four-year-old programs and students in kindergarten. As you write your objectives for your kindergarten students, make sure you emphasize and involve these young students in the fundamental skills that predict later learning in STEAM. Simply to say, "This will help you read." or "This is important." is not enough. Plan objectives that set the stage for further academic achievement.

Your selection of objectives, and procedures must match the physical, social, and mental levels of your students. You must have a strong purpose for the objectives you plan, not just something fun for students to do. In her book on differentiated instruction, Carol Ann Tomlinson (1999, p. 37) wrote about "hazy lessons," lessons without a clear understanding of what students will learn. She gave an example of a 3rd-grade class working on an objective to build a covered wagon. When asked about what students were learning, the teacher said that building the wagon would help them understand western expansion. However, Tomlinson found little evidence that the isolated time-consuming activity of building a covered wagon gave the students a clear and thorough understanding of the westward expansion of the United States.

Think about all the other things students could have learned if building the covered wagon was connected to STEAM content. The teacher could have become an expert on Westward Expansion and planned lessons that connected the building of the covered wagon to clearly planned science, technology, engineering, art, and mathematics objectives. Students who received surface-level instruction on covered wagons had fun, but lost out on so many important learning opportunities.

Vocabulary

Choose words that will help students understand what they read and hear. Nothing stops comprehension faster than a passage with unknown words. Select the words to teach to your students and make sure they have lots of exposure to them through print and speech. Plan two to three words to teach each day and have students use the new words in discussions and conversations. See Chapter 3 for numerous ways to teach vocabulary.

Materials and Resources

Now comes the fun part! With learning objectives in mind, consider relevant real-world resources and other sensory materials to use as aids to learning. Gathering materials for sensory learning does take time, but they are invaluable teaching and learning resources. Often the materials you seek are available inside and outside your home and school and within the community. In our experience, friends, family, and peers were eager to donate materials they no longer need to a worthy purpose. Imagine the materials you could collect when working with other teachers! Garage sales are another source of materials made fun by not knowing what treasures you will find for your classroom!

Today, there are many different sources of instructional materials online and in print. You can find standards and information on the theme and content you are teaching, supplemental visuals, songs, and music to include in your lessons. Local libraries are also a rich source of print and supplemental materials. Keep in mind that the more authentic the materials, the more information and insights students can gain about the topic. Use the HELP Hierarchy for examples of different levels of materials to consider. Give yourself time to gather them and to preview online resources. Look for updated and additional information and current research-based ways to be the best teacher you can be for your students.

Set, Procedures, Closure

Set

In your set, plan ways to capture students' interests and relate new learning to their prior experiences and prior learning. Go over the daily objectives and essential questions to give them a heads-up about the upcoming lesson. Though not every set can be a production, seek ways to make the beginning of your lesson as dramatic as possible with teaser statements, displays, sound effects, and lighting. Consider using, and even wearing, props such as funny hats as you greet students. This is a time you can excite and engage your students!

Procedures

Objectives point to the destination. Procedures describe how to get there. Choose procedures to introduce and reinforce new and learned vocabulary and involve as many of the five senses in your lesson as feasible. Determine whether you want to begin with hands-on exploration and discovery followed by fact finding through reading and direct instruction, or whether you want to begin with the presentation of facts through reading and direct instruction before students explore learning through sensory materials. Use teachable moments that arise that can add interest to your lesson. Adjust your procedures to accommodate them, or use these moments in subsequent lessons. Your goals are for students to acquire a deep knowledge of the facts as expressed in your objectives and an enthusiasm to learn more.

If you have a live animal in the classroom, be sure to communicate specific guidelines on the safe way to approach, touch, and handle it. Our observations of the use of animals in the classroom led us to identify the following procedural pitfalls to avoid:

- Standing in front of the class and holding up a classroom pet or object and describe its features. It is the teacher who gains from the sensory experiences, not the students.
- Giving one student an object or cage with a classroom pet and telling the student to pass it on to the next student without explaining what to look for.
- Placing the classroom pet or object on a table and having the class gather around to see it without telling them what they are looking for. We found that the bolder students crowded in front while other students took a quick peek or touch before returning to their seats.

There should be a difference between procedures written for kindergarten-age students and those written for older students in grades 1–6. The tendency today is to replace play-based activities in pre-K and kindergarten classrooms with mostly academic tasks. Students in kindergarten used to learn behavior, socialization, and basic STEAM content through hands-on interactive activities. Once upon a time, kindergarten classrooms had multiple centers for students to use their imaginations, explore, discover, and learn as they interact with others. We witnessed the kindergarten classroom environment change from a social learning-centered based program to an academic program where students sat at tables and frequently worked on skills independently with few or no manipulatives. Gone are the block centers where students can think like an artist, a scientist, a civil engineer, and a mathematician. Block centers provide opportunities for students to reason as they explore cause and effect and use equation-style thinking to make things equal. Learning and the dispositions of problem solving and perseverance are developed through kitchen, water play, dress-up, and content-area centers, just to name a few. These experiences are especially important for young students when everything is new to them. They are in the early stages of building schema, background knowledge acquired through action upon which to hook new learning. Young students must have a world to explore!

Gray (2015) reported on two notable control-based experimental studies sought to determine whether young students benefited most from early academic instruction versus play-based instruction during their early formative years. A 1970s German study of 100 kindergarten students divided equally between play-based and academic instruction found that students enrolled in play-based programs fared far better on all measures of academic achievement through 4th grade than those who did not. As a result, the German government scrapped the development of an academic kindergarten curriculum in favor of a play-based curriculum.

In 2009, Durkin et al. at the University of Vanderbilt in Tennessee, USA conducted a study of 2,990 low-income students who did and did not attend preschool to measure achievement and behavioral advances through grade six. This study replicated the findings from the earlier German study. The early introduction of academic instruction actually harmed students' later academic performance and behavior. Both the Vanderbilt and German studies indicate that pre-K children are too young to understand the meaning behind what they are trying to learn and therefore have no idea of its importance or how it is applied. For example, if they learn an algorithm for addition, the procedure may have little or no meaning to them. Throughout their preschool and kindergarten years, young children are not ready for structured activities that they cannot relate to their immediate tasks. They need to engage in activities, stories, and songs that actively engage them in the concept of addition. The Vanderbilt study is somewhat controversial, but only because of the surprising results that should affect governments' plans for universal preschools. This study was robust because of the large sample size (2,990) and randomized selection of participants.

The results from both studies align with Piaget's theories of child development where he found that mental and physical development through actions on the environment must occur before a child can learn complex tasks (1950, 1971).

Closure

Closure is a brief part that ends the lesson. Be sure to save time for a closure! You do not want to rush or ignore this important learning time. The closure should contain a review of the objectives and critical information and experiences taught through the lesson. It can also be a time when students seek to answer an essential question. Other parts to the closure are to use informative or teasing statements about the upcoming lesson and have students look for examples of what they learned once they leave school. See examples for sets and closures in Chapter 2.

Formative and Summative Assessment

Formative assessment provides vital information to teachers and students on how well they are meeting the objectives and applying and connecting new learning to previously learned material.

Summative assessment shows teachers and students the degree of learning that took place related to the objective, and how close students came to their destination or final goal.

To plan formative and summative assessments, first check learning objectives to focus on the concepts and skills students were to learn. Keep in mind, the learning objectives in unit plans may take days or weeks to teach, so the assessment must match students' strengths and weaknesses for daily objectives.

Use formative assessment during a lesson to assess current levels of students' attention, interest, and learning. Checks on current learning help you know when to speed up or slow down, reteach, provide interventions, and when to move to the next level.

Plan ways for students to show off their learning. If-Only statements such as "If only I can fly like a bird, I would_____." are a good way to measure students' critical thinking, vocabulary, and learning.

I-Can Statements are formative assessments that ask students to check off what they know and are able to do from a lesson. They empower students to reflect on their learning and mark their progress. Teachers can also use I-Can Statements through individual discussions. One teacher said, that I-Can-Statements provided a time students could talk to her and express their opinions about their learning. The neat thing about I-Can Statements is that students focus on the positive, what they *can* do. Choose just a few key concepts, vocabulary, or skills and use them in terms students understand. For struggling students make sure they can check at least one box about something they can do. Leave time at the end of the lesson for students to mark their I-Can Statements. We found that when left to the very last minute, our students hastily checked off the forms without having an opportunity to process and determine what they learned. Here is an example of an I-Can-Statement: ___ "I can plan ways to include concrete materials in my lessons."

Summative assessment measures the sum total of what students have learned at any point in the lesson through oral and written tests and performance on projects or tasks. After all your planning, hard work, and gathering sensory materials, how well could your students show what they know and how long did the learning last?

Extend Learning

Though meant for highly interested and advanced students, there are ways to extend learning for all students. Look for ways to capitalize on students' interests and academic strengths by not only including their ideas and questions in your lessons, but by offering multisensory ways for them to explore and advance their learning. Students may be interested in and excel in one subject and need help with others. The inclusion of sensory materials gives students fresh learning experiences that can help them understand and use skills and concepts in different ways. Be sure to provide materials and print and online resources for students to research and find interesting facts that advance their learning beyond the scope of the lesson.

Sensory Checklist

Please note that the terms *tactile/kinesthetic*, as listed on the checklist, are frequently combined by most sources. Tactile is the sense of touch students experience through the sensory organ of their skin. Touch is accompanied by movement when students use manipulatives, explore materials, and build or dismantle models or simple machines. Kinesthetics often involves tactile, visual, and auditory senses. It offers a powerful way to teach students through their coordination of muscles, bones, and joints to emulate or demonstrate key concepts and emotions sometimes accompanied by music.

After you have planned your lessons, consider the senses your students will use and mark them on a checklist. Certainly, not all lessons have to involve all five senses, but by marking the sensory chart you may see areas where you could involve your students in a higher level of sensory learning. See Table 4.4.

Table 4.4 Sensory Chart for Lesson Plans

Vision	Audio	Tactile/Kinesthetic	Smell	Taste

Conclusion

You will find online standards for each of the STEAM subjects with an amazing array of content to use in your planning. Research-based information on the use of materials for the K-6 curriculum, science, technology, engineering, art, and mathematics projects is shown in the online references. QR codes for easy access to online references with URL website addresses can help readers quickly identify the ones they want to use.

Sensory information affords students multiple pathways through their five senses for learning. The materials-based, action-based sensory approach to planning a themed unit provides seemingly limitless opportunities for students to experience STEAM learning from a wide variety of perspectives.

To write a themed lesson, become an expert on the content, determine objectives for learning, and use sensory materials. These three early steps to writing themed unit and lesson plans should help you avoid having to answer students' question, "Why do I have to know this?"

Themed learning helps students experience content in multiple ways giving them a more rounded and deeper insight into the information and skills they are learning. Avoid empty lessons that do not have a strong learning purpose, such as an isolated activity of building a covered wagon. Make sure you pack lots of learning into the units and lessons based on planned objectives.

References

Bruner, J.S. (1966). *Toward a theory of instruction*. Cambridge MA: Belknap Press.

Common Core State Standards for Mathematics Practice and Content (CCSS, 2011). Accessed from http://www.corestandards.org/wp-content/uploads/Math_Standards1.pdf. See Figure 4.12.

Durkin, K., Lipsey, M.W., Farran, D.C., &. Wiesen, S.E. (2022). Effects of a statewide pre-kindergarten program on children's achievement and behavior through sixth grade. Accessed from https://pubmed.ncbi.nlm.nih.gov/35007113/. See Figure 4.15.

Gray, P. (2015). Early academic training produces long-term harm: Research reveals potential risks of academic preschools and kindergartens. Facebook. Accessed from https://www.psychologytoday.com/us/blog/freedom-learn/201505/early-academic-training-produces-long-term-harm. See Figure 4.16.

Holmes, K.P. & Holmes, S.V. (2011). Hierarchy for effective lesson planning: A guide to differentiating instruction through material selection. *International Journal of Humanities and Social Science*, *1* (19), 144–151.

International Society for Technology in Education (ISTE, 2016). Accessed from https://www.iste.org/standards/iste-standards-for-students. See Figure 4.8.

Mississippi Department of Education College-and-Career Readiness Arts Learning Standards. Accessed from https://mdek12.org/ESE/Arts. See Figure 4.10.

Mississippi Department of Education Instructional Planning Guides for Science K-8. Accessed from https://www.mdek12.org/secondaryeducation/science/Instructional-Planning-Guides-for-Science-K-12. See Figure 4.7.

Mississippi Department of Education Instructional Planning Guides for Mathematics K-12. Accessed from https://www.mdek12.org/secondaryeducation/mathematics/Instructional-Planning-Guides-for-Mathematics-K-12. See Figure 4.13.

Mississippi Department of Education Mathematics Scaffolding Document Accessed from https://www.mdek12.org/sites/default/files/Offices/Secondary%20Ed/ELA/ccr/Math/04.Grade-4-Math-Scaffolding-Doc.pdf. See Figure 4.14.

National Core Art Standards (2015). National Coalition for Core Arts Standards. Accessed from https://www.nationalartsstandards.org/. See Figure 4.9.

NCTM, National Council of Teachers of Mathematics. Accessed from https://www.nctm.org/standards/. See Figure 4.11.

National Council of Teachers of Mathematics (NCTM, n.d.). Executive summary: Principles and standards for school mathematics. Accessed from https://www.nctm.org/uploadedFiles/Standards_and_Positions/PSSM_ExecutiveSummary.pdf. See Figure 4.17.

NSTA, National Science Teaching Association Position Statements (2022). Accessed from https://www.nsta.org/nstas-official-positions. See Figure 4.6.

NSTA, National Science Teaching Association. Science and Engineering Practices (2014). Accessed from https://ngss.nsta.org/PracticesFull.aspx. See Figure 4.5.

NGSS, Next Generation Science Standards. Accessed from https://ngss.nsta.org/CrosscuttingConceptsFull.aspx. See Figure 4.3.

NGSS, Next Generation Science and Engineering Standards. Accessed from https://www.nextgenscience.org/. See Figure 4.1.

NGSS, Next Generation Science Standards: Engineering Design (2003–2022). Accessed from https://study.com/academy/lesson/engineering-education-national-state-standards.html See Figure 4.4.

The Next Generation Science Newsletter (2022). Accessed from https://www.nextgenscience.org/news/january-2022-ngss-now-newsletter. See Figure 4.2.

Piaget, J. (1950). *The psychology of intelligence.* In M. Piercy & D.E. Berlyne (Trans.). London: Routledge.

Piaget, J. (1971). *Biology and knowledge.* Chicago, IL and Edinburgh, Scotland: The University of Chicago and The University of Edinburgh.

Tomlinson, C.A. (1999). *The differentiated classroom: Responding to the needs of all learners* (p. 37). Alexandria, VA: ASCD.

Wiggins, G. & McTighe, J. (2013). *Essential questions: Opening doors to student understanding.* Alexandria, VA: ASCD.

Part II

Planning Sensory-Rich STEAM Unit Plans

Chapters 5–10
Themed Unit Plans for STEAM Content for Students K–6 Including a Message for Teachers

Chapter 5

Rabbits and Hares

Introduction

The line from the nursery rhyme, "Little Bunny Foo Foo hopping through the forest scooping up the field mice and bopping them on the head," contains serious errors in academic content about rabbits. What are they? Your students will learn what they are through the five STEAM Unit Plans: Science, Technology, Engineering, Art, and Mathematics all focused on the theme of Rabbits and Hares. In addition to the science of diet and nutrition, potential and kinetic energy, and Newton's laws of motion, students will learn technology for finding and representing data, engineering practices for planning, designing, and creating models, ways to engage students in art through music and dramatic movements and realistic gestures of rabbits' and hares' behaviors, and estimation and measurement through mathematics using the English and metric systems. STEAM subjects contain nine steps for unit planning: Become an Expert, Essential Questions, Objectives, Vocabulary, Materials and Resources, Set, Procedures, Closure, Formative and Summative Assessment, Extend Learning, and a Sensory Checklist. Online References contain QR codes that can be optically used to access the websites at the end of each unit plan.

Science Unit Plan > Biology and Physics

Adapt learning for your grade level and the needs of your students and break it down for multiple daily lessons.

Become an Expert

Learn more than you will ever teach about anatomical differences between rabbits and hares, potential and kinetic energy, applied and gravitational force, and Newton's 1st law of motion.

Essential Questions

Determine one to two essential questions for daily lessons to provide a framework for learning, such as:
How could rabbits and hares escape their predators if one leg was injured?
What happens if the force of gravity were to be doubled between two objects?

DOI: 10.4324/9781003290889-8

Objectives

Select or adapt one to three objectives for your daily lesson plans.
Students will learn to:

Contrast physical differences of rabbits' and hares' leg and foot structure.
Compare critical leg positions of rabbits and hares at rest to their leg positions as they apply force to hop.
Determine differences between applied and gravitational force.
Experience the effects of applied and gravitational force.
Determine whether differences in applied force affect the gravitational pull of objects to Earth.
Explore how gravity acts on the speed and direction on the movement of objects.
Relate the effects of gravitational force to the weight of a rabbit and hare.
Relate the mass of the object to the length of time for it to fall to the ground.
Compare the gravitational pull of objects that fall to the Earth from high and low distances.
Compare the length of time it takes for objects of obviously different weights to hit the ground.
Analyze why the effect of gravity is the same on light and heavy objects.
Demonstrate potential and kinetic energy expressed in Newton's 1st law of motion.
Apply potential and kinetic energy to everyday push and pull movements.
Relate potential and kinetic energy to rabbits and hares before and during their hop.
Investigate how stored potential energy changes into kinetic energy aided by gravitational force.

Vocabulary

Choose two to three words to teach in daily lessons. See Chapter 3 for ways to teach vocabulary.

anatomy	femur
physiology	applied force
bone structure	gravitational force
leg joints	Newton's 1st law of motion
muscles	momentum
tendons	vertical and horizontal distance
tibia	potential energy
fibula	kinetic energy

Materials and Resources

Use the HELP hierarchy in Chapter 4 for lists of multisensory materials.

Real-World Experiences

Different weight balls (ping pong, basketball)
Chalk
Computer
Heavy objects
Pendulum
Scale
Slinky

Rabbits and Hares 65

Real-World Artifacts

Caged live rabbit and hare

Representations

Figures
Toys

Visuals

See Online References at the end of this unit plan.

Pictures showing physical differences between a rabbit and a hare, see Figures 5.1 and 5.2.

Figure 5.1 Rabbit Profile.

Figure 5.2 Hare Profile.

Written

See Online References at the end of this unit plan.
PowerPoint
Force, mass, and acceleration
Rabbits, Rabbits, and More Rabbits by Gail Gibbons, ages 4–8
Everything You Should Know About: Rabbits by Anne Richards, ages 5–6
Rabbits and Hares by Dr. Richard A. NeSmith, all ages
The Effects of Force and Energy on Simple Machines by Baby Professor, all ages
Motion: Push and Pull, Fast and Slow by Darlene Ruth Stille, ages 4–10

Set, Procedures, Closure

Read Chapter 2 for multiple ways to plan multisensory sets and closures.

Sample Set

Post a sign telling students to enter the room by hopping directly to their seats. When students arrive at their seats, ask them why some got to their seats before others. Have them describe the effort (force) they put into hopping and the distance they had to travel. Tell them that they will explore the ways force and momentum affects the speed and distance of the movement of rabbits and hares.

Procedures

Plan a variety of instructional strategies that include direct teaching, modeling, guided and independent practice, and inquiry. Include critical thinking, questioning, and investigation.

Match procedures to daily objectives.

View the video *Arctic Hares* (see Online References) and discuss differences between the leg and foot structure of a human and a hare.

Pair students. Have one student hop like a rabbit or hare as slowly as possible and the other observe the student's foot and leg movement. Ask them what movements they made while hopping.

Have students hop with three different levels of applied force (strong, medium, weak) and discuss how the different levels affected speed, distance, and height.

Show a video of a rabbit and hare hopping (see Online References). Pause or slow the video for students to analyze critical leg positions during movement, and qualitatively estimate the amount of force rabbits and hares appeared to apply before their hop.

Have students simulate the force and speed rabbits and hares use to hop for survival, during play, and quietly grazing on grass. Have them use related vocabulary to describe how rabbits and hares changed their force to affect the speed and length of their hops.

Newton's 1st law of motion states that an object at rest remains at rest unless acted upon by an external force. Furthermore, an object in motion also remains in motion with the same speed and direction until acted upon by an external force. Provide varied experiences on the use of force kicking a ball, running, throwing a paper airplane, using a slinky. See Figure 5.3.

Figure 5.3 Newton's 1st Law of Motion Applied to Kicking a Soccer Ball.

To experience the effects of force on distance, have students stand away from an outside wall at different distances and kick a ball toward the wall using varying levels of force. Have students explain what they saw and felt at each distance.

Ask student to define *gravity*. Emphasize that gravity is the force that holds people, animals, and all objects including dust and air on the Earth. The larger the mass of the objects, the larger the gravitational force between them. A scientific definition to teach interested and older students is, "Gravity is proportional to the product of the masses of the object."

Discuss how gravity causes rabbits and hares to land on the ground no matter how far or high they hop. Emphasize that the gravitational force is measured by the weight of their bodies.

Ask students what the strength of the gravitational force would be if it were pulling on a six-pound rabbit or an eight-pound hare.

To demonstrate magnitude of gravitational force, use a kitchen scale to weigh objects. Drop each object and ask students what caused it to fall and have them tell you the magnitude of the gravitational force that caused each item to drop to the floor. Remind students that the gravitational force on each object is equivalent to the weight of the object.

Give students a light and heavy ball. Have them stand in front of the wall holding one ball in each hand at the same height. Ask which ball will hit the ground first. Signal students when to drop the ball and have the class observe when each ball hits the ground. Repeat and have students listen for the sounds of the balls hitting the ground to determine whether they hit at the same time.

Place a slinky at the top of the stairs.

Ask students to explain the potential energy that exists within the slinky before an applied force converts it to kinetic energy. Ask them what force kept the slinky moving downward and what force caused it to cause it to stop. Apply inertia and kinetic energy to a pendulum. See Figure 5.4.

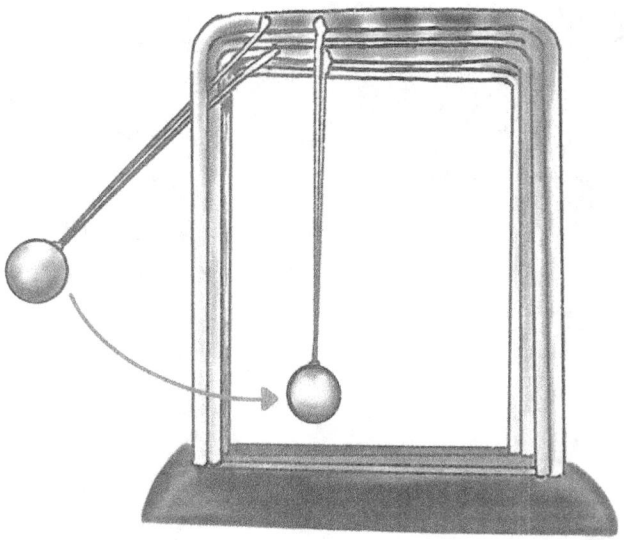

Figure 5.4 Potential and Kinetic Energy in a Pendulum.

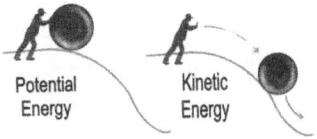

Figure 5.5 Potential and Kinetic Energy.

Ask the students to describe how the potential energy of a ball on a hill is converted to kinetic energy when pushed down the hill. See Figure 5.5.

Have students discuss experiences with the effect of force on potential and kinetic energy such as riding a bicycle, kicking a ball, and riding in a car wearing a seatbelt. Ask them to think of other ways to apply force to objects such as the push and pull movements to push a large object, open and close a drawer, and casting a line with a fishing pole. See Figure 5.6.

Figure 5.6 Force to Produce Kinetic Energy.

Sample Closure

Ask students when they used different forces during the day. Here are some examples to get them thinking: picking up a light or heavy object, running, sharpening a pencil. Have them act out examples of potential energy, inertia, and kinetic energy. Give students the opportunity to briefly review ways gravitational force affected them in just the last hour. Have students demonstrate different ways force is used to their families and friends.

Formative and Summative Assessment

Formative Examples

LET STUDENTS SHOW OFF THEIR LEARNING

Have students act out the way different forces affect the movement of rabbits and hares.

IF-ONLY STATEMENTS

If only I could hop as fast as a rabbit or hare, I would _____.
If only I could become famous and write a law about energy, I would_____.

I-CAN STATEMENTS

_____I can show how potential energy is stored and what kinetic energy looks like.
_____I can explain the types of force rabbits use to hop.

Summative Examples

Projects, oral and written tests

Extend Learning

Explain how gravity transfers kinetic and potential energy on the downward and upward swing of a pendulum.
Experiment with different ways to demonstrate force and motion using Newton's 1st and 2nd laws of motion.

Sensory Checklist

Check the senses students use during your lesson.
See Sensory Chart for Unit Plans, Table 4.4 and downloadable online

Online References

Caution: Select videos carefully. Many were on the mating habits of rabbits and hares and predators catching and eating them.

What Is a Force? See Figure 5.7.
https://www.dkfindout.com/us/science/forces-and-motion/what-is-force/

Forces and Motion. See Figure 5.8.
https://www.dkfindout.com/us/science/forces-and-motion/

Dozens upon Dozens of Pictures of Rabbits and Hares. See Figure 5.9.
https://duckduckgo.com/?q=pictures+of+rabbits+and+hares&iax=images&ia=images&iai=https%3A%2F%2Fwritingexplained.org%2Fwp-content%2Fuploads%2Fhare-vs-rabbit.jpeg

These Are 10 Most Fascinating Facts about Rabbits (4:42). See Figure 5.10.
https://www.youtube.com/watch?v=0Fv4t-28APY

Arctic Hares, (3:20). See Figure 5.11.
https://www.youtube.com/watch?v=hfkS0AzGbXI

Rabbits Body Language: Meaning Behind 15 Strangest Rabbit Behaviors/Rabbit Jaw Dropping Facts (10:16). See Figure 5.12.
https://www.youtube.com/watch?v=dzKY-ZXgwFI

Wild Hare Sprinting and Hopping (0:53). See Figure 5.13.
https://duckduckgo.com/?q=Wild+hare+sprinting+and+jumping+Youtube&iax=videos&ia=videos&iai=https%3A%2F%2Fwww.youtube.com%2Fwatch%3Fv%3Dc7Idvr7BpCE

Cute Rabbits Eating (8:36). See Figure 5.14.
https://www.youtube.com/watch?v=zlg8QmkHPy0

Force, Mass, and Acceleration. See Figure 5.15.
https://www.ducksters.com/science/physics/force.php

Technology Unit Plan > Keywords, Searches, Graphs, and Spreadsheets

Adapt learning for your grade level and needs of your students and break it down for multiple daily lessons.

Become an Expert

Learn more than you will ever teach about searching for information on differences between rabbits and hares on a computer and representing, analyzing, and interpreting data from graphs and spreadsheets.

Essential Questions

Determine one to two essential questions for daily lessons to provide a framework for learning, such as:

How can you determine whether a particular site contains accurate information?
What are the best ways to represent the information on differences between rabbits and hares?

Objectives

Use or adapt one to three objectives for your daily lesson plans.
Students will learn to:

Define the terms *lagomorph* and *species.*
Analyze reasons rabbits and hares are classified in the order of mammals as lagomorphs but are not the same species.
Identify differences in physiological characteristics between rabbits and hares.
Explain why the classification of rabbits and hares is different.
Determine keywords to use in online searches for specific information on the survival and differences in size and weight of rabbits and hares.
Compare and contrast helpful and unhelpful keywords.
Differentiate quality of online sources based on relevance to the search, accuracy, and thoroughness.
Create online tables to organize information on rabbits and hares using rows and columns.
Identify four major characteristics of rabbits and hares to display on a table.
Use tokens to represent information on a graph.
Explain how graphs present patterns of data.
Select the ways rabbits and hares differ that can be represented on a graph numerically, such as ear and leg size or weight.
Define *horizontal* and *vertical axes.*
Experiment with ways to represent numerical information visually on a graph.
Explore ways to use an online spreadsheet such as Excel.
Experiment using steps to create a variety of computer-generated graphs (charts).
Select a chart format and follow instructions to create an online chart using information from computer searches.
Demonstrate the different presentations of data by organizing information on a table and graph.
Distinguish differences between information presented on a table to information presented on a graph.
Compare differences between representing information on a table and graph.
Recognize that both tables and graphs enable readers to observe and analyze data.
Recognize formatting differences between information organized on a table and information charted on a graph.

Vocabulary

Choose two to three words to teach in daily lessons.

lagomorph	spreadsheet
species	cluster and bar graph
physiology	line graph
keywords	horizontal axis
format	vertical axis
column	represent information
database table	data analysis
graph/chart	interpret data

Materials and Resources

Use the HELP hierarchy in Chapter 4 for lists of multisensory materials.

Real-World Experiences

Computer
Bar graph
Tokens
Microsoft Excel Program

Representations

Replicas of tables
Replicas of graphs

Visuals

See Online References at the end of this unit plan.
Pictures of lagomorphs, rabbits, and hares
Board or chart paper
Copy of a 4 × 4 graph with 2-inch/5.08-centimeter squares

Written

Keyword examples
Welcome to the World of Rabbits by Diane Swanson, ages 4–7
Rabbits and Hares by Dr. Richard NeSmith, all ages

Tiger Math: Learning to Graph from a Baby Tiger by Ann Whitehead Nagda and Cincy Bickel, ages 7–10

The Great Graph Contest by Loreen Leedy, ages 5–8

Oral and Aural

Modeling
Explanations
Discussions
Questions

Set, Procedures, Closure

Read Chapter 2 for multiple ways to plan multisensory sets and closures.

Sample Set

List a large number of words on the board related to the physiological differences of leg, body length, and weight of rabbits and hares. Include random unrelated words and phrases in the list. For example: habitat, grasshoppers, food, weight, similarities and differences, cars, hopping force, garage, leg structure, gravity, survival, and myths. Tell students there are many ways to find specific information if they determine sets of essential keywords to use in their search. Ask them to identify possible keywords from the list they can use to find facts on physical differences, hopping, and survival. Tell students there are hundreds of websites on rabbits and hares. Today, they will learn ways to find websites that are most likely to contain the information they need, organize it in a table, and graph it on a spreadsheet.

Procedures

Plan a variety of instructional strategies that includes direct teaching, modeling, guided and independent practice, and inquiry. Include critical thinking, questioning, and investigation.

Match procedures to objectives.

Show pictures of rabbits and hares and ask whether they are the same animals with different names or are they different species with different characteristics? Emphasize they are in the order of lagomorphs, plant-eating mammals with powerful hind legs, fur, stubby tails, and long ears, but are not in the same species.

Ask students to determine which keywords they could use to distinguish the similarities and differences between rabbits and hares. List keywords on the board and have the students identify the ones that would be most and least helpful in their search for information and tell why.

Ask students to think of other words they can use in their search on the physiological differences between rabbits and hares and add them to the list. Cross out unhelpful words. Show images of rabbits and hares and have students name differences they see. See Figures 5.16 and 5.17.

76 Planning Sensory-Rich STEAM Unit Plans

Figure 5.16 Rabbit Profile.

Figure 5.17 Hare Profile.

Inform students that not all sites contain the information they need and that some websites require a subscription and cannot be used. Monitor students carefully as they search different sites!

Relate sifting through information on a computer site to sifting through information in books to find what they need.

As students open sites using different keywords or word combinations, ask them to identify helpful sources.

Show students how to create online tables to organize important information about the differences among rabbits and hares that they found online. To begin the process of developing online tables, first have students draw them on paper to determine the number of rows and columns they need, along with headings.

Ask students to develop an online table with rows and columns using the commands "Insert" followed by "Tables." Have them enter information using numbers, pictures, or tally marks in each column for a visual display of data.

Have students compare information from a table and a graph to note differences in the presentation of data. Model how to transfer information from a table to a graph.

Ask the students to state which of the following animals is their favorite: rabbits, hares, turtles, or snakes. Or, alternatively, ask the students to provide their own list of animals. Count the students' choices and write the numbers on the board. This data can be put onto a graph.

Give students a copy of a 4 × 4 graph with each square being 2 inches (5.08 centimeters) and 16 tokens. See Figure 5.18.

Figure 5.18 4 × 4 Graph with Two-Inch Squares.

Let them have a minute to handle the tokens and explore placing them on the graph. Show and explain the horizontal and vertical axes and have students use the terms as they manipulate their tokens along each axis. Emphasize that they will be comparing two different sets of information: the names of the animals and the numbers of students who favor each animal. Put the names on the horizontal axis and the numbers vertically above the names. Use tokens to indicate the numbers. That is, if rabbits are the favorite animal of seven students, put seven tokens on the column marked "rabbits." You may have to create a scale for the vertical axis, starting at zero and increasing to the maximum.

Ask the students to look up how much rabbits and hares weigh. Record the answers. Ask the students to find what other animals similar to the size of rabbits and hares weigh, and record the answers. Be careful to use only adult male weights or adult female weights since they can differ by sex. Record the answers.

After students name four or five species of animals of similar sizes to rabbits and hares, tell them they are going to make it easy to determine visually which animals are larger and which are smaller by graphing the species by weight.

Open an Excel workbook page. Enter the data at any convenient location on the spreadsheet. Enter the species under one column and the weights under an adjacent column. Any labeled column will do. Then darken the cells.

On the Toolbar, click "Insert." Then press "Recommended Charts". For these purposes, "charts" refer to the same thing as graphs. Investigate the "Charts" that are recommended. The students can experiment with the various kinds of charts. To get a full list of the kinds of charts available, press "All Charts" in the box that pops up after pressing "Recommended Charts". There the students will see numerous types of charts, including column, line, bar, pie, box, and so forth. There is an example for each kind of chart.

Although the students can choose any of the charts, ask which makes sense in this specific case to display the weights of multiple species of animals. Does the order make any difference? It would if this were a chart of *sequential* data. But, in this case, it doesn't matter what the order of the animals is.

The students will probably come to the conclusion that a "clustered column" chart fits their purposes. Then simply press the "clustered column" chart. The chart will "pop up."

Ask the students to read the Excel instructions to find out how to put titles onto the graph related to speed and hopping, move the graph around on the screen, and how to save it.

Discuss the data represented on the students' completed graphs and have them explain possible reasons for differences in weight.

Sample Closure

Ask students what helped them and the problems they encountered during their online search for information. Refer them to the list of keywords from the beginning of the lesson and note which combinations helped them in their search. Review differences between rabbits and hares from the information recorded on students' graphs and how these differences affect survival. Review ways to represent information on a table, graph, and spreadsheet. Ask students about the advantages and disadvantages of reading data from a table or graph. Have them look for examples of tables and graphs in printed materials at home. The sports page of the newspaper is a good place to look.

Formative and Summative Assessment

Formative Examples

LET STUDENTS SHOW OFF THEIR LEARNING

Have students share the keywords they listed for their search and explain why some worked better than others and why.

IF-ONLY STATEMENTS

If only I had a rabbit as a pet, I would _____.

I-CAN STATEMENTS

I can create a graph with two axes that would show the differences in weights among my favorite animals.

Summative Examples

Oral and written tests and projects

Extend Learning

Explore different types of graphs that represent the same information and compare their effectiveness of for providing specific data.

Explain differences in the types of information provided by qualitative and quantitative graphs.

Sensory Checklist

Check the senses students use during your lesson.
See Sensory Chart for Unit Plans, Table 4.4 and downloadable online

Online References

Pictures of Rabbits and Hares. See Figure 5.19.
https://duckduckgo.com/?q=pictures+of+rabbits+and+hares&iax=images&ia=images&iai=https%3A%2F%2Fwritingexplained.org%2Fwp-content%2Fuploads%2Fhare-vs-rabbit.jpeg

Images of Skeletons of Rabbits and Hares. See Figure 5.20.
https://duckduckgo.com/?q=rabbits+skeleton&t=ffab&atb=v320-1&iax=images&ia=images&iai=https%3A%2F%2Fi.pinimg.com%2Foriginals%2F8e%2Fa1%2F92%2F8ea192624c305c1f2f62a529d0a6bb83.jpg

Engineering Unit Plan > Mechanical Engineering

Adapt learning for your grade level and the needs of your students and break it down for multiple daily lessons.

Become an Expert

Learn more than you will ever teach about physiological differences between rabbits and hares, the unique qualities of rabbits and hares for mobility, materials for creating a model of the rabbits and hare's hind legs, and the purpose of building models.

Essential Questions

Determine one to two essential questions for daily lessons to provide a framework for learning, such as:

Why is a physical model of a mobile system needed?
What materials are needed to create a physical model?

Objectives

Select or adapt one to three objectives for your daily lesson plans.
Students will learn to:

Measure the relevant lengths of specific bones that are useful in hopping using English or metric system units.
Analyze the rabbits' and hares' feet and legs from pictures.
Estimate the size of the model to be built and a realistic scale for the measurements.
Determine the materials that must be collected prior to constructing the model of a rabbit or hare's feet and legs.
Compare and contrast English and metric system units in building a model.
Use mathematical thinking that involves measurement, ratio and proportion, and geometry and angles to build a model.
Interpret mathematical data during the construction of a model of a rabbit's and hare's foot and leg structure.
Construct a model that shows the size and movement of a rabbit or hare's foot and leg and describe the approximations that were used.
Analyze features of the model.
Sketch improvements to the model based on feedback.
Recognize the importance of asking questions when working on their model.
Respond to questions about possible changes to the model.
Defend reasons for the design of the model.

Vocabulary

Choose two to three words to teach in daily lessons. See Chapter 3 for ways to teach vocabulary.

tibia	equal
fibula	fractions
femur	whole numbers
ilium	estimate
scale	ratio
rulers	proportions
inches	angles
feet	data
centimeters	interpret
meters	approximation

Materials and Resources

Use the HELP hierarchy in Chapter 4 for lists of multisensory materials.

Real-World Experiences

Rabbits and hares in their native environments
Measurements of rabbits' and hares' leg bones

Real-World Artifacts

Classroom rabbits and hares
Rabbits and hares in a zoo or pet store

Representations

Models of a rabbit and hare
Adhesive foam
Jumbo Craft Stick
Dowl
Scotch tape
Fasteners (brads)
Heavy duty hole punch
Small hole punch
Scissors
Pipe cleaners

Visuals

See Online References at the end of this unit plan.
Pictures of rabbits' and hares' skeletons

Written

See Online References at the end of this unit plan.
All Things Rabbits for Kids by Animal Reads, ages 6+
All About Mechanical Engineering by Don Herweck, ages 9+
Engineered: Engineering Designs at Work by Shannon Hunt, ages 8–12

Set, Procedures, Closure

Read Chapter 2 for ways to plan sets and closures.

82 Planning Sensory-Rich STEAM Unit Plans

Sample Set

Ask the students what makes a rabbit's hind leg unique? How does a hare's leg and foot structure enable the animal to elude its enemies? How do the rabbit's hind legs enable him to stand up so that he can more easily detect a predator approaching? Could we build a model of his hind legs so that we could test the animal's capabilities? Tell students that today they will make a model that shows the length of rabbits' and hares' legs and how they move.

Procedures

Plan a variety of instructional strategies that include direct teaching, modeling, guided and independent practice, and inquiry. Include critical thinking, questioning, and investigation.

Match procedures to daily objectives.

Show a video (see Online References) of rabbits and hares hopping and have students determine which set of legs propel the rabbit or hare quickly to escape from predators and enable the animal to stand to see approaching enemies better. Also have them study the size and movement of their feet.

Display the materials students will use and describe possible ways to use them.

Tell the students that one-half the class is going to build a model of a rabbit's hind legs and one-half the class is going to build a model of a hare's hind legs.

Have students measure in English or metric units the relative sizes of the rabbit and hare's foot, lower leg, and upper leg from pictures of a skeleton of a rabbit and hare. Ask students to note details of the bones in the toes which enable the animal to jump quickly and accurately.

Using a picture of the skeleton of a rabbit, have students compare the length of the long lower leg bone, the tibia, to the bones in the foot of a rabbit. Then have them compare the length of their foot and tibia.

The bone in the upper leg is the femur. Ask the students to measure the relative lengths of these components of the hind leg by looking at the skeletal structure. See Figures 5.21 and 5.22.

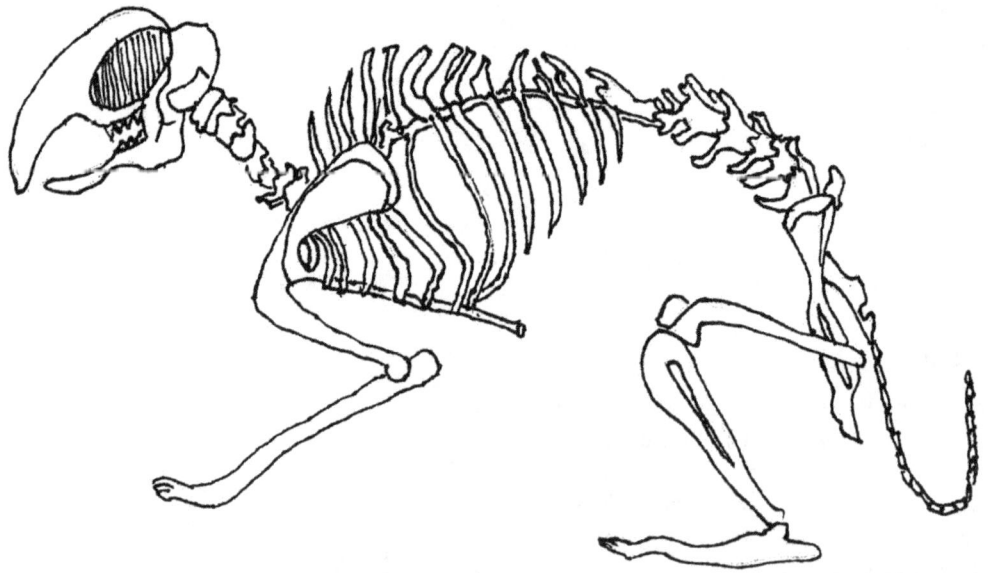

Figure 5.21 Rabbit Skeleton.

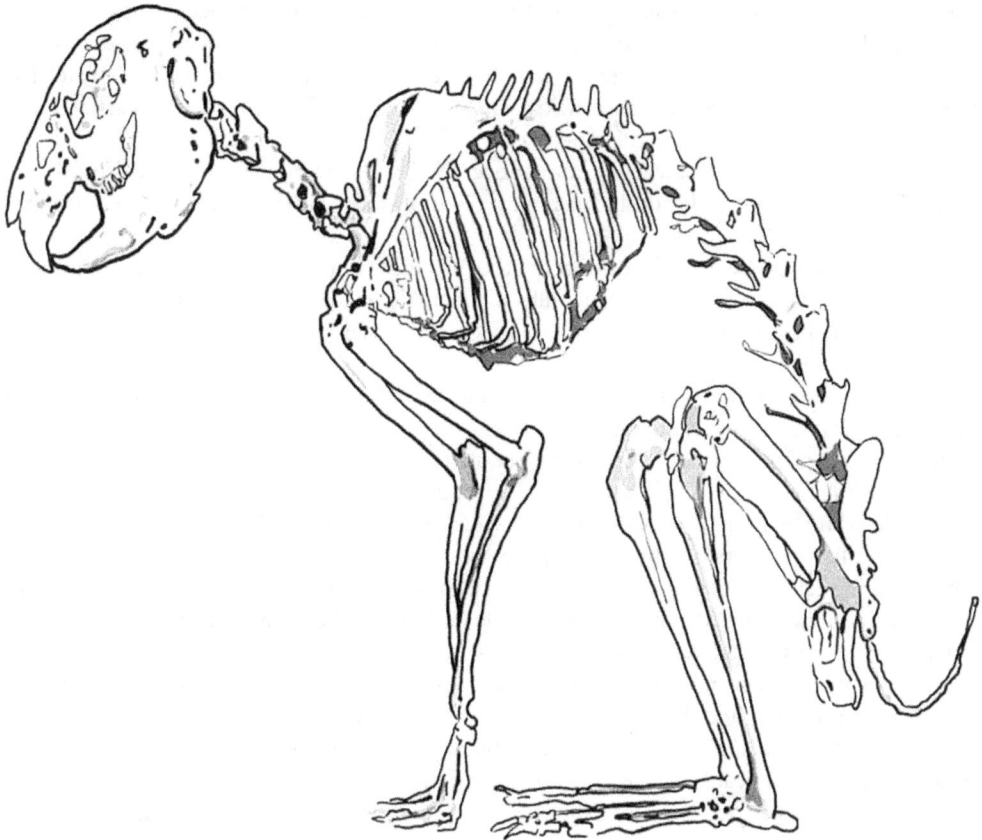

Figure 5.22 Hare Skeleton.

Use measurements of the leg and foot bones of a rabbits or hares when experimenting on ways to construct a model.

How many toes does a rabbit and hare have? Ask the students to look up the answer or inspect the skeleton of a rabbit and hare from imagery found on the web. Cut as many strips of foam as needed for the toes. Remember, there are two hind legs. Don't take the adhesive backing off the foam until the design is complete.

Have students build a model of the leg structure of rabbits and hares making sure the measurement of each bone is accurate to the nearest inch or centimeter and the model is built to scale. If the students found that the foot was four inches, the tibia was six, and the femur was four, that's close enough. Thus, the ratio of foot-to-tibia-to femur is 1:1.5:1.

Now that the students know the ratio of the length of the parts of the hind legs, the students decide what the size of the model will be. Choose a convenient length for the feet. One convenient length may be the width of the adhesive foam sheets, but any reasonable length will do. Make sure that once students selected a length for the parts of the legs and feet, they will construct their model to scale.

The tibia, then, could be modeled by one of the Jumbo Craft Sticks. But, it must be connected to the foot in a way that projects the tibia into the vertical dimension so, it must be perpendicular to the plane of the foot. This step is not easy, but tell the students to persevere.

(Hint: It may be necessary to cut an additional strip off the adhesive foam sheet and use it to wrap the ankle of the model in such a way that the Craft Stick can be projected upward.)

The model must be hinged at both the ankle and the knee. So, if the students decided to use the Craft Sticks for the tibia and the femur, it will be necessary to punch three holes. One for the tibia stick at the ankle, one for the tibia stick at the knee, and one for the femur stick at the knee. Use a heavy-duty hole punch for this purpose.

The students must think ahead because once the adhesive is in place, it cannot be removed. Thinking through the design prior to assembly is essential to save materials, time, and cost.

Fasteners (brads) can be used to connect the foot assembly to the tibia, but the important idea is to produce a tibia that is movable vertically at the ankle just as a human ankle that joins the foot to the human tibia is movable. Then, at the knee, another fastener can be used to connect the femur to the tibia.

Have the students check to make sure that the length of the tibia is 1.5 times the length of the foot and the femur is the same length as the foot.

When one leg of the model is complete, see if it will stand up alone. If not, that's okay, because every rabbit/hare has two hind legs! The students should complete the other leg just as they completed the first one and connect them together with another Craft Stick or dowel. The skeletal bone that connects one hind leg to the other is called the ilium.

Once the model has been constructed, it is possible to move the hind legs carefully and demonstrate the motion that the rabbit uses when it jumps. The long foot and powerful tibia and femur give the strength that the rabbit needs for survival.

Have students use their measurement from the data they collected on the sizes of rabbits and hares' legs to construct models of a rabbit and a hare's leg using pipe cleaners. Ask students to compare the structures and sizes between a rabbit and a hare for both sets of legs.

Students from 8–12 years often wish to build the model to their own design. The materials provided in this unit provide flexibility and the teacher can encourage unique designs so long as the end goal remains a model of the hind legs of a rabbit or hare.

Ask students to write their questions about their experiences as they go through the process of building a model of a rabbits or hare's foot and leg to share with the class.

Have students demonstrate their models and describe any questions or problems they faced and identify the angles and measurements used.

Sample Closure

Building models of physical objects, especially of living things, can bring appreciation of the amazing adaptations that animals and plants have undergone over the lifetime of the species. The extraordinary construction of the rabbit's hind legs is a product of thousands of years of adaptation to the rabbit's environment, including the threats of predators, weather, and disease.

Formative and Summative Assessment

Formative Examples

LET STUDENTS SHOW OFF THEIR LEARNING

Ask the students to explain how they built their model and especially some of the challenges that they overcame.

IF-ONLY STATEMENTS

If only I could hop like a rabbit, I would _____.

I-CAN STATEMENTS

___ I can build a scale model showing the important parts of the animal's skeleton.

Summative Examples

Projects, oral and written tests

Extend Learning

Determine physical characteristics and bone structure of other mammals and reptiles, gather materials, and build scale models of them.

Advanced students can use more sophisticated materials including wood, glue, screws, and other fasteners.

Sensory Checklist

Check the senses students use during this lesson.
See Sensory Chart for Unit Plans, Table 4.4 and downloadable online

Online References

Images of skeletons of rabbits and hares. See Figure 5.23.
https://duckduckgo.com/?q=rabbits+skeleton&t=ffab&atb=v320-1&iax=images&ia=images&iai=https%3A%2F%2Fi.pinimg.com%2Foriginals%2F8e%2Fa1%2F92%2F8ea192624c305c1f2f62a529d0a6bb83.jpg

Habits and physical characteristics of rabbits and hares. See Figure 5.24.
https://onekindplanet,org/animal/rabbit/

Rabbit Body Systems. See Figure 5.25.
https://thepetvet.com/rabbit-anatomy/

Rabbit Anatomy: Understand Bunnies from Ear to Tail. See Figure 5.26.
http://lionheadrabbitcare.com/rabbit-anatomy/#Rabbit_Hind_Legs

Art Unit Plan > Visual, Music, and Drama

Adapt learning for your grade level and the needs of your students and break it down for multiple daily lessons.

Become an Expert

Learn more than you will ever teach about the underlying skills of drawing such as observation, angular and curved lines, proportion, and shading related to the features of rabbits' and hares' body structure. Know different ways to teach drama and movement such as creative and realistic gestures, motions, imitations related to the behavior of rabbits and hares, and musical compositions that can be used to set the mood for the actions of rabbits and hares.

Essential Questions

Determine one to two essential questions for daily lessons to provide a framework for learning, such as:

What characteristics can you show through drawings that distinguish rabbits from other animals?
How can you use gestures and other movements to show characteristics of rabbits and hares at rest, play, eating, and in danger?

Objectives

Use or adapt one to three objectives for your daily lesson plans.
Students will learn to:

Recall facts about the differences of rabbits' and hares' anatomy and behaviors to use in drawing and drama.
Examine the sizes of rabbits' and hares' legs and feet and find exact measurements with a ruler.
Draw the bone structures of rabbits and hares.
Compare the phalanges (fingers and toes) of humans to the number of phalanges on a rabbit and hare's feet and count the number of joints for each finger and toe.
Sketch a rabbit or hare's feet and the way they look in motion.
Analyze the use of curved and angular lines in drawings.
Experiment with different proportions of different parts of rabbits' and hares' anatomy.
Use shading to show dark and light spaces and to create interest.
Investigate different art tools to use to color pictures.
Create realistic and creative line, free-form, doodle, and cartoon drawings.
Mimic the different ways rabbits and hares hop.
Demonstrate differences between the way rabbits and hares jump and hop to ways humans jump and hop.
Improvise ways rabbits and hares act and sound when frightened, uncomfortable, and happy.
Experiment with jumping and hopping using different levels of force.
Mimic the ways rabbits and hares hop.
Read the book, *The Tale of Peter Rabbit* by Beatrix Potter and have students select parts to act out, being as true to the characters as possible.

Vocabulary

Choose two to three words to teach in daily lessons. See Chapter 3 for ways to teach vocabulary.

cranium (skull)	mirror images
tibia	pantomime
fibula	improvisation
femur	scenario
ankle joint	sketch
phalanges (toes and fingers)	perspective
spinal cord	proportion
vertebrae	shading
characterization	line art
mannerisms	curved and angular lines
diagram	shading
drama	

Materials and Resources

Choose materials from the list below for science lessons. Use the HELP Hierarchy in Chapter 4 for more examples of concrete and abstract materials.

Real-World Experiences

Live rabbit and hare
Drawing pad
Pencils: water color, graphite, charcoal, carbon
Props for drama and movement
Disposable gloves

Real-World Artifacts

Caged live rabbit and hare
Skeleton of a rabbit and hare

Representations

Realistic replicas of a rabbit and hare (figures, toys)
Model of a rabbit and hare skeleton

Visuals

See Online References at the end of this unit plan.
Ruler
Moving and still pictures of a rabbit and hare
Copies of a profile picture showing differences between a rabbit and a hare. See Figures 5.27 and 5.28.

Rabbits and Hares 89

Figure 5.27 Rabbit Profile.

Figure 5.28 Hare Profile.

I'm a Hare There! by Julie Rowan-Zoch, ages 5–8
Rabbit Breeds: The Pocket Guide to 49 Essential Breeds by Lynn M. Stone, no ages (colors)
Book-*Basics of Drawing: The Ultimate Guide for Beginners* by Leonardo Pereznieto, no ages

Written Descriptions

See Online References at the end of this unit plan.
Notebook and pencil
PowerPoint, Prezi, Visme
Lyrics to the story of *Peter and the Wolf* Op. 67, Sergei Prokofiev
Teaching Drama: The Essential Handbook by Denver Casado, no ages
On Stage: Theater Games and Activities for Kids by Lisa Bany-Winters, ages 7–11
The Tale of Peter Rabbit by Beatrix Potter, ages 5–7
The Velveteen Rabbit: How Toys Become Real by Margery Williams, no ages

Oral and Aural

Microphone for speaking and singing
Peter and the Wolf, Op 67 by Sergei Prokofiev 26:14 (with score and narration)
https://www.youtube.com/watch?v=ki0xu6Gl9Nc

Set, Procedures, Closure

Read Chapter 2 for multiple ways to plan multisensory sets and closures.

Sample Set

Greet students wearing rabbit ears and work up the courage to hop or at least run around the room. Have *Peter and the Wolf* by Sergei Prokofiev playing as students enter the classroom. Tell them that the music tells a story about Peter, a little boy, in danger of being chased by a wolf. The birds, ducks, and a cat are also fearful of the wolf. Tell students they will pretend they are rabbits or hares and use all the energy and force they can to escape the wolf as they listen to the music. They will experience how rabbits and hares hop to escape danger and create scenarios through pictures to dramatize.

Procedures

Plan a variety of instructional strategies that include direct teaching, modeling, guided and unguided practice, and inquiry. Include critical thinking, questioning, and investigation.

Match procedures to daily objectives.
Review the story told through the music of *Peter and the Wolf* about survival. Have students listen as each theme of the story is played by different orchestra instruments that include the flute, oboe, clarinet, bassoon, French horn, percussion, woodwinds, and stringed instruments.
Discuss the way the sounds of the instruments create a mood for the action in the story.
With the music playing, ask students to suggest different versions of the story told through *Peter and the Wolf* that they could dramatize.
Have students determine different ways they can move to dramatize the fear and the actions rabbits and hares would take to escape a wolf.
Turn up the music and have students in groups, or as a class, dramatize the movements of rabbits and hares.

Review the movements the students chose to represent rabbits and hares and the force they needed to apply to their feet to move quickly.

Select one or both books, *The Tale of Peter Rabbit* by Beatrix Potter and *The Velveteen Rabbit: How Toys Become Real*, to read to the class. Have students describe their favorite parts, and from these parts, have them select ones to act out for the class.

To introduce mimicry, choose one person to be a rabbit or hare moving in some way (e.g., hopping, eating, playing, hiding). Have the rest of the class mimic the "rabbit's" or "hare's" actions.

Have students design and create props for the dramatizations.

Show pictures of rabbits and hares and ask students to observe the differences they see between the size of their feet, legs, bodies, and ears.

Relate how the bone structure of rabbits and hares aid jumping and hopping.

Have students measure the size of the rabbit's and hare's feet, ears, body, and tail and sketch a rabbit and hare using the measurements. Encourage students to emphasize parts of their picture through their choice of lines, angles, curves, and shading.

Model ways students can draw proportional sketches from their measurements. Have students draw proportional sketches of the feet of rabbits and the feet of hares and compare the lengths of the feet from both sets of sketches.

From these sketches, have students make a realistic, creative, or cartoon drawing using color and shading to emphasize the individual parts of the rabbit's and hare's feet. See Figure 5.29.

Figure 5.29 Cartoon Drawing.

Have students create fanciful rabbits and hares by changing the proportion of one or more of their parts.

Ask students to draw a picture of themselves and the way they would look if they had the same ratio of their body length to foot length as a rabbit or hare. Have them demonstrate how this ratio impacts the movement of humans and rabbits and hares.

Ask students for ways they can draw what rabbits see from their perspective when finding food, sensing danger, and sitting in tall grass. Solicit other ideas students could draw.

Have students demonstrate their knowledge of rabbits and hares through improvisations of the various movements they make.

Ask students to suggest reasons that rabbits and hares would change their movements and locations and use them as a basis to create scenarios. Some examples could be hunger, fear, survival, and playfulness. Ask students to act out their movements on actual mannerisms of rabbits and hares as seen on videos.

Sample Closure

Review key information on rabbits and hares related to the size of legs and feet on movement. Provide disposable gloves and have students try hopping, walking, and running by using their hands and feet. Review ways they dramatized characterization and used mimicry. Have students share the drawings they made and review the different techniques they used to change proportions.

Formative and Summative Assessment

Formative Examples

LET STUDENTS SHOW OFF THEIR LEARNING

Have students use one of the characteristics of drama, mimicry, improvisation, characterization, mirror imaging, and pantomime to demonstrate specific facts about rabbits and hares.

IF-ONLY STATEMENTS

If only I could run and jump like a rabbit, I would _____

I-CAN STATEMENTS

_____I can calculate the ratio between the relationship of foot size and the distance rabbits and hares hop.

Summative Examples

Presentations, projects, oral and written tests

Extend Learning

Analyze the techniques of professional painters and the ways they represented rabbits and hares. Here is one site we found interesting, ASTOR, Hopping through culture: the rabbit in art. See Online References at the end of this unit plan.

Find other instrumental music that can be used to support dramatic scenes about rabbits and hares.

Sensory Checklist

Check the senses students will use during your lesson.
See Sensory Chart for Unit Plans, Table 4.4 and downloadable online

Online References

Online videos of rabbits and hares
Wild Hare Sprinting and Hopping (0.53). See Figure 5.30.
https://duckduckgo.com/?q=Wild+hare+sprinting+and+jumping+Youtube&iax=videos&ia=videos&iai=https%3A%2F%2Fwww.youtube.com%2Fwatch%3Fv%3Dc7Idvr7BpCE

Rabbit Body Language: Meaning Behind 15 Strangest Rabbit Behaviors/Rabbit Jaw Dropping Facts (10:16). See Figure 5.31.
https://www.youtube.com/watch?v=dzKY-ZXgwFI

Still Picture of Rabbits and Hares. See Figure 5.32.
https://duckduckgo.com/?q=pictures+of+rabbits+and+hares&iax=images&ia=images&iai=https%3A%2F%2Fwritingexplained.org%2Fwp-content%2Fuploads%2Fhare-vs-rabbit.jpeg

94 Planning Sensory-Rich STEAM Unit Plans

Lyrics to the story of *Peter and the Wolf* Op. 67, Sergei Prokofiev. See Figure 5.33.
https://genius.com/Sergei-prokofiev-peter-and-the-wolf-op-67-lyrics

ASTOR, Hopping through culture: the rabbit in art. See Figure 5.34.
https://www.artstor.org/2015/04/02/hopping-through-the-centuries-rabbits-in-art/

Mathematics Unit Plan > Measurement, Data, and Statistics

Adapt learning for your grade level and the needs of your students and break it down for multiple daily lessons.

Become an Expert

Learn more than you will ever teach about physiological differences between rabbits and hares, estimation, use of and conversion of metric and English systems, ways to represent data, and statistical quantities, such as mean, median, and mode.

Essential Questions

Determine one to two essential questions for daily lessons to provide a framework for learning, such as:

What arithmetic operations do you use to make an estimate?
What is a reasonable estimate for how far a rabbit or hare can hop?
What is a reasonable estimate for how many hops a rabbit or hare takes before resting?

Objectives

Select or adapt one to three objectives for your daily lesson plans.
Students will learn to:

Compare the length of two of the leg bones of rabbits and hares to determine whether they are longer, shorter, or equal.
Order a variety of objects by their length.
Estimate lengths of objects using metric and English units.
Use a variety of nonstandard and standard tools to measure the length of rabbits' and hares' legs beginning with ordinary objects and advancing to rulers and yardsticks.
Calculate length in whole numbers followed by fractions in metric and English units.
Contrast the anatomy of rabbits' and hares' leg and foot structure.
Explain ways that differences in rabbits' and hares' leg and foot structures affect hopping distance and speed.
Determine the mean number of hops made by rabbits and hares by counting the number of hops for a specified distance.
Measure and record distances rabbits and hares can hop in feet or meters.
Transfer data from recorded measurements on the hopping distances of rabbits and hares to a graph: real (concrete objects), picture, line, or bar graph.
Analyze data from a graph to verify the relationships between the distances rabbits and hares hopped.
Represent data on the mean number of hops made by rabbits and hares on the apparent speed (fast, medium, slow) and distance on the real, picture, bar, and line graphs.
Interpret data from the graph on the effects leg size and speed have on distance.

Vocabulary

Choose two to three words to teach in daily lessons. See Chapter 3 for ways to teach vocabulary.

addition/sum	gravitational force
percent	applied force
subtraction/difference	line segment
trajectory	centimeter
multiplication	meter
ratio	inch
division	foot
data	gram
fraction	horizontal distance
mean/average	vertical distance
numerator	proportional
denominator	

Materials and Resources

Use the HELP hierarchy in Chapter 4 for lists of multisensory materials.

Real-World Experiences

Rabbits and hares in their native environments
Ruler with English and metric system markings
Full-page graph paper
Computer
Pipe cleaners
Chalk
Scale

Real-World Artifacts

Rabbits and hares as classroom pets
Rabbits and hares in a pet store, farm, or zoo

Representations

Different types of graphs

Visuals

See Online References at the end of this unit plan.
Illustration of skeletons of rabbits and hares
Profile picture showing differences between rabbits and hares

Written

See Online References at the end of this unit plan.
Hare and Rabbits: Comparing Animal Differences by Ryan Gale, ages 5–8
Rabbits and Hares by Dr. Richard A. NeSmith, all ages
Ants Rule: The Long and the Short of it by Bob Barner, ages 4–8
Amazing Visual Math by DK, ages 8–12

Set, Procedures, Closure

Read Chapter 2 for ways to plan sets and closures.

Sample Set

Ask the students to guess how many hops a rabbit or hare makes in 10 minutes. Ask how far each hop will take the rabbit or hare. Ask about the animals' speed at hopping and why it is necessary for rabbits and hares to hop so fast. Ask how high a rabbit or hare can jump. Is height important as well as distance? Today we will work to learn the answers to these questions.

Procedures

Plan a variety of instructional strategies that include direct teaching, modeling, guided and independent practice, and inquiry. Include critical thinking, questioning, and investigation.

   Match procedures to daily objectives.
   Ask the students to look closely at a hare's skeleton. See Figure 5.35.

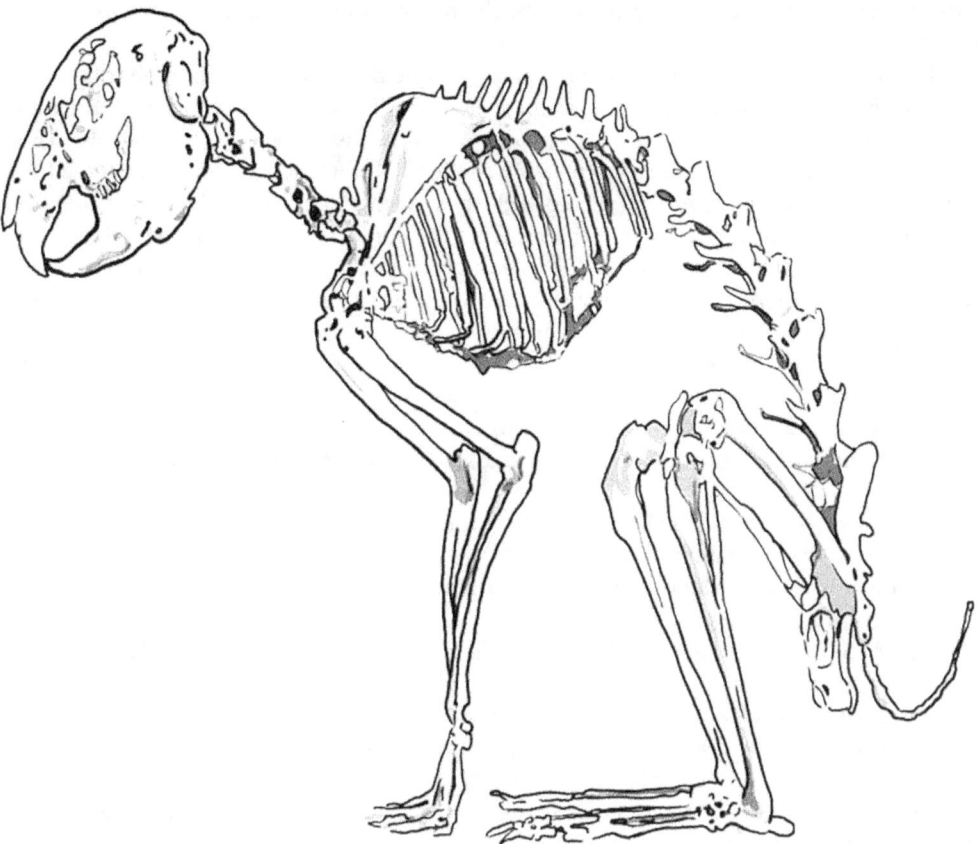

Figure 5.35 Hare Skeleton.

Ask them to locate the two leg bones. After finding the leg bones (tibia and femur), ask them to measure the length of the bones using a separate piece of paper for each leg and rabbit or hare. Mark on the paper the length of each leg.

Tell students to arrange the pieces of paper in order of increasing length. That is, put the smallest at the top of the page and the largest at the bottom. Label the pieces of paper as to "rabbit femur," "hare tibia," and so forth.

Ask the students to substitute a ruler for the pieces of paper and remeasure the lengths of the legs. Write down the measurements on the board. Emphasize that the measurement by ruler is a convenient way to measure lengths because everybody understands what a meter or foot is. Measure the lengths of legs in centimeters and in inches (metric and English systems of length).

Have students observe rabbits' and hares' foot movement and the force they used just before they hopped and after they leave the ground before beginning the next hop. Students can observe live rabbits and hares on video.

Pair students. Have one student hop like a rabbit or hare slowly and the other observe the student's foot and leg movement.

Have students hop high and low, fast and slow. Mark distances with chalk. With a rule, record the distances they went with each hop.

Have students find the mean (average) value of the distance of each hop by adding the distances of each hop and dividing the sum by the number of hops. Have students record data on a classroom chart.

Call on students two at a time to use rulers to measure the legs and feet of rabbits and hares from real skeletons or models and record them. Rarely will the measurements result in whole numbers. First, instruct the students to round off the measurements to the nearest whole number. Then, instruct the students to measure to the nearest fraction as identified on the ruler. Remember, a fraction is a part of a whole. Tell the students how to use the ruler to find the fractional part of an inch. Finally, tell the students top convert the fractions they obtained by measurement to decimals. Review the conversion process of changing fractions to decimals.

Have students compare foot and leg sizes between rabbits and hares and relate this information to the video clips of rabbits and hares hopping.

Have students draw proportional sketches of the feet of rabbits and the feet of hares and compare the lengths of the feet from both sets of sketches.

Have students measure the length of their own feet and the height of their body and compare the ratio of length and height to the ratio of length and height of the rabbits' and hares' feet and bodies.

Ask students to draw a picture of the way they would look if they had the same ratio of length of feet to body size as a rabbit or hare.

Have students research the running speeds of humans and the running speeds of hares and rabbits. Compare the differences between them.

Compare the distance rabbits and hares can hop to the 2019 long jump of Taja Gayle of Qatar: 28'6" (8.69 meters).

Have students run as fast as they can for 10 seconds. Have them mark where they started and stopped and measure the distance they ran. View a live rabbit or hare, or a video of one hopping for a 10-second period of time. Have students estimate the distance the rabbit or hare hopped, based on landmarks, and compare it to the distance they traveled. Discuss and have students explain reasons for differences in speed and distance between humans, rabbits, and hares using knowledge of the bone structure of rabbits' and hares' legs and feet.

Have students hop and run at different speeds for different purposes and review principles of applied and gravitational forces to their speed and eventual return to the ground.

Have students experiment using different levels of force (weak, medium, strong) when kicking a ball and measure the differences the ball traveled for each level of force. Relate the force applied to kicking a ball to the force applied for hopping and running. Mark starting and ending points with chalk to measure lengths. Record the data.

Have students graph two or three levels of force (weak, medium, strong). Have them display information on hopping on a scaled graph. Students may begin with a real graph where they display information with concrete objects before moving to pictures in a picture graph followed by bar and line graphs.

Have students make inferences on the length of rabbits' and hares' hopping distances when they use maximum force to escape a predator compared to hopping for play and to find food.

Study the hopping trajectory of rabbits and hares on a video. This is NOT going to be all in a straight line, but instead will be a series of straight-line segments. Have students hop in a series of straight-line segments to emulate a rabbit or hare. Mark line segments with chalk.

Distribute a picture of a rabbit and hare and have students measure the body from the nose to the tail. Calculate the ratio of the size of the body to the length of the hind feet using knowledge of measurement, multiplication, division, fractions, and decimals. Have students calculate and graph the differences they found between the ratio of the size of the body to the length of the feet between rabbits and hares. See Figures 5.35 and 5.36.

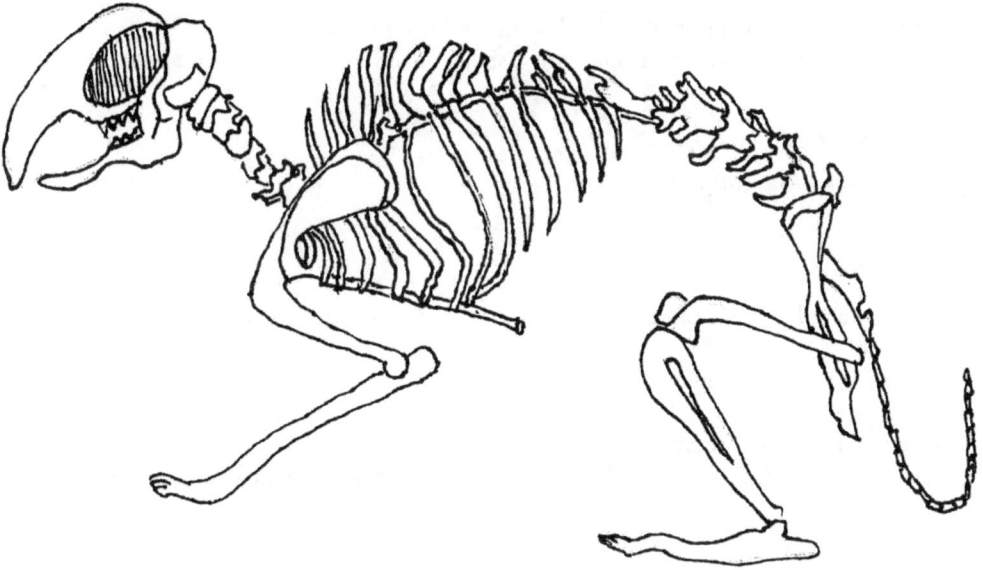

Figure 5.36 Rabbit Skeleton.

Sample Closure

Post the graphs on the bulletin board. Summarize what the graphs say about the hopping characteristics of rabbits and hares (i.e., how many hops do the animals make and how far do they go in a single hop).

Formative and Summative Assessment

Formative Examples

LET STUDENTS SHOW OFF THEIR LEARNING

Ask students to explain their graphs of hopping distances.
Let students define the characteristics of the anatomy of rabbits and hares and how those characteristics enable the animal to escape predators.

IF-ONLY STATEMENTS

If only I could hop as fast as a rabbit or hare, I would _____.
If only I could measure every hop a rabbit or hare made, I would _____.

100 Planning Sensory-Rich STEAM Unit Plans

I-CAN STATEMENTS

___ I can compare the lengths of rabbits' and hares' leg and foot structure.
___ I can explain how force affects hopping distances from information viewed on graphs.

Summative Examples

Oral and written tests and projects

Extend Learning

Compare the length of the front and hind legs of rabbits and hares to the length of the front and hind legs of other mammals.
Research survival skills among animals, especially the effects of speed, distance, and height on escaping prey.
Explore different ways to represent data on graphs.
Calculate the standard deviation to determine how close measurements are to the mean.

Sensory Checklist

Check the senses students use during this lesson.
See Sensory Chart for Unit Plans, Table 4.4 and downloadable online

Online References

Caution: Select other YouTube videos for students carefully. Many of the videos were on the mating habits of rabbits and hares and predators catching and eating them.
Images of rabbit skeletons. See Figure 5.37.
https://duckduckgo.com/?q=rabbits+skeleton&t=ffab&atb=v320-1&iax=images&ia=images&iai=https%3A%2F%2Fi.pinimg.com%2Foriginals%2F8e%2Fa1%2F92%2F8ea192624c305c1f2f62a529d0a6bb83.jpg

Images of hare skeletons. See Figure 5.38.
https://duckduckgo.com/?q=hares+skeleton&t=ffab&atb=v320-1&iar=images&iax=images&ia=images

YouTube Multiple Images of Rabbits and Hares Jumping. See Figure 5.39.
https://duckduckgo.com/?q=Youtube+pictures+of+hares+and+rabbits+jumping&iax=images&ia=images

YouTube Multiple Images of Wild Hare Sprinting and Hopping. See Figure 5.40.
https://duckduckgo.com/?q=Wild+hare+sprinting+and+jumping+Youtube&jax=video&ia=videos&iaihttps%3A%2F=&atb=v320-1&iax=videos&iai=https%3A%2F%2Fwww.youtube.com%2Fwatch%3Fv%3Dc7Idvr7BpCE

Chapter 6

The Water Cycle

Introduction

The Itsy Bitsy Spider, a popular song with accompanying finger actions, engages students in three of the four stages of the water cycle. Which one is missing? Once your students have been taught the STEAM content, Science, Technology, Engineering, Art, and Mathematics from the five unit plans, they will be able to identify the missing stage and relate the four stages to their dependency on the Sun. This chapter contains ways to teach important content about the water cycle across the curriculum. Science, the S in STEAM, enables students to learn about the causes and effects of the water cycle. Technology, the T in STEAM, provides information on ways to conduct computer searches, create QR Codes, and game templates related to the water cycle. Engineering, the E in STEAM, focuses on processes of analyzing and building dams important to the collection stage of the water cycle. Art, the A in STEAM, promotes the visual arts, drama, and movement to represent and re-enact stages of the water cycle. Mathematics, the M in STEAM, teaches students how to record and evaluate data on the changing stages of the water cycle.

Each STEAM subject contains nine steps for unit planning: Become an Expert; Essential Questions; Objectives; Vocabulary; Materials and Resources; Set, Procedures, and Closure; Formative and Summative Assessment; Extend Learning; and a Sensory Checklist. Online References have QR codes that can be optically used to access websites.

Science Unit Plan > Chemistry and Physics

Adapt learning for your grade level and the needs of your students and break it down for multiple daily lessons.

Become an Expert

Learn more than you will ever teach about the stages of the water cycle and its effects on landforms and all living things.

Essential Questions

Determine one to two essential questions for daily lessons to provide a framework for learning, such as:

How might a decaying dead animal make its way into your drinking water?
What would happen if the wind did not blow air over the ocean?

DOI: 10.4324/9781003290889-9

Objectives

Select or adapt one to three objectives for your daily lesson plans.
Students will learn to:

Explore properties of the three states of water: solid, liquid, and gas.
Demonstrate how water vapor, combined with tiny dust particles, saturates clouds and falls to Earth as rain, sleet, or snow.
Show the molecular structure of water.
Analyze natural causes of water movement.
Locate water sources on a map.
Determine where water drained from the bathtub, drunk from a glass, and rained on plants ultimately goes.
Identify four major stages of the water cycle: evaporation, condensation, precipitation, and collection.
Evaluate the importance of each stage of the water cycle.
Determine the interrelationships between the parts of the water cycle.
Research evidence that the water cycle is a continuous process driven by the Sun.
Research how the four stages of the water cycle affect temperatures on the Earth.
Explain the importance of water on all living things.
Determine what happens to water when plants and animals die and decompose.
Explore ways plants seek water.
Describe the effects of heat on cold water.
Formulate reasons cataclysmic events deep within the Earth affect the four stages of the water cycle.

Vocabulary

Choose two to three words to teach in daily lessons. See Chapter 3 for ways to teach vocabulary.

water/ H_2O	erosion
solid	run off
liquid	landform
gas/water vapor	glacier
condensation	crevice
evaporation	infiltrate
transpiration	collection
precipitation	reservoir
atmosphere	ocean
stratosphere	spring
drought	ground water
flood	organic material
dew point	wilt
molecule	dehydrate
atom	decompose
saturated	decay

Materials and Resources

Use the HELP hierarchy in Chapter 4 for lists of multisensory materials.

Real-World Experiences

Container of water
Small bottles of cold water
Ice cubes
Outdoor weeds and plants
Grapes (2-4 per student)
Raisins
Plastic knives and spoons
Plastic cups
Clay
Sharpies
Teapot, water, and heat source

Real-World Artifacts

Small paper plates
Large sheet of newsprint or butcher paper
Blue tape
Colored markers

Representations

Clear wide-mouth plastic cups
Large and small gumdrops
Straws
Dominoes
Sponges

Visuals

See Online References at the end of this unit plan.
Markers
World map

Written

See Online References at the end of this unit plan.
Observation logs
National Geographic Readers: Water by Melissa Stewart, ages 6–9
What's Inside the Water Cycle by William B. Rice, ages, 8–12
A Drop Around the World by Barbara Shaw McKinney, 5–12

Set, Procedures, Closure

Read Chapter 2 for multiple ways to plan multisensory sets and closures.

The Water Cycle   105

Sample Set

As students enter the classroom give each one a wide-mouth cup marked at the halfway point, and a cup of ice cubes. Tell them to set both cups on a table or window sill and fill one cup half full with water from the sink or a water container. Inform students that the ice cubes and water will disappear over the next few days without even touching them! Tell students they will be studying the three states of water, solid, liquid, and gas, that are a part of the water cycle.

Procedures

Plan a variety of instructional strategies that include direct teaching, modeling, guided and independent practice, and inquiry. Include critical thinking, questioning, and investigation.

Match procedures to daily objectives.

Give students a cup of water and have them take a sip. Ask them where they think the water came from. Then tell them that the water they are drinking likely came from a dinosaur that died over 200 million years ago. See Figure 6.1.

Figure 6.1 Decayed Dinosaur.

Ask students to name other sources that could have contributed to the water they drank, the grosser the better.

A Norwegian geologist recently found footprints of a prehistoric animal that possibly predates the dinosaurs in a large boulder at the Grand Canyon in Arizona, USA. Ask what happened to the fluids that were once inside the animal.

Introduce the continuous movement of water through four stages of the water cycle: evaporation, condensation, precipitation, and collection that are driven by the Sun and occur over all areas of the Earth. Have students name the molecular structure of the three states of water: solid, liquid, and gas. See Figures 6.2 and 6.3.

106 Planning Sensory-Rich STEAM Unit Plans

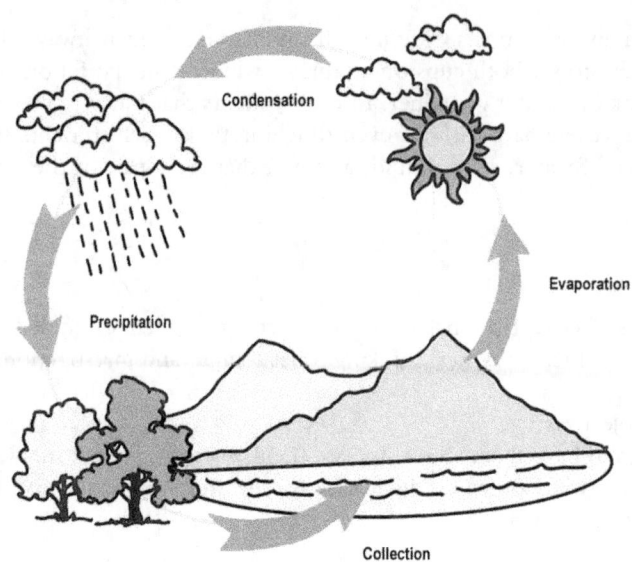

Figure 6.2 Water Cycle.

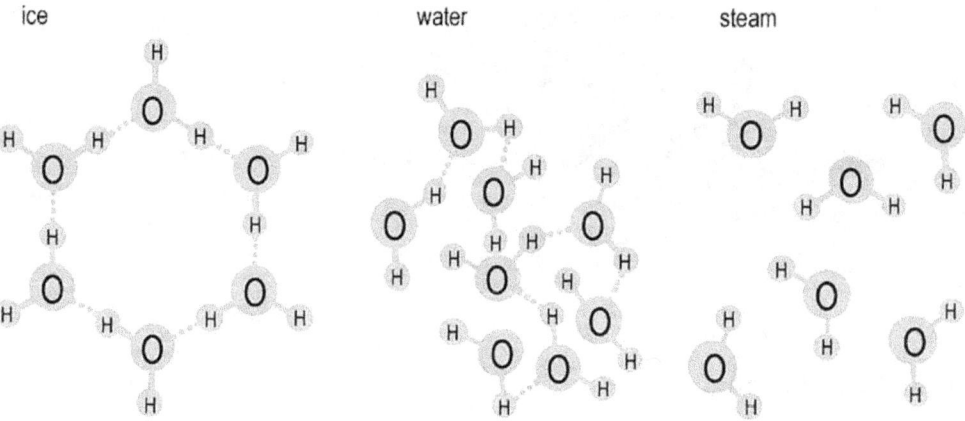

Figure 6.3 Molecular Structure of Three States of Water.

Have students explore different ways water goes through the four stages of the water cycle. Drive home the point that water comes from many sources before it eventually ends up as drinking water.

Have students research differences in the rates surface water evaporates compared to water in deeper bodies of water and from deep within the Earth.

Direct students to research how long it takes water from oceans and glaciers to go through the four stages of the water cycle in different parts of the world.

Discuss the effects of heat and cold on water molecules. Explain that a molecule is made of atoms that when bonded together display the properties of the matter. Have students make a model of a water molecule using two small gumdrops, one large gumdrop, and two straws. Two gumdrops should be the same color to represent hydrogen atoms. The large gumdrop of a different color represents one oxygen atom. See Figure 6.4.

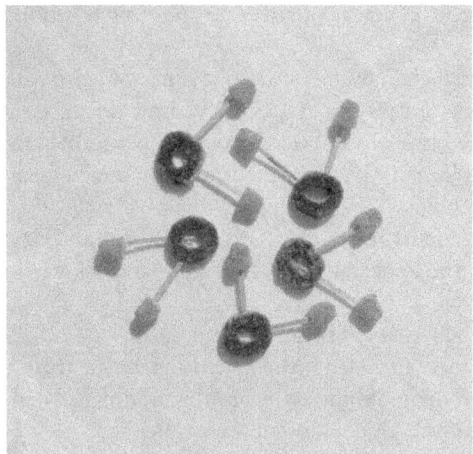

Figure 6.4 Water Molecule Gumdrop Model.

Ask students to explain the role of the Sun in each stage of the water cycle.

Have students illustrate four stages of the water cycle and explain how they are interrelated.

Have students explore cause and effect by standing dominoes in a line or circle. Direct them to look at the *effect* that is *caused* when one domino is pushed.

Relate cause and effect, as shown by the dominoes, to the water cycle where condensation is formed by the difference of hot and cold temperatures. Give students a bottle or glass of very cold water. Ask them where the water comes from that coats the outside of their container. Relate this water to the dew point, where the hotter air in the classroom meets the cold container, causing the water to condense and form on the outside of the glass or cup. Ask students what the water that has collected on the outside of their glass or bottle is called.

Demonstrate how water can change its form when heated and explode when confined. Heat cold water in a teapot and *have students watch from a safe distance* how the heat changes water into water vapor that escapes through the spout.

Have students consider how water and heat create steam by having them read information on the Tonga Hunga-Hunga Ha'api volcanic eruption that happened in January 2022. Provide online accounts of the volcanic eruption that spewed a trillion grams of water vapor into the Earth's atmosphere. Ask students to consider the effects of this massive explosion of water vapor on the stages of the water cycle. Have students relate similarities and differences between the erupting steam-from-the-teapot demonstration to the volcanic eruption.

Investigate natural landforms created by water, such as gorges and gullies carved out by rivers and waterfalls.

Ask students to investigate natural water collection places such as oceans, rivers, lakes, and ponds on Earth through pictures and maps to describe where collection sites are located and how they were formed.

Ask students to identify a location with famous landforms and have them create landform shapes from clay. Have them use their models to explain how the natural landforms were shaped by water.

To show cause and effect of water on plants, take students outside after a dry period and have them examine weeds and other plants that show signs of wilting. Tell them that the plants have been losing water through their leaves (transpiration) and ask where the water went. Inform students that transpiration is often considered another stage of the water cycle and ask whether they want to include it in their descriptions and diagrams of the water cycle.

Have students carefully pull up weeds that grow in cracks of concrete and note how long the tap root has grown in its search for water.

Have students experience how organic material changes form when it is no longer nourished or watered. First, have students smell and eat one or two grapes and notice how the juice smells, feels, and tastes. Next, have students use plastic knives to cut one or two grapes in half and lay them out with the cut part exposed. Have them keep a written or picture log of their appearance over many days.

After the grapes have dried over time, ask students to squeeze and smell them and describe how they feel and smell. Discuss differences in the appearance of the grapes and ask where the juice went and relate it to the water cycle.

Give students raisins and have them relate their characteristics to grapes.

Before they leave class each day, remind students to check the level of water in their cups, mark the level if it has changed, and record it in a log. As the water level goes down, ask where the ice and liquid water went. Discuss results of the grape and cup experiments.

Sample Closure

After the students take one final measurement of the water in the cups with liquid and ice and logged the information, remind them that because the water cycle can cause water to move thousands of miles over millions of years, they might be drinking water that came from decayed dinosaurs or the same water that Julius Caesar, Jesus, and Napoleon drank! If it has been raining, ask students to look at puddles left behind and think about the sources of the water that created them.

Formative and Summative Assessment

Formative Examples

LET STUDENTS SHOW OFF THEIR LEARNING

Describe the four stages of the water cycle using information from their log.

IF-ONLY STATEMENTS

If only I could be a water source that creates landforms, I would _____.

I-CAN STATEMENTS

____I can explain how the water I drink could have come from a dinosaur.

Summative Examples

Projects, oral and written tests

Extend Learning

Explore elements of the water cycle that occur simultaneously, evaporation, sublimation, transpiration, and infiltration.
Explain the statement that water is neither made nor destroyed.

Sensory Checklist

Check the senses students use during your daily lesson.
See Sensory Chart for Unit Plans, Table 4.4 and downloadable online

Online References

Multiple online accounts of the Tonga Hunga-Hunga Ha'api volcano that spewed enough water to fill 58,000 Olympic-size swimming pools into atmosphere. (One of many websites.) See Figure 6.5.
https://www.foxnews.com/science/tonga-volcano-spews-enough-water-fill-olympic-size-swimming-pools-stratosphere

What Is the Water Cycle and Can the Water Cycle Be Disrupted? See Figure 6.6.
https://www.iweathernet.com/educational/what-is-the-water-cycle

Disruptions to the Water Cycle: The Dust Bowl. See Figure 6.7.
https://www.istockphoto.com/search/2/image?phrase=dust+bowl

Diagram of Water Cycle. See Figure 6.8.
https://byjus.com/biology/diagram-of-water-cycle/

The Water Cycle. See Figure 6.9.
https://www.khanacademy.org/science/biology/ecology/biogeochemical-cycles/a/the-water-cycle

Dinosaur Stock Photos: Fossil Dinosaur Fight, Tyrannosaurus and Triceratops. See Figure 6.10.
https://www.dreamstime.com/photos-images/dead-dinosaur.html

Technology Unit Plan > Computer Operations, Searches, QR Codes, and Game Templates

Adapt learning for your grade level and the needs of your students and break it down for multiple daily lessons.

Become an Expert

Learn more than you will ever teach about computer operations, searches, QR code sheets, and game template operations.

Essential Questions

Determine one to two essential questions for daily lessons to provide a framework for learning, such as:

What reason would you have to develop QR codes to represent information?
How would you use technology to create a *Jeopardy* game that uses information about the water cycle?

Objectives

Use or adapt one to three objectives for your daily lesson plans.
Students will learn to:

Review computer and iPad operations.
Review printer and scanning operations.
Determine different keywords to use for a search.
Explore ways to search for information on the water cycle.
Analyze information from sources and tutorials for relevancy, authenticity, and lack of bias.
Represent information on the computer on the water cycle in different ways.
Determine uses for Quick Response (QR) codes.
Recall experiences scanning QR codes in stores.
Explore apps for generating and reading QR codes.
List key words to use in a search for game templates.
Explore ways to search for tutorials on making and using game templates.
Outline steps to create an online *Jeopardy* game using a water cycle theme.
Determine sites on ways to create a *Jeopardy* game, save it, and play the game.
Explore ways to make a *Jeopardy* game with different programs (PowerPoint, Word, Excel).
Demonstrate understanding of the water cycle by creating a *Jeopardy* game using a template and technology.
Describe the four stages of the water cycle.
Explain why the water cycle is a continuous process.
Identify the interrelationships among the stages of the water cycle.

Vocabulary

Choose two to three words to teach in daily lessons. See Chapter 3 for ways to teach vocabulary.

precipitation	gravity
collection	scanner
condensation	app
evaporation	Uniform Resource Locator (URL)
transpiration	iPad
gas/water vapor	download
solid	smart devises
liquid	Quick Response QR Code
circulate	QR Code Generator
percolate	QR Code Reader
clouds	QR Log Sheets
dew	template
ground water	software
infiltration	slides
seepage	categories
runoff	tutorials
accumulation	sound effects
sublimation	

Materials and Resources

Use the HELP hierarchy in Chapter 4 for lists of multisensory materials.

Real-World Experiences

Smart devices (iPad or cell phone)
QR code generator and reader
Printer and paper
Class iPad with *Decide Now* app that downloaded from the App Store

Real-World Artifacts

Computer or iPad with *Jeopardy* template

Visual

See Online References at the end of this unit plan.

Written

See Online References at the end of this unit plan.
Pearl the Raindrop: The Great Water Cycle Journey by Rana Boulos, ages 3–8
I Am the Rain: A Science Book for Kids About the Water Cycle and Change of Seasons by John Paterson, ages 3–8
Evaporation, Transpiration, and Precipitation: Water Cycle for Kids Children's Water Books by Baby Professor, all ages
The Little Panda and His Blue Feet: With QR Code Animations by Paul Boschen and Rudson Nick (use Kindle version to share with large groups), all ages

Five Little Frogs in QR Code: A Children's Book for Tech Savvy Kids by Harris Tobias, all ages
Coding for Kids in Scratch 3: The Complete Guide to Completing Art, Artificial Intelligence, and Computer Games for Beginners by Raj Sidhu, ages 8–12

Set, Procedures, Closure

Read Chapter 2 for ways to plan multisensory sets and closures.

Sample Set

Search online, https://www.teachjunkie.com/language-arts/qr-code-learning-activities-free, to find and put free level-appropriate fun QR code activities on the white board. (See Online References for the QR code for this website.) For young students, read the Kindle version of *The Little Panda and His Blue Feet: With QR Code Animations,* to use on smart devices or a white board so that the whole class can see.

Tell students they will be doing activities to learn how to make and read QR codes.

Procedures

Plan a variety of instructional strategies that include direct teaching, modeling, guided and independent practice, and inquiry. Include critical thinking, questioning, and investigation.

Match procedures to daily objectives.

Before allowing students to use the Internet, talk about Internet safety, copyright issues, plagiarism, and proper conduct online. Find appropriate websites and bookmark them for use with younger students. Check with your school district's policies for using and downloading information from the Internet.

Check with your school district technology person before generating and reading QR Codes. See Figure 6.11.

They may have advice for your project and suggestions for apps to use with available technology.

Have pairs or small groups of students use an iPad with a QR code reader to scan and complete activities. Print log sheets for each group. Many free QR code activities are available online (Materials and References). After everyone has had a chance to do the activities, ask them what their favorite ones are and why.

If a white board is not available, the QR code activities can be printed and placed on a table for pairs or small groups to use.

Directions for QR Log Sheets

Students will research the water cycle online and find websites, YouTube videos, and other information.

Download a Quick Response (QR) code generator and reader from the app store to your smart devices (iPads and smartphones).

Have students create Quick Response (QR) codes to share with their classmates. These QR codes can be done in groups or individually. Students will follow the directions of websites like https://www.schrockguide.net/qr-codes-in-the-classroom.html or other tutorials appropriate for the ability level of the students. (See Online References for the QR code for this website.) Teachers can model the steps and guide the students through the process.

The following website contains ideas for activities related to the water cycle: https://www.teachjunkie.com/sciences/8-fast-free-water-cycle-resources-and-activities.

(See Online References for the QR code for this website.)

Have the students save their QR codes and print a copy.

Have students share their QR codes with classmates, other classrooms, collaborative schools, parents, principals, and their families.

In preparation for creating a game, have students review the four stages of the water cycle.
Ask students to describe the stages and give examples of each.
Using a diagram of the water cycle, have students observe that it is a continuous process.
Have students discuss how the parts of the water cycle relate to each other.
Use the following lesson on game templates after the class has demonstrated basic knowledge about the water cycle. Provide books and time for students to review and learn factual information. Ask students to take notes on facts about the water cycle to use in their *Jeopardy* game.
Find a fun online *Jeopardy* game on a topic the class is familiar with and display it on the whiteboard. Divide the class into groups and let them play the game. After the game, ask the students what they liked about the game and other topics and categories they could use to create a game.

Directions for Game Templates

Research and find game templates with tutorials to make a *Jeopardy* game appropriate for the ability level of the students. Check available software on your class computers that matches the tutorial. Choose one and preview it to confirm its appropriateness.

Divide the class into groups for the project and have them brainstorm a list of categories with questions and answers they could use for the water cycle *Jeopardy* game.

Use the tutorial to assist them in creating a *Jeopardy* game about the water cycle using the brainstormed categories, questions, and answers. When completed, have the students save it and email to the teacher.

Allow each group to use the whiteboard to display its game and have their classmates play. The group that earned the most money, wins.

Discuss what they liked and disliked about creating the *Jeopardy* game using a game template, and what other topics they would like to use to make another *Jeopardy* game.

Divide the class into groups and have them swap iPads, so they have a different water cycle *Jeopardy* game. Some groups may have to swap twice to be sure they have a game that is not their own. Allow the students to play the game they have. They can jot down questions so they can go back and review and answers they think the game creators got wrong, so they can fix them.

Sample Closure

Print the QR codes linked to information and videos, and place on a centrally located table. Ask students to come in small groups and scan them. After viewing, ask the students to tell what they liked about some of the QR codes and describe some of the difficulties they had making them. Have students look for QR codes when shopping.

Formative and Summative Assessment

Formative Examples

LET STUDENTS SHOW OFF THEIR LEARNING

Have students show their list of search words on the water cycle and game templates.

IF-ONLY STATEMENTS

If only I could lead a group to create an QR code and a *Jeopardy* game about the water cycle, I would _____.

I-CAN STATEMENTS

____I can use a QR code generator to make and share information about any topic.

Summative Examples

Projects, presentations, oral and written tests

Extend Learning

Add other STEAM content to the *Jeopardy* game wheel. Collaborate with another class or school. Create a water cycle YouTube video.

Sensory Checklist

Check the senses students will use during your lesson.
See Sensory Chart for Unit Plans, Table 4.4 and downloadable online

Online References

The Water Cycle for Schools and Students: Advanced Students. See Figure 6.12.

https://water.usgs.gov/edu/watercycle-kids-adv.html

Water Cycle. See Figure 6.13.
https://www.britannica.com/science/water-cycle

8 Fast Free Water Cycle Resources and Activities. See Figure 6.14.
https://www.teachjunkie.com/sciences/8-fast-free-water-cycle-resources-and-activities

Discover Water: The Role of Water in Our Lives. See Figure 6.15.
https://www.discoverwater.org

The Water Cycle 117

Examples of Color Words. See Figure 6.16.
https://whatihavelearnedteaching.com/using-qr-codes-in-the-classroom

Using QR Codes in the Classroom. See Figure 6.17.
https://www.schrockguide.net/qr-codes-in-the-classroom.html

QR Code Activities. See Figure 6.18.
https://cdn.shopify.com/s/files/1/0725/1285/files/Sight_Word-QR_Code_Flash_Cards.pdf?v=1576685200

Water Cycle: See Figure 6.19.
https://www.teacherplanet.com/content/water-cycle

Internet 4 Classrooms: Tutorial for Microsoft Office. See Figure 6.20.
http://www.internet4classrooms.com/on-line_powerpoint.htm

Fun QR code activities. See Figure 6.21.
https://www.teachjunkie.com/language-arts/qr-code-learning-activities-free

Engineering Unit Plan > Civil Engineering

Adapt learning for your grade level and the needs of your students and break it down for multiple daily lessons.

Become an Expert

Learn more than you will ever teach about the many types of dams, hydroelectric energy, the forces that impact dams, the materials that are used to build dams, and the terrible consequences of dam failure.

Essential Questions

Determine one to two essential questions for daily lessons to provide a framework for learning, such as:

How can a dam convert hydroelectric potential energy to useful electrical energy?
What prior calculations are necessary to determine the size and shape of a dam?
What are the appropriate materials for building a dam?

Objectives

Select or adapt one to three objectives for your daily lesson plans.
Students will learn to:

Relate the building of dams to the water cycle, most notable the collection stage.
Develop a plan to build a model dam.
Create a model of a dam.
Create simple dams with rocks and dirt.
Investigate how water held back by a dam seeks to escape and ways to prevent it.
Analyze the force of water that is let loose from a dam when a rock or rocks are removed from the dam.
Recognize why we use dams to provide hydroelectric energy to light our homes and warm/cool our houses, run medical equipment, and pump gas.
Recall how dams store potential energy.
Describe how dams create electrical energy from the potential energy of the water stored behind a dam.
Describe common types of dams that are used all over the world.
Show how dams can be used for flood control as well as electricity development.
Determine what fraction of total energy produced in the United States is produced by dams and hydroelectric installations.
Compare helpful and harmful effects of dams.

Vocabulary

Choose two to three words to teach in daily lessons. See Chapter 3 for ways to teach vocabulary.

potential energy	magnetic field
kinetic energy	Michael Faraday
hydroelectric energy	magnetism
force	rotate
dam	shaft
turbine	conductor
current	reservoir

Materials and Resources

Use the HELP hierarchy in Chapter 4 for lists of multisensory materials.

Real-World Experiences

Field trip to the nearest earthen or concrete dam, preferably one that was built to provide hydroelectric power to the neighboring community.
Logbook to record engineering activities involved in the construction of the hydroelectric power station.

Real-World Artifacts

Visit a local dam
Dirt or sand
Rocks of different sizes, bricks
Large water-proof container

Representations

Water
Popsicle sticks
Long plastic box
Small rocks (gravel)
Water

Visual

See Online References at the end of this unit plan.

Written

See Online References at the end of this unit plan.
Energy from Water by Nancy Dickmann, ages 10–13
Hydroelectric Power by Josepha Sherman, ages 8–10
Hydroelectric Energy by Tamra B. Orr, ages 9–adult
Michael Faraday: Spiritual Dynamo (Trail Blazers) by Derick Bingham, ages 8–14
Renewable Energy Sources –Wind, Solar, and Hydro Energy by Baby Professor, ages 7–12
Canals and Dams: Investigate Feats of Engineering by Donna Latham, ages 8–12

Set, Procedures, Closure

Read Chapter 2 for ways to plan sets and closures.

Sample Set

Have music playing, flick the lights, and then ask the students what these phenomena have in common. Where do they get their electrical power? How does the electricity get to the school room to light the lights, heat the space, run the air conditioner, play the TV or radio, and even ring the bell? We use electricity for almost everything, but where does it come from? Tell students that they are going to learn about one source for electricity, dams.

Procedures

Plan a variety of instructional strategies that include direct teaching, modeling, guided and independent practice, and inquiry. Include critical thinking, questioning, and investigation.

Match procedures to daily objectives.

Tell students that one way to produce electricity is by use of the hydroelectric systems that store water in huge reservoirs and release a little at a time to drive turbines that, in turn, generate electricity. That electricity is delivered to businesses, homes, factories, and every stationary place where electrical power is needed.

Ask the students to research the components that go into a hydroelectric power plant system through print and online sources.

While they are researching those components show them how water can be used to drive (rotate) a shaft. Using Tinkertoys, have students construct a small "fan" with the multiple (the more the better) fan blades connected to a circular block by short Tinkertoy sticks. Be sure that the fan is free to move on the shaft. Now take a pitcher of water and pour the water on the fan blades. That will drive (rotate) the shaft, assuming that the shaft rotates freely. Hold the pitcher low to the blades, then lift the pitcher so that it attains a height over the blades of about six feet. Notice that the shaft rotates faster as the pitcher is held higher. See Figure 6.22.

Figure 6.22 Tinkertoy Turbine.

One principle that the students should take away from this demonstration is that the water in the pitcher has "potential" energy, and we can convert that "potential" energy to "kinetic" (movement) energy by pouring it down to earth. The greater the height of the pitcher pouring the water, the faster the water moves and the faster the shaft will turn. The faster the shaft turns, the greater the electrical output.

So, the fast water rotates the shaft, but how does that create electricity? Ask the students to look up Michael Faraday, a British scientist of the 19th century in print and online sources.

Have students list important facts they learned about Faraday, magnets, and generating electric current. Faraday showed that moving a magnet around a copper conductor generated electric current in that conductor. Thus, he showed that magnetism and electricity were parts of the same phenomenon. Ask the students to imagine a rotating conductor shaft surrounded by a permanent magnet. The rotation of the conductor shaft generates current in the shaft because of its movement in the magnetic field.

Tell students that one of the major features of hydroelectric power is the dam. A dam is a structure that holds water in a reservoir higher than the turbine/power plant. See Figure 6.23.

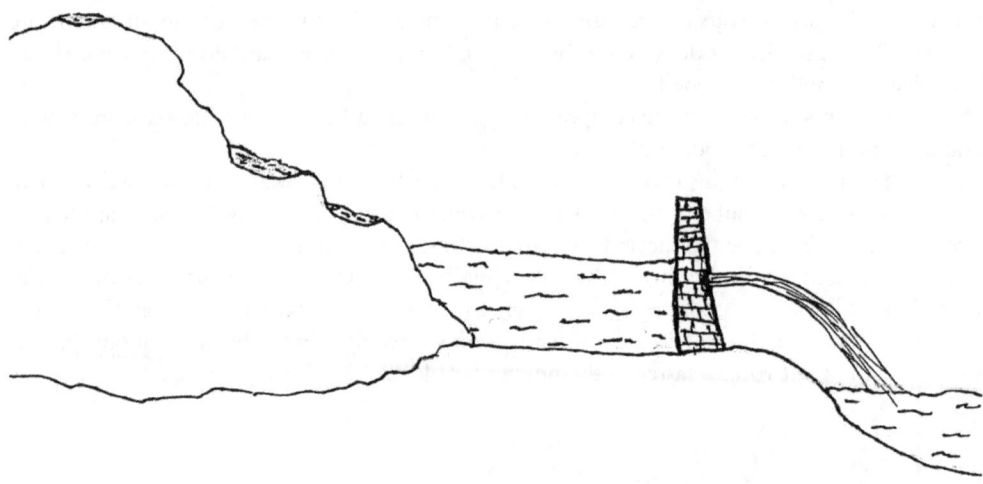

Figure 6.23 Dam.

It is typically fed by rainfall and rivers. The dam is used for flood control as well as electrical power generation. It depends for its operation on the difference in height between the water in the reservoir and the turbine below. Remember, the potential energy of the water contained in the reservoir must be converted to the kinetic energy of flowing water in order to rotate the turbine's shaft.

Ask students why dams are important. Have them look up information on various dams: Grand Coulee Dam in Washington State; the Wilson Dam in Florence, Alabama; the largest dam in the world, the Guri Dam in Venezuela; and the second largest, the Aswan Dam in Egypt. Some of these dams are earthen dams (constructed by massive amounts of dirt) and some are concrete dams.

Ask students to read about the worst dam disaster in U.S. history, the breaching of the South Fork Dam near Johnstown, Pennsylvania, in 1889, when the dam collapsed and sent the entire reservoir of water racing through the town on a 40-foot wave front a half mile wide.

In order to gain some understanding about dams, ask the students to build one. Here are two ideas for building a dam. Remember, the students will require two water levels (one for the reservoir, one for the turbine). The two levels will be separated by a dam. The dam can be constructed of any available material.

One possibility is two plastic boxes.

Obtain a long plastic box and fill it with sand and small rocks (gravel). Students need a river, so have them scoop out the sand and rocks to produce a river bed with banks on each side. The river can be as deep as the box. Then construct a dam across the river. What shall the dam be made of? The students can bring popsicle sticks and glue them together to produce about a 4-inch width for the dam. Insert the popsicle stick dam into the sand and rocks on either side of the "banks" of the river. Finally, carefully pour the water upstream of the dam and watch as the water fills up the portion of the "river" on the reservoir side of the dam. Don't pour the water on the sand … just on the part of the river that the students have dredged. Some of the water will leak through the dam. That's okay. Dams are not supposed to be water tight.

Observe the leakage of the water on the other side of the dam. This is the water that will drive the turbine to create electricity.

If the dam is too leaky, ask the students what they should do. They may have to reinforce the bottom of the dam. Simply use more than one layer of popsicle sticks at the bottom of the dam.

Have students keep track of actions they take in a logbook.

Here is the second idea for dam-building: break students into groups, or have a few students at a time work on a build-a-dam project.

Use a plastic swimming pool or other large container filled about halfway with water. Have students use dirt, rocks, bricks, and other hard materials to build a dam. Have them dig a trench in the dirt and place the hard materials somewhere along the trench to block the water. Have students observe the properties of water that tend to change course to move past obstacles. The students' job is to build a dam to stop the flow of water.

During the dam building project, have students ask questions about why the water changes course and seeks to go past the dam. From their questions, have them plan and try multiple solutions until they are able to stop the water.

Once the water is stopped from flowing, have students move rocks to let the water flow and observe the amount of initial force it uses as it seeks to continue its flow.

Sample Closure

Review parts of a hydroelectric power plant. Require students to use the vocabulary words when they answer questions. There are two parts to producing a hydroelectric power plant: the dam and the turbine. The dam provides a reservoir of water with potential energy and the turbine produces electricity from the kinetic energy of the falling water. Suggest that next time students are near a dirt or sand source, they could build a dam with solid materials.

Formative and Summative Assessment

Formative Examples

LET STUDENTS SHOW OFF THEIR LEARNING

Ask students to name the two major parts of a hydroelectric power plant.
Ask students to describe their experiences in building a small dam.

IF-ONLY STATEMENTS

If only I had access to a super large reservoir and a huge dam, I would _____.

I-CAN STATEMENTS

____ I can build a small dam and explain the advantages of hydroelectric power generation.

Summative Examples

Projects, oral and written tests

Extend Learning

Explain the differences in earthen dams and concrete dams and describe the advantages of each.
Explore the attributes of the use of wind, solar, and hydroelectric power as well as nuclear and fossil fuel to create electricity and provide it to society.
Research how we get most of our electrical energy.

Sensory Checklist

Check the senses students use during this lesson.
See Sensory Chart for Unit Plans, Table 4.4 and downloadable online

Online References

An Overview of the 1889 Tragedy. See Figure 6.24.
https://www.jaha.org/attractions/johnstown-flood-museum/flood-history

Reclamation/Projects & Facilities/Dams. See Figure 6.25.
https://www.usbr.gov/projects/facilities.php?type=Dam

10 Largest Dams in the World. See Figure 6.26.
https://largest.org/structures/dams/

Hydroelectric Power: How It Works. See Figure 6.27.
https://www.usgs.gov/special-topics/water-science-school/science/hydroelectric-power-how-it-works

Saturday Science: Build a Dam. See Figure 6.28.
http://www.childrensmuseum.org/blog/saturday-science-build-a-dam

Art Unit Plan > Visual Art and Drama

Adapt learning for your grade level and the needs of your students and break it down for multiple daily lessons.

Become an Expert

Learn more than you will ever teach about creating diagrams and ways to use puppets and drama to express the four stages of the water cycle.

Essential Questions

Determine one to two essential questions for daily lessons to provide a framework, such as:

What elements of visual art can be distinguished in a diagram/representation of the water cycle?
What motions could a puppeteer use to dramatize the stages of the water cycle?

126   Planning Sensory-Rich STEAM Unit Plans

Objectives

Select or adapt one to three objectives for your daily lesson plans.
Students will learn to:

Connect scientific knowledge about the water cycle and artistic practice through the visual arts.
Observe and distinguish different stages of the water cycle.
Understand how lines, shapes, and colors can be used to represent the stages of the water cycle.
Experiment with a variety of art materials to draw and represent the water cycle.
Demonstrate how a diagram can represent the cycling of water due to temperature variations caused by the Sun and the wind.
Represent scientific knowledge about the stages of the water cycle through drama.
Make puppets that have simple movements controlled by hand and complex movements controlled by transition mechanisms such as rods and string.
Distinguish properties of water in various states and express them through simple and complex movements with puppets.
Vary voice, emotions, and movement through puppets to show the effects that are caused when the duration of one of the stages of the water cycle is prolonged or delayed.
Use vocabulary related to each of the stages of the water cycle when speaking through their puppets.
Use music and sound effects during dramatization of the water cycle.

Vocabulary

Choose two to three words to teach in daily lessons. See Chapter 3 for ways to teach vocabulary.

water cycle	illustrate
precipitation	sketch
collection	lines
evaporation	color names
condensation	shape names
water vapor	diagram
circulate	mediums
solid	schematic
liquid	outline
gas	drama
clouds	theater
sublimation	stage
de-sublimation	puppetry
infiltration	puppeteer
accumulation	spectators
seepage runoff	plot or sequence
transpiration	interpretation
dew	projection
percolation	animation
ground water	transition mechanism
gravity	improvisation
represent	

Materials and Resources

Use the HELP hierarchy in Chapter 4 for lists of multisensory materials.

Real-World Experiences

Clouds and other weather conditions seen from the classroom
Glass with condensation
Crayons
Colored markers
Sharpie markers
Paint brushes
Pastel chalk
Drawing paper
Cardboard
Transparency film
Scissors
Glue
Jumbo craft sticks or tongue depressors
Socks
Paper lunch bags
Felt pieces
Googly wiggle eyes
Yarn

Real-World Artifacts

Water faucet and sink
Empty container

Representations

Bracelet activity for the water cycle. (See Online References for the QR code for this website.)
  https://www.bgsu.edu/content/dam/BGSU/COSMOS/Documents/waterCycleBracelet-envirn.pdf

Visuals

See Online References at the end of this unit plan.
Diagrams
Pictures
Videos

Copies of a simple water cycle diagram: See Figure 6.29.

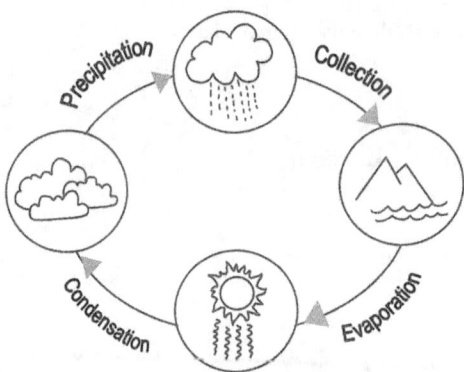

Figure 6.29 Water Cycle.

Easy Water Cycle Drawing (3:35) (See Online References for the QR code for this website.)
https://m.youtube.com/watch?v=9iOarozb9E4&feature=youtu.be

Written

See Online References at the end of this unit plan.
Pearl the Raindrop: The Great Water Cycle Journey by Rana Boulos, ages 3–8
I Am the Rain: A Science Book for Kids About the Water Cycle and Change of Seasons by John Paterson, ages 3–8
Evaporation, Transpiration, and Precipitation: Water Cycle for Kids Children's Water Books by Baby Professor, all ages
The Great Big Water Cycle Adventure by Kay Barnham, ages 5–8
The Water Cycle at Work by Rebecca Jean Olien, ages 6–8
Easy to Make Puppets and How to Use Them by Fran Rottman, ages 2–12
Puppet Mania! by John Kennedy, ages 8–10
Making Puppets Come Alive: How to Learn and Teach Hand Puppetry by Larry Engler, all ages

Oral and Aural

Water Cycle Song: Sing Along GoNoodle. (See Online References for the QR code for this website.)
https://www.youtube.com/watch?v=KM-59ljA4Bs

Set, Procedures, Closure

Read Chapter 2 for multiple ways to plan multisensory sets and closures.

Sample Set

Put a picture that shows the four stages of the water cycle: precipitation, collection place, evaporation, and condensation in a prominent place in the classroom. Or, if you have a water source in your classroom, number the parts of the water cycle. 1. Faucet as precipitation, 2. Sink full of water as collection site, 3. Empty container to show evaporation, and 4. Glass covered with condensation. Point out each feature and ask students what they think the stages of the water cycle have in common. Build on their ideas and tell them they will be making a diagram of the water cycle and an articulated puppet to move and explain how water moves through each of the stages.

Procedures

Plan a variety of instructional strategies that include direct teaching, modeling, guided and independent practice, and inquiry. Include critical thinking, questioning, and investigation.

Match procedures to daily objectives.

Students will view videos, and collect factual information from the Internet about the water cycle that will help with a diagram representation. Be sure they include evaporation, condensation, precipitation, and water collection in their search. More stages such as transpiration can be added for older students.

Once students have reviewed the information, have them write down features they want to include in their representation of the stages of the water cycle.

Provide each student with a simple printed outline copy of a diagram of the water cycle, a blank transparency film, and a fine black sharpie. Ask them to place the transparency film over the printed version and trace the outline of the stages (evaporation, precipitation, condensation, collection) of the water cycle diagram. Ask students to look at the lines and shapes and think about ways color and pictures could make the diagram even better.

Have students use a variety of art materials to add details to the outline and pictures of the representations of each of the stages of the water cycle.

Pair students and have them compare their diagram representations of the water cycle. Tell them to discuss how the diagrams are the same and how they are different, but still represent the water cycle correctly. Ask them to pick one thing they like about the other person's representation of the water cycle. Tell them to think of two things they could add to their diagrams to make them more effective for representing the water cycle.

Before the lesson on puppetry, select and read books to the students and leave them where students can have access to them during their free time to review information on the water cycle.

Put a variety of materials students can use to make a puppet in a pillow case. Ask students one at a time to come up and pull something out of the pillow case. After about the fifth student has pulled out something from the pillow case, ask the class what they think they will be doing during the lesson. Continue having students pull out materials until the class has guessed that they will be making something. Pour out the remainder of the materials and ask if anyone has an idea how these materials can be used in the lesson on the water cycle.

Tell students that they are going to create a simple or articulated (jointed) water drop puppet to dramatize one of the four stages of the water cycle (precipitation, collection, evaporation, and condensation) using materials from the pillow case. Have students select the stage of the water cycle they want to dramatize. Have them use cardstock paper and other materials to design a puppet and attach it to a tongue depressor or jumbo craft stick. To make an articulated puppet, help students, if necessary, attach wooden dowls to the legs so they can manipulate them. See Figures 6.30 and 6.31.

Different Types of Puppets

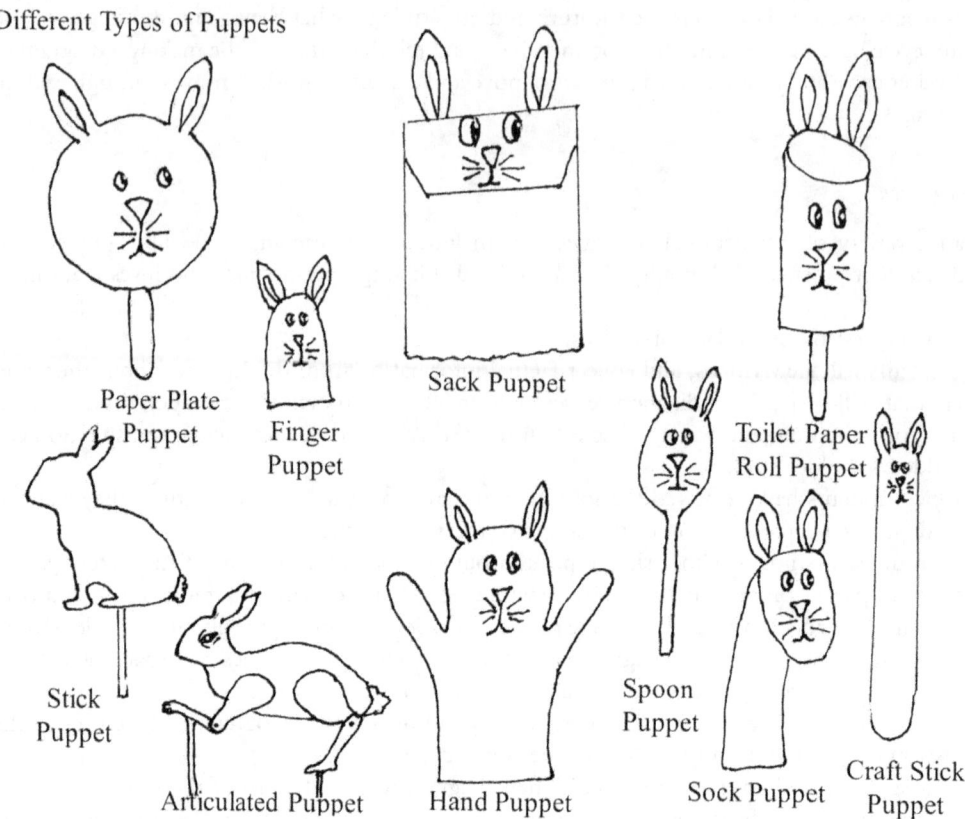

Figure 6.30 Different Types of Puppets.

Figure 6.31 Example of a Simple and Articulated Water Drop Puppet.

Let students work individually or in small groups to create their puppets and have them write a fact-based script about the adventure their little water drop will have as it goes through the four stages of the water cycle. Give students time to practice their parts using their puppets. Show them how to vary their voices in pitch and loudness and remind them that voices and motions help their puppet characters come alive.

A variation is to combine four students, each with a different stage of the water cycle, to practice using their puppets to show and explain the importance of each of the stages.

Have students use their puppets to practice their parts with the Water Cycle Song: Sing Along GoNoodle https://www.youtube.com/watch?v=KM-59ljA4Bs to practice using improvisation, music, movements, and puppets. (See Online References for the QR code for this website.)

Sample Closure

Have each group stand together and ask students to explain why their stage of the water cycle is important. Have students debate why their stage is the most important and conclude with the fact that all the stages are necessary to work together.

Formative and Summative Assessment

Formative Examples

LET STUDENTS SHOW OFF THEIR LEARNING

Act out one or more stages of the water cycle.

IF-ONLY STATEMENTS

If only I could make my puppet talk about the water cycle it would say,_____.

I-CAN STATEMENTS

___I can use drawings to create a diagram of the water cycle.

Summative Examples

Projects, presentations, oral, and written tests

Extend Learning

Explore the parts of the Earth that receive the most and least precipitation and represent information on a diagram.

Investigate disasters caused by weather such as hurricanes, tornadoes, and droughts and create a proportional image of the water cycle that represents the weather patterns in these areas.

Sensory Checklist

Check the senses students use during your lesson.
See Sensory Chart for Unit Plans, Table 4.4 and downloadable online

Online References

Bracelet activity for the water cycle. See Figure 6.32.
https://www.bgsu.edu/content/dam/BGSU/COSMOS/Documents/waterCycleBracelet-envirn.pdf

Easy Water Cycle Drawing (3:35). See Figure 6.33.
https://m.youtube.com/watch?v=9iOarozb9E4&feature=youtu.be

H_2O – The Mystery, Art, and Science of Water. See Figure 6.34.
http://witcombe.sbc.edu/water/music.html

Teaching the Water Cycle: Activities, Resources, and a Freebie. See Figure 6.35.
https://elementarynest.com/teaching-water-cycle-activities

BrainPop Jr. Water Cycle. See Figure 6.36.
https://jr.brainpop.com/science/weather/watercycle

Teacher Planet: Water Cycle. See Figure 6.37.
https://www.teacherplanet.com/content/water-cycle

Exploring the Water Cycle Through Music! See Figure 6.38.
https://www.artsmendocino.org/wp-content/uploads/sites/www.artsmendocino.org/images/2016/08/2013gaspmodelprojectalimiller.pdf

Water Cycle Song: Sing Along GoNoodle. See Figure 6.39.
https://www.youtube.com/watch?v=KM-59ljA4Bs

Mathematics Unit Plan > Measurement, Data, and Statistics

Adapt learning for your grade level and the needs of your students and break it down for multiple daily lessons.

Become an Expert

Learn more than you will ever teach about the three states of matter, the four stages of the water cycle, evaporation, freezing, melting, condensing, and the purposes of observation, recording, and evaluation of physical phenomena.

Essential Questions

Determine one to two essential questions for daily lessons to provide a framework for learning, such as:

What are some good ways to measure the amount of water evaporation?
How much water passes a river landmark in an hour on its way to the sea?

Objectives

Select or adapt one to three objectives for your daily lesson plans.
Students will learn to:

Describe measurable features of each stage of the water cycle.
Calculate the measurement of liquid volumes in milliliters and liters.
Order the depth of water collected in a glass, bucket, and puddle in inches or centimeters.
Differentiate between the measuring depth of water to the volume of water in a container.
Determine the variables that affect the amount of water that evaporates from water collection sites.
Investigate how the Sun is a vital part of the water cycle.
Estimate the length of time it will take for total evaporation to occur from a glass, bucket, and puddle.

The Water Cycle

Measure the amount of water that evaporates from each source each day.
Document the level of sunshine that shines on the water in a glass, bucket, and puddle.
Determine what meteorologists do when they measure rainfall.
Calculate the amount of water that a river distributes to the sea in a day or hour.
Relate the evaporation rate of water in your area to the rainfall in the same area.
Learn and use measures of fluids (fluid ounces, pints, quarts, liters, cubic centimeters).
Describe how much water humans should drink in one day.
Formulate the path water goes from human consumption throughout the four stages of the water cycle.
Calculate averages of consumption of water by drinking and averages of rainfall.
Record and transfer data to spreadsheets.

Vocabulary

Choose two to three words to teach in daily lessons. See Chapter 3 for ways to teach vocabulary.

precipitation	cup
drought	ounces
dehydrate	fluid ounces
evaporation	pint
water vapor	quart
condensation	gallon
flood	liter (l)
flood plain	milliliter (ml)
consumption	cubic centimeter (cc)

Materials and Resources

Use the HELP hierarchy in Chapter 4 for lists of multisensory materials.

Real-World Experiences

Plastic water glasses of different sizes
Several containers with graduated marks on the side in milliliters and ounces with different-sized openings at the top (measuring cups are a good start).
Water source
Notebook for observations of the levels of water in each container
Logbook

Visual

See Online References at the end of this unit plan.

Written

See Online References at the end of this unit plan.
National Geographic Readers: Water by Melissa Stewart, ages 6–9
What's Inside the Water Cycle by William B. Rice, ages 8–12

A Drop Around the World by Barbara Shaw McKinney, ages 5–12
What is a Forecast? by Jennifer Boothroyd, ages 5–8
Inside Science: Forecast the Weather by Sue Gibbison, ages 8–11

Set, Procedures, Closure

Read Chapter 2 for ways to plan sets and closures.

Sample Set

Tell the students, "Today we are going to learn about water: how much you drink, how much is in the atmosphere, how much falls as rain or snow." Ask students how much water they drink each day. A simple question, perhaps, but if the answers are "six glasses" or "eight glasses," then repeat the question and focus on how much water is in each glass. Have several different-sized glasses available to hold up. Hold the biggest one up: "Do you mean glasses this size?" Hold the smallest one up: "Or glasses this size, or something in between?"

Procedures

Plan a variety of instructional strategies that include direct teaching, modeling, guided and independent practice, and inquiry. Include critical thinking, questioning, and investigation.

Match procedures to daily objectives.

We know that we need some robust way to measure how much water we drink. So, tell the students that we are going to determine how much water is in each of the different-sized glasses. Fill up each glass with water. Show a transparent container that has graduated marks on its side and explain that the students will determine how much water is in each glass by pouring the water into the graduated container and measuring its volume. Demonstrate this measurement process. Ask what the unit of measure is.

Explain that one convenient unit of measure for volume of fluids is the "fluid ounce," not to be confused with "ounce" which is a unit of weight. Remember, 16 ounces equals 1 pound in weight, but 16 fluid ounces equals 1 pint in volume: 32 fluid ounces equals 1 quart, and 128 fluid ounces equals 1 gallon. Students should understand that "ounce" and "fluid ounce" don't even measure the same thing. In the metric system, cubic centimeters and liters measure fluid volume. One thousand cubic centimeters equals 1 liter.

Pour each glass of water into the graduated container. Measure the number of fluid ounces. If the graduated container is too small to hold all the water from one of the glasses, ask the students to figure out a way to measure it anyway. Write down all the measurements.

Now, ask again, "How much water do you drink each day?" This time insist that the answer be given in fluid ounces, cups, or pints. The students are unlikely to know at first, but ask them to keep track of the amount of water over the next several days and have an answer for the next few days.

Questions are sure to arise concerning other liquids and drinking from a fountain. Since most liquids (orange juice, soda, and so forth) are mostly water, tell the students to count everything they drink over the next 24 hours as water. Or call it liquids or fluids. Tell them to measure the time that they drink from a drinking fountain and have a conversion table that converts the time they stand drinking from the fountain to the amount in fluid ounces they consume. This may take some experimentation.

One way to keep the students involved is to ask them to keep a logbook, just like researchers and experimentalists, for how much they drink. The logbook can be used to record the water they drink for five days or longer.

When the recording time the students compiled is complete, look at the logbooks they compiled. Put the amounts on a daily basis on the board. Leave the names off for privacy purposes. Note the largest and smallest amount of water recorded. The difference between these two numbers is called the "range" of the data. Discuss the *range*.

Ask what the average amount of water that students drink per day is. Show the students how to make the calculation and ask them to calculate the average that they drank per day over the experiment.

Using several graduated containers, pour into each the same number of fluid ounces. Be sure that some of the containers have different-sized openings at the top. Place the containers in different parts of the room without lids. If the room has windows, place both a container with a large "mouth" and one with a smaller "mouth" near a window. Mark the level of the water and ask the students to record the level for each container in their logbook.

Do this for several days. At the end of the experiment, record how much water was lost by evaporation from each container. Ask students where the water went.

Discuss reasons for the differences. (Temperature, amount of surface area exposed to the Sun, atmosphere, and so forth.) For advanced students, calculate the surface area of each container.

Review the four stages of the water cycle and emphasize how heat from the Sun causes water to be in constant motion.

Consider Figure 6.40.

Figure 6.40 Bodies of Water: Collection.

Extrapolate the results to the bodies of water that the students are familiar with: lakes, rivers, seas, oceans. How much water evaporates from these sources each day? How many fluid ounces of water evaporate into the atmosphere each day and eventually returns to the Earth's surface in the form of rain?

Sample Closure

Ask students some challenging questions: What would happen to the oceans if the temperature were increased significantly? Would evaporation increase or decrease? Would rain increase or decrease? We often talk about conservation of water. What do we really mean? Can we really destroy water? Or, are we talking about simply changing the form of water or its location? Tell the students to share this information with family and friends.

Formative and Summative Assessment

Formative Examples

LET STUDENTS SHOW OFF THEIR LEARNING

Ask each student to describe the two experiments with water with emphasis on how much water they drank on average per day and the average amount of water that evaporated per day.

IF-ONLY STATEMENTS

If only the water in my body would evaporate, I would _____.

I-CAN STATEMENTS

___ I can keep a logbook and determine average amounts of water that evaporate each day.
___ I can calculate how much water will be evaporated from a lake if I know the temperature and the surface area.

Summative Examples

Oral and written tests and projects

Extend Learning

Find out what percentage of one's body is made up of water.
Calculate the variance and standard deviation of the amount of water lost by evaporation over several weeks.

Sensory Checklist

Check the senses students use during this lesson.
See Sensory Chart for Unit Plans, Table 4.4 and downloadable online

Online References

Climate Kids: What is the Water Cycle? See Figure 6.41.
https://climatekids.nasa.gov/water-cycle/

National Oceanic and Atmospheric Administration: Water Cycle. See Figure 6.42.
https://www.noaa.gov/education/resource-collections/freshwater/water-cycle

Water Cycle. See Figure 6.43.
https://byjus.com/biology/water-cycle/

NASA Precipitation Education. See Figure 6.44.
https://gpm.nasa.gov/education/water-cycle

Chapter 7

Nutrition and Health

Introduction

"Little Jack Horner" a nursery rhyme about a little boy eating a plum pie, describes nutritious and non-nutritious ingredients and how they are often combined into one delicious dish. Through STEAM content, Science, Technology, Engineering, Art, and Mathematics, students will learn science facts on the effects of natural and manmade ingredients in food and use them to make healthy eating choices. Students will learn technology as they follow the step-by-step directions to search for information and present this information on tables and through avatars. Through the engineering chemical process of heat transfer, students will learn about temperature and the three forms of chemical elements and compounds in foods: gas, liquid, and solid. Students will learn ways to use art to represent nutritious foods through sculpture and pastel chalk drawings. From selecting nutritious foods to planning healthy diets, mathematics is vitally important for students to compute the percentages of nutrients in foods. The five unit plans follow a nine-step format: Become an Expert; Essential Questions; Objectives; Vocabulary; Materials and Resources; Set, Procedures, and Closure; Formative and Summative Assessment; Extend Learning; and a Sensory Checklist. Online References contain QR codes that can be optically used to access the websites at the end of each unit plan.

Science Unit Plan > Biology and Chemistry

Adapt learning for your grade level and the needs of your students and break it down for multiple daily lessons.

Become an Expert

Learn more than you will ever teach about specific nutrients: proteins, carbohydrates, fats, vitamins, minerals, and water for healthy meal planning, and safe handling of food.

Essential Questions

Determine one to two essential questions for daily lessons to provide a framework for learning, such as:

How do nutrients in foods affect our body?
What are differences between healthy and unhealthy foods?

DOI: 10.4324/9781003290889-10

Objectives

Select or adapt one to three objectives from the lists below for your daily lesson plans.
Students will learn to:

Recognize the names of the five food groups: fruits, vegetables, grains, dairy, and protein.
List each of the food groups from high to low based on the recommended amounts that should be eaten each day.
Plan menus for healthy snacks and meals.
Determine the total number of calories people should eat in a day.
Describe reasons to drink water instead of sugared drinks.
Explain benefits and harmful effects salt and sugar have on health and development.
Describe effects vitamins and minerals found in foods have on health and development.
Define the terms *saturated* and *unsaturated fats*.
Recognize names of healthy oils: olive, walnut, sesame, grapeseed, and sunflower.
Recognize names of unhealthy oils, coconut, partially hydrogenated, and palm oil.
Determine levels of healthy and unhealthy nutrients in foods from the labels on packages and cans of food.
Define *carbohydrates* and why they can be healthy and unhealthy in our diets.
List healthy and unhealthy carbohydrates.
Explain benefits and harmful side effects of carbohydrates.
Identify sources of protein.
Relate the effects of proteins on the body.
Identify sources of fiber.
Relate the effects of fiber on health and digestion.
Compare differences in nutritional values of processed and unprocessed foods.

Vocabulary

nutrient	cholesterol
vitamin	protein
mineral	fiber
sodium/salt	calorie
natural and unnatural sugars	carbohydrate
natural and added fats	fiber
saturated and unsaturated fats	unprocessed food
cooking oils	processed food

Choose two to three words to teach in daily lessons. See Chapter 3 for ways to teach vocabulary.

Materials and Resources

Use the HELP hierarchy in Chapter 4 for lists of multisensory materials.

Real-World Experiences

Empty cans of soup, fruit, vegetables, beans, and packages of cookies, nuts, and cereal with nutrition facts listed on the back
Examples of solid saturated fat found in meat and dairy sources
Examples of unsaturated fat found in cooking oils, nuts, avocados, and peanut butter
Examples of natural and unnatural sugars
Examples of foods from the five food groups
Bags of food samples
Individual pieces of donuts, cooked sausage, potato chips, raw carrots, apples, and grapes
Paper towels
Canned and packages of processed and unprocessed foods
Front pages of popular magazines that feature information on diets
Markers
Drawing paper

Visuals

See Online References at the end of this unit plan.
What's on My Plate? Choosing from the Five food Groups by Jennifer Boothroyd, age 6–9.
Super Foods for Super Kids Cookbook: 50 Delicious (and Secretly Healthy) Recipes Kids Will Love to Make by Noelle Martin, ages 8–12.

Written

See Online References at the end of this unit plan.

Set, Procedures, Closure

Read Chapter 2 for ways to plan sets and closures.

Sample Set

Important! *Check with parents and guardians for food allergies before bringing food into the classroom. Nuts are notorious for harming children with allergies, even if they are around them without eating them.*
 Give students a baggie each with a slice of fruit, piece of a vegetable, grain product, dairy product, and meat slice. Do *not* include nuts or food with nuts. Tell students they have a bag of vitamins, minerals, sugar, salt, carbohydrates, and fiber. Ask students to tell what their favorite snacks are. Tell them they will be learning about the nutritional ingredients in the foods they eat.

Procedures

Plan a variety of instructional strategies that include direct teaching, modeling, guided and independent practice, and inquiry. Include critical thinking, questioning, and investigation.

 Match procedures to daily objectives.
 Ask students to sample the food in their bags and have them note whether they taste sweet, salty, or fatty. Inform students of the healthy and unhealthy effects of salt, sugar, and fat and

have them determine which one of their favorite foods contains large amounts of salt, sugar, and fat and which ones they think are the healthiest.

Hang a large piece of chart paper in front of the class with five divisions labeled for each of the five main food groups: fruits, vegetables, grains, dairy, and protein. Ask students to name foods that would go into each category and write them on the chart. Discuss foods students eat at each meal and for snacks. With their help, use a different color to write their favorite foods in each of the categories on the food chart. Discuss the foods the students like to eat and determine how many they think are healthy. Periodically, revisit the information on the chart and add foods to each category. Select up to three words on nutritional facts to teach directly each day (see Chapter 3).

Have students look at the grain food group on the chart and name foods they may not have thought of such as cereals, cookies and cakes, pasta, rice, and oats. Ask if they want to add other favorite foods to the grain food group.

Have students consult online or print resources to determine whether fruit juices are as healthy, less healthy, or healthier than a piece of fresh fruit and discuss their findings. Guide students as they work and need help finding sources to consult.

Provide online and print sources for students to research the types of food high in protein. Different types of meat vary in the fat content. Have students determine meat, cheese, eggs, beans, and other foods that are high in protein and contain various amounts of saturated and unsaturated fats. Have students learn the recommended amounts of both types of fat in a healthy diet and determine the types of proteins they would recommend be a part of a healthy diet.

Introduce the terms *saturated* and *unsaturated fat* and have students study the differences between them. To show the high fat content in some favorite foods, bring in examples of saturated and unsaturated fatty foods such as donuts, cooked sausage, and potato chips for students to see, taste, and feel. Give students a paper towel and ask them to put the fatty food samples face down on the paper towel to see whether the fat leaves a mark on the towel.

Give students small pinches of sugar and salt and ask them to put a few granules on their tongue and describe how each one tastes. Discuss the unhealthy effects of consuming too much salt and sugar.

Provide a collection of canned and packaged processed and unprocessed food that have clearly written nutrition facts and ingredients for students to study. See Figure 7.1.

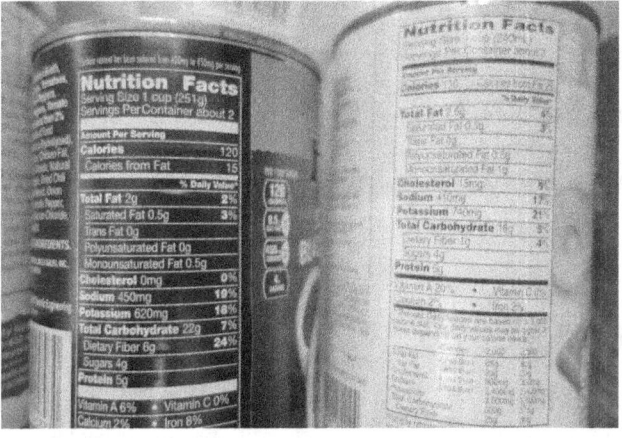

Figure 7.1 Nutritional Facts.

Ask students to evaluate differences of the amounts of salt, sugar, saturated and unsaturated fats, vitamins, and minerals listed for each product. Have students compare the nutritional differences between processed and unprocessed foods.

From the labels on food cans and packages, have students determine healthy food portions and compare the serving size found on food packages to the serving size they normally eat.

Guide students to find information on the importance of vitamins and minerals in a diet and why they are necessary for health and development.

Identify sources of carbohydrates and have students research the effects that carbohydrates have on their bodies and discuss how they contribute to weight gain, weight loss, and energy levels.

Tell students the definition of a calorie and have them compare the number of calories in a variety of processed and unprocessed foods. Have older students determine the number of calories they should eat in a day.

Have students explore ways they can burn up calories through physical activity. Ask for volunteers to demonstrate different ways they could exercise and lead the class in simple movements.

Challenge students to explain how excessive amounts of minerals, vitamins, fat, fiber, sugar, salt, carbohydrates, and protein can harm them.

Bring in headlines on diet information from popular magazines. Have students connect the diet information from the headlines to what they have learned in class.

Provide books and online sites for students to read and/or look at pictures about the food groups. Have them determine the foods they should eat in a day from each food group.

Show students a menu from a restaurant that contains a wide assortment of food options. Have them analyze the menu and write and illustrate their own menu for a healthy, breakfast, lunch, and dinner. In groups, have students share their menus and discuss the balance of healthy and unhealthy foods.

Sample Closure

Ask students to describe their favorite healthy snack and why they like it. Ask whether their favorite snack is processed or unprocessed. Review nutritional information about the snacks students like. Tell them to think about healthy eating and changes they should make in their food choices to grow strong healthy bodies. Relate to the puzzling facts that the same food nutrients can help or hurt students' health based on the amount they eat. Have students evaluate the foods they eat during the day to determine whether they are getting too much or too little of the essential ingredients from their food.

Formative and Summative Assessment

Formative Examples

LET STUDENTS SHOW OFF THEIR LEARNING

Ask students to look at healthy eating from the viewpoint of their body and share three pieces of advice their body would tell them.

IF-ONLY STATEMENTS

If only I could plan a healthy menu for lunch, I would_____.

I-CAN STATEMENTS

___I can name three healthy proteins.

Summative Examples

Oral and written tests and projects

Extend Learning

Determine differences among polyunsaturated and monounsaturated fats, omega-3 fatty acids. Explain how nutrients affect different parts of the body.

Sensory Checklist

Check the senses students use during your lesson.
See Sensory Chart for Unit Plans, Table 4.4 and downloadable online

Online References

USDA My Plate: Protein Foods. See Figure 7.2.
https://www.myplate.gov/eat-healthy/protein-foods

Enkimd (2018). Vegetables and Fruits High in Sodium. See Figure 7.3.
https://www.enkimd.com/high-sodium-vegetables.html

Barrie, L. (2020). Everyday Health: 11 Best and Worst Oils for Your Health. See Figure 7.4.
https://www.everydayhealth.com/news/best-worst-oils-health/

Mayo Clinic (2022): Nutrition and healthy eating. Carbohydrates: How carbs fit into a healthy diet. See Figure 7.5.
https://www.mayoclinic.org/healthy-lifestyle/nutrition-and-healthy-eating/in-depth/carbohydrates/art-20045705

Technology Unit Plan > Search, Keywords, Avatar

Adapt learning for your grade level and the needs of your students and break it down for multiple daily lessons.

Become an Expert

Learn more than you will ever teach about computer operations on searches, keywords, tables, and avatars.

Essential Questions

Determine one to two essential questions for daily lessons to provide a framework for learning.
How would you create an avatar to share information about health and nutrition, save it, and present it?
What personal traits could you use to show the personality of the avatar?

Objectives

Use or adapt one to three objectives from the list below in your daily lesson plans.
Students will learn to:

Explore ways to conduct an online search on the nutritional value of the five food groups.
Research different programs for creating a table.
Investigate different ways to create a table to represent nutritional information for the five food groups.
Determine ways to format a table to display information on the nutritional value of food in a graphical display.
Compare and contrast nutritional differences among the five food groups using an Excel spreadsheet.
Understand the meaning of an avatar as a personal web-based character.
Recognize the different types of avatars that can be created online.
Explore ways to conduct a search on creating an avatar.
Distinguish character and personal traits that can be represented through an avatar, like emotions, physical traits, movement, and personal items they like to use for play.
Determine different steps to design and create an avatar.
Explore different ways to design and create an avatar.

Vocabulary

Choose two to three words to teach in daily lessons. See Chapter 3 for ways to teach vocabulary.

diet	deficiency
fitness	cursor
nutrient	drag
calorie	columns
minerals	rows
carbohydrates	click
vitamins	insert
calcium	drop
trans fat	categories
saturated fat	data
polyunsaturated fat	mouse
sodium	headings
protein	slide
glucose	avatar
cholesterol	search engine
electrolytes	keywords
fiber	email
blood	save
additives	generator
malnutrition	tutorials
dehydration	representation

Materials and Resources

Use the HELP hierarchy in Chapter 4 for lists of multisensory materials.

Real-World Experiences

Computer with Microsoft PowerPoint
Avatar

Visuals

See Online References at the end of this unit plan.
Completed online table of the five food groups
PowerPoint

Written

See Online References at the end of this unit plan.
Nutrition Facts for Kids: Teaching Children the Facts about Nutrition by Maryse A. Rouffaer, ages 8–12
How to Teach Nutrition to Kids by Connie Liakos Evers, all ages
Jack and the Hungry Giant Eat Right with MyPlate by Loreen Leedy, ages 4–8 yrs.
Get Your Dragon to Eat Healthy Food: A Story About Nutrition and Healthy Food Choices by Steve Herman, ages 4–10
Avatar: The Last Airbender, the Search by Michael Dante, Bryan Konietzko, and Gene Luen Yang, ages 8–11

Set, Procedures, Closure

Read Chapter 2 for numerous ideas on ways to plan multisensory sets and closures.

Sample Set

The teacher will create an avatar and have it introduce the lesson for the class on the whiteboard. Tell students in the presentation that they will be building their own avatars, keeping in mind the theme of health and nutrition.

Procedures

Plan a variety of instructional strategies that include direct teaching, modeling, guided and independent practice, and inquiry. Include critical thinking, questioning, and investigation.

Match procedures to daily objectives.
Ask students how they can remember information about nutrition and health. Show students a large table you created online that includes foods from the five food groups and their nutritional values. Encourage them to point out the advantages of organizing information on a table and tell them they will learn how to create their own online table to record important information they can use for their avatar.

Before allowing students to use the Internet to search for health and nutrition information about the five food groups, make sure you have talked with the students about Internet safety, copyright issues, plagiarism, and proper conduct online. You can find appropriate websites and bookmark them for use with younger students. Check with your school district's policies for using and downloading information from the Internet.

Check with technology experts in your school district if you do not have Microsoft PowerPoint. They may have suggestions for the technology available.

Before the lesson, search online and find several tables with different topics, designs, and types of information, and print out multiple sets. Divide the students into groups of no more than four members. Give each group a set of the different ways to create tables. Provide time for students to peruse and discuss the tables and write down what they liked and disliked about them. Call on volunteers to share some of their findings with the class.

Tell the students they will be creating a table of the five food groups with categories of food examples, nutritional information, and suggested daily portions.

Have students research information on health and nutrition information for the five food groups online or in books to find examples of foods, daily suggested portions, and nutritional content.

Open Microsoft PowerPoint by double-clicking the icon and choose Blank Presentation. Then, click on Layout from the home ribbon and choose title and content.

In the center of the slide are faded icons. Roll the cursor over them and click on the one that says "Insert Table." Then decide the number of columns (6) and rows (5), and click OK.

> At top, click to add title and type "Five Food Groups."
>
> Click on the table and see table design at top and change to a plain design with no shading or color by using the up and down arrow to find and click on it. The table on the slide will change to it. This is done to save printer ink, if you print them.
>
> Click the first cell under the title and type "Food Group."
>
> Label the five remaining columns by clicking on the cells and type "fruit," "vegetable," "grain," "protein," and "dairy" in each cell. Demonstrate how to do this for those who need it.
>
> On the next row, first cell, type "Food Examples." Fill cells on that row with examples of that type of food. For example, under fruit you could type "apples," "oranges," or fruits of your choice.
>
> On the next row, first cell, type "Daily Portion." Type the suggestions for each food group.
>
> On the next two rows, type "Important Facts" in the first cell. Type two important facts about each food group in the remaining cells, one per row.
>
> Save the table, then print.

Once students have completed their tables on the five food groups, have them share their tables with their classmates by having them print a copy of their table and staple a blank piece of paper behind it. Place the tables on a centrally located table, face down. Ask students to read at least three of the tables and write two nice things they liked about it on the blank page on the back and return it to the table face down. When finished, have students pick their Five Food Groups tables and read the positive comments their classmates wrote.

Be sure to check with the school district about rules for creating an account or downloading files to build an avatar. For this lesson, the computer-generated avatar was built using the website, https://www.voki.com. For QR code, see Figure 7.6.

Have students design and manipulate computer-generated avatars using voki.com to share information about health and nutrition with their classmates.

Direct students to go online and research important information about health and nutrition. Tell students to write facts they think are important for a healthy life.

Once the students have the facts they need, guide them as they go to the website voki.com and follow the directions for creating their avatar.

When their avatar is completed, you can have the students name their avatar and ask them to type or record their voice to share important information about health and nutrition.

Have students review the appearance of their avatar and the information it expressed to be sure it is satisfactory to them. Assure students it is okay to make adjustments or even redo parts or all of their avatar.

The teacher or students can share each avatar with the class using the whiteboard.

After the presentations, ask the students what they liked and disliked about the project and what they would do differently next time if they were going to make another avatar.

Ask the students what other lessons they think would be effective using an avatar and what other things avatars could be used for, like teaching vocabulary words and definitions.

Make sure students save their avatar and email it to the teacher. Review each avatar, before asking students to send them to their parents or guardians. Check with school officials about their policies before sending online information to parents and guardians.

Invite other classes, grades, administration, or parents and guardians to come to your classroom and have the students present their avatars. You may break their presentations into several sessions by having three to five students present at a time.

Sample Closure

Review key steps for making an avatar beginning with the planning of the avatar and creating it into a digital character that they customized by including facial features, movements, and speech. Ask students which key facts about the five food groups they think are important to include in a written statement or by having their avatar talk to the class.

Formative and Summative Assessment

Formative Examples

LET STUDENTS SHOW OFF THEIR LEARNING

Have students show the avatar they created and describe how they designed and created it.

IF-ONLY STATEMENTS

If only I could lead a group to create a table about the five food groups, I would _____.

I-CAN STATEMENTS

___I can search, find, and download information on any topic using the Internet, safely.

Summative Examples

Projects, presentations, oral and written quizzes

Extend Learning

Create and advertise a healthy diet to send to popular magazines that would promote growth and development.

Create a graphic organizer of the food groups using Microsoft PowerPoint that includes examples, portions, and nutrients.

Sensory Checklist

Check the senses students will use during your lesson.
See Sensory Chart for Unit Plans, Table 4.4 and downloadable online

Online References

Computer-Generated Avatar. See Figure 7.6.
https://www.voki.com

My Plate from the United States Department of Agriculture. See Figure 7.7.
https://ChooseMyPlate.gov

United States Department of Agriculture. See Figure 7.8.
https://www.nutrition.gov/topics/nutrition-age/children/kids-corner

USDA My Plate. See Figure 7.9.
https://www.myplate.gov/life-stages/kids

5 Online Resources for Great Nutrition Lessons. See Figure 7.10.
https://www.educationworld.com/a_lesson/5_online_resources_great_nutrition_lessons.shtml

Engineering Unit Plan > Chemical Engineering

Adapt learning for your grade level and the needs of your students and break it down for multiple daily lessons.

Become an Expert

Learn more than you will ever teach about what chemistry and chemical engineering are and the differences between them. Learn about heat; heat transfer; the three forms of chemical elements and compounds (gas, liquid, and solid); and how to change one form into another.

Essential Questions

Determine one to two essential questions for daily lessons to provide a framework for learning, such as:

What is "heat"?
How is heat transferred from one substance to another?
How does heat transform a substance from solid to liquid to gas states?
How are heat and refrigeration used in the preparation of food and, especially, the sanitation and purity of our food?

Objectives

Select or adapt one to three objectives for your daily lesson plans.
Students will learn to:

Identify the three states of substances (gaseous, liquid, solid).
Describe the properties of the three states.
Identify everyday substances (elements and compounds) that are in the three states.
Compare the differences of molecular motion in the three states of liquids.
Describe heat as a form of energy.
Recognize that all matter has heat energy.
Transform substances from one state to another by the use of heat transfer.
Experiment with ways heat can transfer energy from one form of matter to another.
Slow or stop growth of bacteria in food and other decomposition (rotting) by cold temperatures.
Reduce levels of bacteria infestation by cooking food with a high temperature.
Observe the effects of prolonged exposure to ambient temperature and air on food.
Describe the units that measure temperature (heat).
Use both metric and English scales to measure temperature.
Explain the molecular action that occurs during the conduction of heat.
Relate molecular action to kinetic energy.

Vocabulary

Choose two to three words to teach in daily lessons. See Chapter 3 for ways to teach vocabulary.

Nutrition and Health 155

element	kinetic energy
compound	ambient temperature
gas	refrigeration
liquid	contamination
solid	bacteria
heat	atoms
heat transfer	molecules
energy	molecular motion
centigrade	random
Fahrenheit	conduction
Celsius	

Materials and Resources

Use the HELP hierarchy in Chapter 4 for lists of multisensory materials.

Real-World Experiences

Food coloring
Cold water
Hot water
Drinking glass
Dark clothing
Light (color) clothing
Ice
Dry ice
Thermometer

Visuals

See Online References at the end of this unit plan.

Written

See Online References at the end of this unit plan.

Set, Procedures, Closure

Read Chapter 2 for ways to plan sets and closures.

Sample Set

As students enter the classroom have a setup on a table that includes an inflated balloon, a glass of water, and a tray of ice cubes. Ask the children what is in the balloon, glass, and ice tray. The answers will be "air", "water", and "ice". Challenge the children to imagine how some of the material in the balloon, glass, and tray can be put into one of the other containers. That is, can they imagine putting the ice into the glass, the water into the tray, and either the ice or water into the balloon?

Procedures

Plan a variety of instructional strategies that include direct teaching, modeling, guided and independent practice, and inquiry. Include critical thinking, questioning, and investigation.

Match procedures to daily objectives.

It's all a question of heat. Have the students note what the temperature is in the room. This should lead to a discussion about how heat is measured. Ask the students to research how heat is measured and what the commonly used scales are.

Inform students that there are two common scales: Fahrenheit and Celsius. Find out about these names and why they are applied to temperature scales. Have students look up these names on various websites and get brief answers.

Have students determine that the Celsius scale has, as its zero point, the freezing point of water and as its 100-degree point, the boiling point of water. Ask whether the students can imagine why these numbers are used and why water is used as a standard?

Review with students that the Fahrenheit scale uses the freezing point of water as 32 degrees and the boiling point of water as 212 degrees. So, the scales are quite different, but the heat they measure is the same. That is, 0°C = 32°F and 100°C = 212°F.

Ask the students which degree is larger, a Celsius degree or a Fahrenheit degree. A little mathematical inspection will lead the students to the conclusion that the Celsius degree is larger, by a factor of 1.8 (9/5).

Return to the statement at the start of this procedure: *It's all a question of heat.* If the temperature in the classroom is, say 78°F (=25.6°C), then the temperature of the water in the glass is close to 78°F. The air in the balloon is also close to 78°F. But the ice can't be the same temperature. Ask the students why.

Ask the students to wait overnight and then inspect the ice in the ice tray. It will probably be completely melted. Use a thermometer to measure the temperature in the melted ice tray. It will probably be close to 78°F or whatever the ambient temperature is in the room.

Ask the students to dip their finger into either the glass or ice tray. Ask students whether the water is cool or warm to the touch. Despite the fact that the water is the same temperature as the air, it feels cool. Explain that our bodies' normal internal temperature is about 98.6°F.

Challenge students to summarize what they learned from touching warm and cold substances. Help them to grasp the important principle that heat travels from hot bodies to cold bodies and the difference in temperatures of the two bodies determine which way heat travels. So, when students dip their finger in the water, the heat leaves the students' bodies and goes into the water because the students are hotter than the water.

Now that students know how to measure heat (temperature) and know one of its characteristics, ask the students, "What is heat?" A number of definitions can be found. We chose the physics definition of heat from the website, https://wonders.physics.wisc.edu/what-is-heat/. For QR code, see Figure 7.11.

> "The study of heat is really the study of the atoms and molecules that make up an object. The faster the atoms are moving, the hotter the temperature because they have more energy."

The movement of atoms and molecules is consistent with the kinetic energy of moving objects.

Tell the students they are going to witness a demonstration that shows that heat and molecular motion are the same concept. Put hot water in one transparent glass and cold water in another. Make the temperatures as different as possible. Then, with an eyedropper, put a drop of food coloring into each glass. Direct students to note the differences in the time it took to color all the water each glass. Have them describe how the food coloring in the hot water moved

Nutrition and Health 157

quickly to color the entire contents of the glass, while the food coloring in the cold water moved more slowly. Have students discuss reasons why the molecules in the hot water circulated and moved faster than the molecules in the cold water.

Ask the students, "How many states of water are there?" They have worked with ice (solid water) and liquid water. Is there a third state? The answer that the students should offer is, yes, there is a gaseous state, which is why we have the balloon. Ask the students what the gaseous state of water is. It is water vapor.

Emphasize that all chemical elements have three states, and *it's all a question of heat* as to whether a substance exists as a solid, liquid, or gas. If a substance is solid, then it is below its freezing point and is cold. If a substance is a gas, then it is above its boiling point and is hot. Water and a few other substances are liquid at everyday temperatures. Ask the students to make a list of substances that are normally solid, liquid, and gaseous.

Show students a balloon is filled with air (gas). Ask them what the temperature of the air in the balloon is. It's around 78°F, the ambient temperature in the classroom. Ask the students what would happen if the air inside the balloon were heated.

One way to find out is to place the mouth of the balloon over a plastic water bottle. Fill a bowl with ice and water (make it as cold as possible) and another bowl with hot water from the tap. Then place the bottle into the hot water. What happens? Take it out of the hot water and insert the bottle into the ice water. Again, what happens? See Figure 7.12.

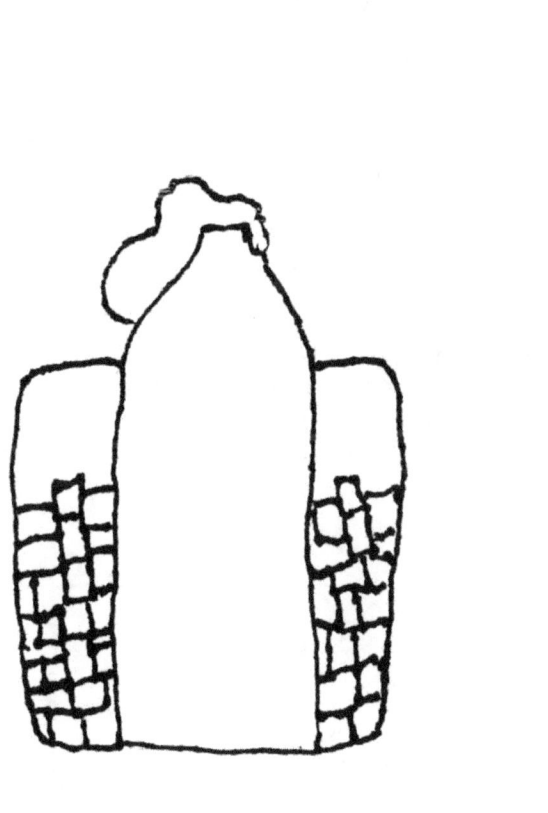
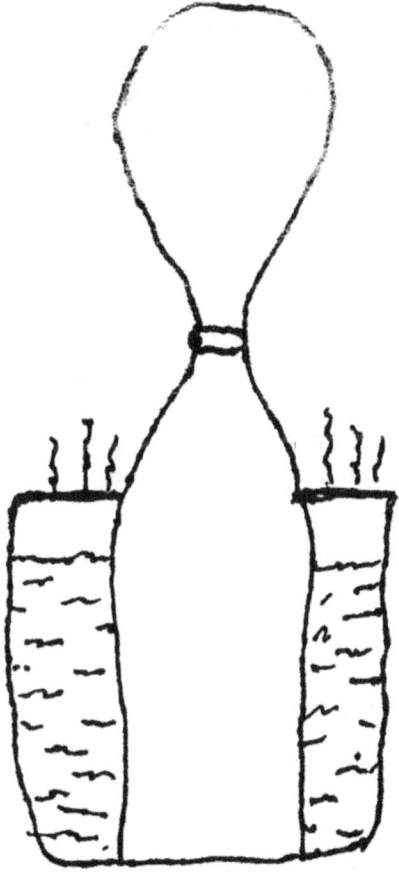

Figure 7.12 Bottles of Cold and Hot Water with Balloons.

Demonstrate another principle concerning heat. The principle is that as the molecules of the air get hotter, their velocity increases and they hit each other and the sides of the bottle with more energy. This force expands the balloon. But when the balloon is withdrawn from the hot water and placed in cold, the water molecules immediately slow down and the balloon is again deflated. Ask students to come up with one notable point about this demonstration. The demonstration can be done over and over again until the hot water cools and the ice water melts.

Leave out a scoop of ice cream overnight and compare it with some refrigerated ice cream. Write the results in a logbook.

Leave out a fresh banana, an apple, and a slice of bread in the classroom for two weeks and at the same time, put a fresh banana, apple, and slice of bread into a refrigerator. Compare the degradation of the fruits and bread left at room temperature with the refrigerated food. Write the results in a logbook.

Do the same for a piece of meat while putting another piece into the refrigerator for several days. Compare the degradation of the meat at room temperature with the refrigerated meat. Write the results in a logbook.

Ask students to conclude whether refrigeration is necessary to reduce contamination and to provide for the sanitation and purity of foods.

Sample Closure

Remind the students that water has three states: gaseous (water vapor), liquid, and solid (ice). Remind them that all three are very important for the water cycle. The gaseous state results from evaporation from oceans, seas, rivers, and every other body of liquid water. We drink the liquid state and we cool our drinks with the solid state (ice). Have students notice the three states of matter as they are at home or play outside.

Formative and Summative Assessment

Formative Examples

LET STUDENTS SHOW OFF THEIR LEARNING

Ask students to describe the three states of water and how each is important to us.
Ask students what *heat* is and how heat flows from one body to another.
Have students dramatize how molecules move in the three states of matter.
Ask students how refrigeration helps to keep food pure and sanitized.

IF-ONLY STATEMENTS

If only I could blow up balloons with hot air, I would _____.

I-CAN STATEMENTS

___ I can determine whether substances are solid, liquid, or gaseous.
___ I can describe what heat is and how it moves from body to body.

Summative Examples

Projects, oral and written tests

Extend Learning

Research which metals are liquid at room temperature. What are some uses of these metals? Explore how heat helps or hinders the breeding of bacteria in food.

Sensory Checklist

Check the senses students use during this lesson.
See Sensory Chart for Unit Plans, Table 4.4 and downloadable online

Online References

What Is Heat? See Figure 7.11.
https://wonders.physics.wisc.edu/what-is-heat/

How does sunscreen work? See Figure 7.13.
https://www.livescience.com/32666-how-does-sunscreen-work.html

Hot and Cold Science Experiments for Kids. See Figure 7.14.
https://www.mombrite.com/hot-and-cold-balloon-experiment/

Art Unit Plan > The Visual Arts

Adapt learning for your grade level and the needs of your students and break it down for multiple daily lessons.

Become an Expert

Learn more than you will ever teach about integrating sculpture and pastel chalk with nutrition and health.

Essential Questions

Determine one to two essential questions for daily lessons to provide a framework for learning, such as:

What upcycled objects can be used to make a sculpture that represents the five food groups?
What techniques can be used to create an illusion of space and depth in a 2-D still life of fruit?

Objectives

Select or adapt one to three objectives for your daily lesson plans.
Students will learn to:

Connect scientific knowledge of nutrition to artistic practice.
Investigate ways additive, subtractive, and relief methods can be used to create a sculpture that represents the five food groups.
Discover the use of different methods to assemble a sculpture from upcycled, found objects, and art media to represent food from one or more of the five food groups.
Produce an original work using upcycled and found objects along with other materials and art media to represent the five food groups.
Demonstrate ways to create depth in a chalk pastel still life.
Recognize ways the illusion of space or depth can be created through color and value, placement, size, overlapping, perspective, and the amount of detail with chalk pastels.
Connect scientific knowledge and artistic practice.
Understand the connection between artwork and other content knowledge.
Explore connections of a fruit still life with health and nutrition.
Demonstrate the use of chalk pastels in the creation of artwork.

Vocabulary

Choose two to three words to teach in daily lessons. See Chapter 3 for creative ways to teach vocabulary.

fruits	three-dimensional
vegetables	upcycled materials
starches	recycled materials
dairy	found objects (natural, paper)

Nutrition and Health

protein: animal-based
protein: vegetable-based
essential nutrients
vitamins
minerals
phytochemicals (color)
sculpture
collage
additive methods
subtractive methods
relief methods
form
symbolic shapes

air-dry clay
paper clay
rhythm
illusion of space
depth
linear perspective
blending
feathering
fixative
overlapping
value
scumbling

Materials and Resources

Use the HELP hierarchy in Chapter 4 for a list of multisensory materials.
Collect the following materials related to the five food groups ahead of time over a couple of months: grain-cereal box, dairy-milk jug, fruit-basket, protein- meat container, and fat-butter wrapper.

Real-World Experiences

Upcycled materials (fabric scraps, yarn, magazines, envelopes, pipe cleaners, cardboard boxes, tissue paper, newspaper)
Recycled materials (containers, variety of paper, and cardboard)
Variety of fruit (all shapes and colors)
Pastel chalk
Air-dry clay
Paper clay
Props for pictures (bowls, pitchers, non-breakable plates, cup and saucer, drinking glass, tablecloth)
Plastic bags, quart size or plastic grocery bags
Sketching tools (plastic fork, whisk broom, brush, straw, sponge)
Art tools (scissors, pencils, crayons, markers, washable acrylic paints, brushes, glue, staples and stapler, colored construction paper, tape, brads, water, pencils paper towels)

Real-World Artifacts

Found materials (natural leaves, acorns, sticks, pebbles)
Flexible hose neck desk lamp
Famous fruit and vegetable paintings

Representations

Plastic fruit and vegetables

Visuals

See Online References at the end of this unit plan.
Pictures of pastel drawings by famous artists

Written

See Online References at the end of this unit plan.
Board, chart paper
Chalk, markers, charcoal pencil, pencil
Post-it notes
Nutrition Facts for Kids: Teaching Children the Facts about Nutrition by Maryse A. Rouffaer, ages 8–12
How to Teach Nutrition to Kids by Connie Liakos Evers, all ages
Cézanne by Mike Venezia, ages 8–9
Paul Cézanne: Activities for Kids by Marisa Boan, ages 6–10
Children's Book of Art: An Introduction to the World's Most Amazing Paintings and Sculptures by DK, ages 4–8
A Child's Introduction to Art: The World's Greatest Paintings and Sculptures by Heather Alexander, ages 9–12
The Encyclopedia of Pastel Techniques: A Unique Visual Directory of Pastel Painting Techniques With Guidance on How to Use Them by Judy Martin, all ages
Pastels for the Absolute Beginner by Rebecca de Mendonca, all ages

Set, Procedures, Closure

Read Chapter 2 for multiple ways to plan multisensory sets and closures.

Sample Set

Place a variety of fruit, upcycling materials such as bits and pieces of fabric, bottle caps and tops, straws, combs, and other everyday items, and art tools in multiple plastic bags. Display bags. Shake one of the bags and ask students what they think is inside. Tell them that they will be making a sculpture of one or more of the foods from the five food groups using the upcycled materials in the bags. They will then use chalk pastels to create a picture of their sculpture.

Procedures

Plan a variety of instructional strategies that include direct teaching, modeling, guided and independent practice, and inquiry. Include critical thinking, questioning, and investigation.

Match procedures to daily objectives.
Divide students into groups of no more than four. Give one bag of fresh or plastic fruit, art tools, and upcycled materials on each table to each group and have them empty their bags and study the materials.

Tell students to examine their items and write ways they can use the materials to create a collage sculpture about one of the food groups. Encourage students to share and swap items from their bags if needed by other groups.

Show students ways to research information about the five food groups through printed sources and the Internet that will help them plan and design their collage sculpture.

Review information students learned about the categories within the five food groups and the effects they have on health and development. Engage them in a class discussion.

Have students plan a design, collect items, and construct a collage sculpture using themes from the five food groups. Have them choose a variety of upcycled and found natural materials and encourage them to use a variety of tools to add interest and realism to their sculptures. Provide paper towels for cleanup.

Use upcycled food containers to make a variety of fish. See Figures 7.15 and 7.16.

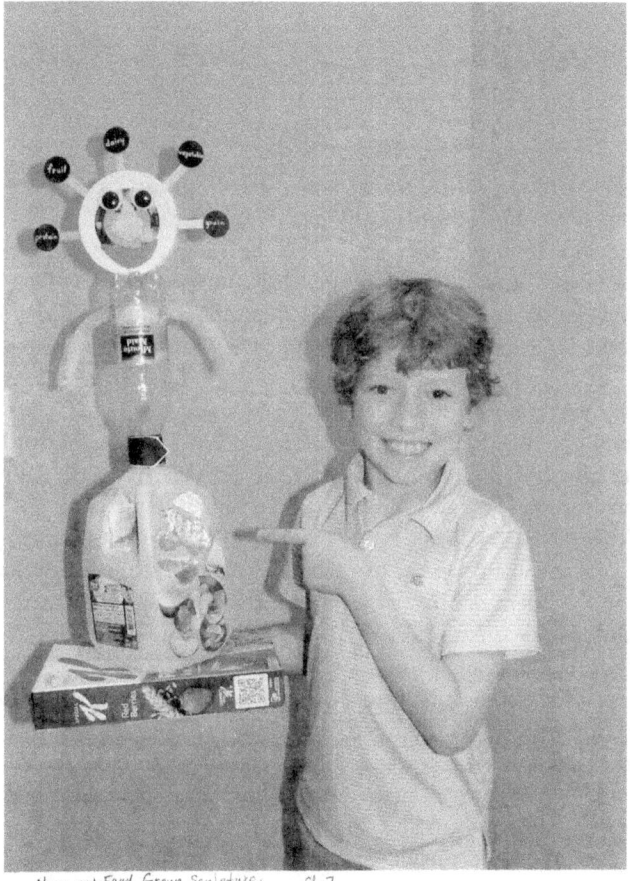

Figure 7.15 Jett Pointing to Upcycled Food Group Sculpture.

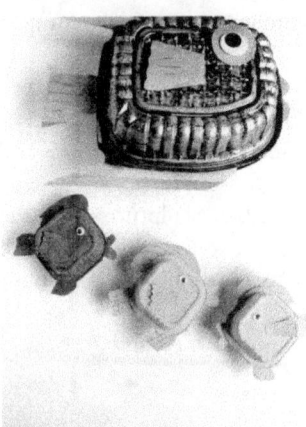

Figure 7.16 Food Container Made into Fish.

Have students examine each other's sculptures and make suggestions for additions or give structural advice.

Have students practice what they will say when they present their sculptures to the class and explain why they chose objects to represent food from the five food groups.

Search and find famous pastel drawings in books and online and make them available to students. Artists to consider are Paul Cézanne, Pierre-August Renoir, Mary Cassatt, Pablo Picasso, Jean Francois Millet, Eugene Delacroix, and Henri de Toulouse-Lautrec. Show work by famous artists. Their artwork will serve to inspire students as they draw and use pastels such as a Paul Cézanne–inspired pastel.

Ask students to share what they see in terms of lines, colors, shapes, and textures. Have them tell where their eye first went as they looked at the picture and where it moved. Ask students what they think the artist wants them to focus on and what the artist is trying to say. For questions that lead students to analyze artwork, go to https://drawpaintacademy.com/analyze-art. For QR code, see Figure 7.17.

View the picture and write important words on the elements of art such as line, color, value, shape, space, form, and texture on the board or chart paper. Leave them there. You may need to define or show examples of some of these elements.

Bookmark websites that spotlight Paul Cézanne and his work. Show pictures and tell students about the style of his artwork and his inspiration and read children's books about him. Discuss ways students can use Cézanne's ideas to create their own pictures.

Give small groups of students fruits and props to experiment with ways to create a still-life fruit display that will become a model for their still-life painting. Other food group items can be used to add interest and address the theme, health and nutrition the students are studying. For ideas and inspiration suggest that students consult the websites or books for pictures of Cézanne's artwork. See Figure 7.18.

Figure 7.18 Imitation of Cézanne's Pastel Chalk Still Life.

    Place sets of art materials for each group at the student tables for the project. Have extra art materials and clean-up items in a place that is easily accessible to the students. Each table should have a box of chalk pastels (Moore breaks the sticks in half, so more students can use a color and it gives nice edges to use), art paper, sketching tools, blending tools, and clean-up items. Be sure to have extra art paper and clean-up items in case of mistakes and accidents.

    Tell the students to study the still life and use a pencil or charcoal pencil to make a light outline sketch of the vignette. Have them put their name on the back of the paper before they add colors. Remind them as they begin to think about the chalk pastels to remember Paul Cézanne's artwork they viewed.

    When they are happy with their sketches, they will find chalk pastel colors they want to use. Remind them, that they may not have a chalk the exact color they want, but they can mix other colors and make it.

The students will begin to lay in the colors they want in their still-life picture. They can use techniques like blending, layering colors, use scumbling to add texture, and use feathering so the new color and the color underneath shows. Some students prefer to use their fingers to blend, so that is why extra paper towels are necessary. Encourage the students not to overwork their chalk pastels.

Using a flexible hose neck desk lamp, show students how changes in light create light and dark spots on objects.

Ask students to stop, look away, and then look back at their artwork to see if they need to add more techniques. Remind them of creating highlights and shadows by keeping in mind where the light source would be. When students are happy with their chalk pastel still life, lightly mist the artwork with a fixative such as hairspray or purchased sealers. Allow it to dry in a safe place.

Hang students' pastel pictures around the room at eye level for the students to view. Provide Post-it notes for students to write brief descriptions of the work. Encourage students to study each picture and write at least three things they see, feel, or think about the artwork.

Sample Closure

Set up the classroom as an art exhibition of the sculptures and pastel drawings. Have the students stand by their artwork and be ready to talk with classmates, friends from other classes, and families and guests about their work and how it relates to the five food groups. You could divide the class in half with each half taking turns being the audience and artists.

Formative and Summative Assessment

Formative Examples

LET STUDENTS SHOW OFF THEIR LEARNING

Have students share a list of search words they used to find ways to make collage sculptures from upcycled, found, and natural objects.

IF-ONLY STATEMENTS

If only I could be a famous artist like Cézanne, I would _____.

I-CAN STATEMENTS

___I can use a variety of materials and methods to represent the five food groups.

Summative Examples

Projects, presentations, oral and written tests

Extend Learning

Determine the use of additive and subtractive methods to create realistic or interesting spatial relationships in sculptures.

Nutrition and Health 167

Compare differences in technique between the work of impressionist artist, Claude Monet and post-impressionist artist Paul Cézanne.

Sensory Checklist

Check the senses students use during your lesson.
See Sensory Chart for Unit Plans, Table 4.4 and downloadable online

Online References

Analysis of Artwork. See Figure 7.17.
https://drawpaintacademy.com/analyze-art.

Famous Fruit and Vegetable Paintings. See Figure 7.19.
https://www.artst.org/famous-fruit-paintings/

See Figure 7.20.
https://duckduckgo.com/?q=famous+still+life+paintings+of+vegetables&t=chromentp&iax=images&ia=images

Cezanne's Still Life Art Work. See Figure 7.21.
https://duckduckgo.com/?q=pictures+of+Cezanne%E2%80%99s+still+life+artwork&iax=images&ia=images

Sculpture Project Ideas for Preschool and Kindergarten Kids. See Figure 7.22.
https://tinkerlab.com/sculpture-project-ideas-for-preschool-and-kindergarten-kids

3D Art & Sculpture. See Figure 7.23.
https://artfulparent.com/activities/sculpture

Eric Carle Museum: Painting with Found Materials. See Figure 7.24.
https://carlemuseum.org/education/making-art-together/painting-found-materials

Mathematics Unit Plan > Fractions, Percent, and Decimals

Adapt learning for your grade level and the needs of your students and break it down for multiple daily lessons.

Become an Expert

Learn more than you will ever teach about fractions, percents, and decimals, including addition, subtraction, multiplication, and division of fractions and the physical meanings. Learn the purpose of fractions, how they are used in the description of foods.

Essential Questions

Determine one to two essential questions for daily lessons to provide a framework for learning, such as:

What is a fraction and what does it mean?
How are fractions represented in normal everyday usage?
How can the arithmetic operations of addition, subtraction, multiplication, and division be implemented with fractions?
How can fractions be used to help us eat in a healthy way?
How can fractions be converted to percents?
How can fractions be converted into decimals?

Objectives

Select or adapt one to three objectives for your daily lesson plans.
Students will learn to:

Recognize that fractions are parts of a whole.
Recognize differences in whole numbers and fractions.
Represent fractions through drawings and in written form.
Identify equivalent fractions.
Understand the algorithm for creating equivalent fractions.
Reason about the size of individual fractions.
Name fractions on a number line.
Identify the numerator of a fraction.
Identify what the denominator of a fraction is.
Describe what is meant by 1/2, 1/3, 1/4, and so forth, by use of manipulatives.
Add and subtract fractions with the same denominator.
Add and subtract fractions with different denominators.
Convert fractions to percents and to decimals.
Convert percents and decimals to fractions.
Multiply fractions.
Divide fractions.

Vocabulary

Choose two to three words to teach in daily lessons. See Chapter 3 for ways to teach vocabulary.

whole number	divisor
fraction	dividend
equivalent	multiplicand
decimal equivalent	multiplier
product	common denominator
numerator	least common denominator
denominator	sector
repeating decimal	nutrient
quotient	recommended daily allowance
percent	(RDA) or Daily Value (DV)

Materials and Resources

Use the HELP hierarchy in Chapter 4 for lists of multisensory materials.

Real-World Experiences

Assorted cans of vegetables, fruits, meats, soup, and so forth
Notebook for recording parameters of recommended daily consumption of various foods

Visuals

See Online References at the end of this unit plan.

Written

I Can Halve Even Numbers by Clara Rose, ages 4–6
Good Enough to Eat: A Kids Guide to Food and Nutrition by Lizzy Rockwell, ages 5–9
Nutrition Facts for Kids: Teaching Children the Facts about Nutrition by Maryse A. Rouffaer, ages 8–12
Fractions Decimals & Percents by Chris McMullen, ages 9–12
Fractions, Decimals, and Percents by David A. Adler and Edward Miller, ages 6–9
Big Book of Math Practice Problems, Fractions & Decimals by Stacy Otillio and Frank Otillio, ages 9–11
Fractions and Decimals by Erin Muschla, ages 8–12

Set, Procedures, Closure

Read Chapter 2 for ways to plan sets and closures.

Sample Set

Give younger students a rectangular shape of paper. Ask how many rectangles they have. Then show the students how to fold the rectangle in half. Ask how many rectangles they have. Ask whether the two rectangles are larger, smaller, or the same size as the unfolded rectangle. Tell them that today we will learn about parts of a whole. Give older student or pairs of students one or two colorful tins of canned food. One tin should contain a vegetable or fruit and the other should contain meat, peanut butter, or soup. Ask them to read the labels of the cans and write down the nutrients and the percent of the daily values of various nutrients that are contained in a serving of the food. Tell them today we are going to learn some interesting things about fractions.

Procedures

Plan a variety of instructional strategies that include direct teaching, modeling, guided and independent practice, and inquiry. Include critical thinking, questioning, and investigation.

Match procedures to daily objectives.

For young students, hold a small pie in front of the class. Describe the pie and then cut the pie into two pieces. Ask the students how many pieces of pie they see. Tell the students that the *whole* pie has been cut into two pieces. Each piece is only a part or *fraction* of the original pie. Note that if the two pieces were put together again, they would constitute the whole pie.

Now cut the pie again and create a third piece. Tell students that the three pieces of pie would again reconstitute a whole pie if they could be put back together. The pieces are *fractions* of the whole pie. Have students observe that the more pieces (two, three, four, and so forth) of the pie, the smaller the pieces are. But they add up to a whole pie every time.

Tell the students that if we represent the whole pie by the number one (1), then each piece can be represented by a fraction. A fraction is always written with a numerator and a denominator, separated by a horizontal or slanted line (/). The number atop the line is called the numerator and the number below the line is called the denominator. The students can recognize fractions as distinct from whole numbers by that horizontal or slanted line separating the numbers. Whole numbers don't have that line.

Tell students to draw a circle. Then have them draw a line cutting through the circle. Tell them that the line cuts the circle into two pieces and each piece is a fraction of the whole circle.

To help students understand that the denominator represents the number of pieces of pie and the numerator represents the number of pies, write fractions 1/2, 1/3, 1/4, on the board and again ask students which amount of pie they would like to have.

A procedure for older students is to ask them what equivalent fractions are. Using the pie example, have the students cut the pie into four equal pieces. Ask how many pieces constitute half a pie. When they respond with the answer "two," encourage them to observe that two pieces out of four constitute half a pie, and, of course, if the pie were cut just once, making two pieces, that, too, would constitute half a pie.

Write the fractions 2/4 and 1/2 on the board. Explain that the denominators indicate how many pieces of pie were cut from the whole pie and the numerators show how many of those pieces would be equal to half a pie. Then write

$$2/4 = 1/2.$$

If the pie were cut into 4 pieces, it would take 2 to make half a pie. If the pie were cut into just 2 pieces, 1 piece would make a half pie.

Then show older students an amazing trick. All that they have to do is multiply the numerator and denominator by the same number to get equivalent fractions. For instance, if we take 1/2 and multiply both the numerator and denominator by 2, then we get 2/4, which, as they have already seen, equals a half pie.

Tell the students that they can multiple the numerators and denominators by any number and the trick will still work. For example, if we multiply the numerator and denominator of 1/2 by 3, we get 3/6, also equivalent to 1/2.

Ask students to find the total fat contained in each serving of the product in the meat, peanut butter, or soup can. The answers will range from 1 gram (2%) to about 20 grams (25%) where the number in the parenthesis corresponds to the Daily Value of RDA. Also have them note the number of calories contained in a serving.

Ask the question, "What does percent mean?" Percent is a part of a whole. What part? Percent is that amount of the nutrient (fat) per hundred units of the product. That is, "cent" is Latin for 100 and 20% (20%) means that the amount of the nutrient in 100 pounds, grams, or bucketfuls (!) is 20 pounds, grams, or bucketfuls. Every time the student takes a spoonful of the product, 20% of the spoonful consists of the nutrient (fat). Since the total is *always* 100%, the 80% (100% − 20% = 80%) isn't fat, but is something else.

Draw a pie chart on the board showing a circle with the product (meat, vegetable) written inside. This is the amount of the product shown in graphical form. Now draw a "sector" in the circle and write "fat, 20%" inside. Outside that sector, write "other, 80%." See Figure 7.25.

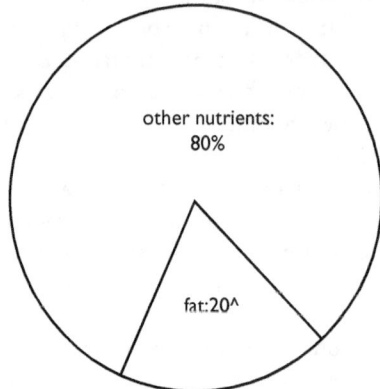

Figure 7.25 Pie Chart: Nutrition Percentages.

Ask the question, "Is there another way we could represent (write, discuss, talk about) how much fat is in this product?" One other way would be to represent the amount of fact as a fraction of the product. How can we do that? The appropriate method would be to divide 20% by 100%. That is, we would divide the total amount of fat by the amount of the product. 20% divided by 100% is 1/5. One-fifth. So, we know that 1/5 of this product is fat.

Ask the students, "If you ate two servings of this product, how much of the DV would you have eaten?" The answer should be made explicit:

$$1/5 + 1/5 = 2/5$$

Have students note that the number above the slant line (which indicates division) is called the numerator and the number below the slant is called the denominator. The numerator indicates the "amount or number of objects" (in this case, fat) and the denominator shows the number of objects it would take to make a whole. Five one-fifths would make a whole.

Since the answer is 2/5 DV of fat in the two servings, we can use the slant line to divide 2 by 5 and multiply by 100% to get the total percent of fact consumed with respect to the daily value:

$$2/5 \times 100\% = 40\%$$

Have students study the label of another canned product: Ask students how much total fat they think is contained in a single serving. It tells us that the total fat contained in a serving of that product is 25% of DV. Going through the same process, have students find that ¼ of this new product is fat. So, if they eat one serving of product 1 and one serving of product 2, they have eaten 1/5 + ¼ =? of their daily allowance.

Ask why adding 1/5 to 1/5 was easy. Make sure students understood that to arrive at the answer, they simply added numerators. We could do that because the denominators were the same. But here, we cannot. So, what can we do?

Remind students that they can add numerators, but only if the denominators are the same. Ask whether there is a way to convert these fractions (1/5 and 1/4) to fractions that have the same denominator? Yes. Tell students they must find a *common denominator* of the two fractions. Model how to do this by multiplying the denominators together (5 × 4 = 20) and use 20 as the common denominator. Tell students they must change the numerators as well

$$\frac{\text{Numerator 1} + \text{Numerator 2}}{20} =$$

Ask students how many ways they can represent one of something.

Have students explain the mathematical rule that says "When you multiply a quantity by one, the result has the same value you started with." That is, if you multiply 5 by 1, you get 5. But 1 can be written in many ways: 1, 1/1, 2/2, 3/3, 16/16, and so forth.

Tell students if we multiply 1/5 by 20/20, we get 20/100 and if we multiply ¼ by 25/25 we get 25/100. Now we have the two fractions we started with (1/5 and 1/4) but in different forms (20/100 and 25/100). These new forms have the same denominator, so the numerators can be added.

20/100 + 25/100 = 45/100

Have students determine how to convert to percent. We get 45/100; 100% = 45% which is the answer to how much of our daily recommended allowance of fat we would get in one serving of each of these two products.

The next question is "How many servings of one of these products would you have to eat to get your daily value (allowance) of fat?" Have students calculate the answer using multiplication and division.

Sample Closure

Emphasize that fractions measure parts of a whole. Fractions are numbers just like integers (1,2,3, …), but they are used when we wish to measure a part of a whole. Which would you rather have, 1/5 of a delicious chocolate pie, or 1/6 of it? Tonight at dinner tell your family that you only want 1/2 of the pie instead of 1/8th and try to trick someone into thinking you are only getting 2 pieces rather than 8.

Formative and Summative Assessment

Formative Examples

LET STUDENTS SHOW OFF THEIR LEARNING

Ask students to determine how many servings of a certain product would be required if each serving provided 10% of their daily value. 30%? 50%?

IF-ONLY STATEMENTS

If only I knew how much of my daily value (DV) of fat, protein, and carbohydrates ice cream would fulfill, I would_____.

I-CAN STATEMENTS

___ I can read labels to determine recommended daily allowance (RDA) or daily value (DV) of various nutrients.

___ I can calculate how much of my RDA/DV I have eaten today.

Summative Examples

Oral and written tests and projects

Extend Learning

Multiply mixed numbers and fractions by other fractions.
Divide mixed numbers and fractions by other fractions.
Explain why when we multiply two fractions (both less than one), the result is a product less than either of the fractions involved in the operation.
Determine why when we divide a number by any fraction less than one, the result is a quotient that is greater than either the dividend or the divisor.

Sensory Checklist

Check the senses students use during this lesson.
See Sensory Chart for Unit Plans, Table 4.4 and downloadable online

Online References

3rd Grade: Understand Fractions. See Figure 7.26.
https://www.khanacademy.org/math/cc-third-grade-math/imp-fractions

3rd and 4th Grade: Get Reading for Fractions. See Figure 7.27.
https://www.khanacademy.org/math/get-ready-for-4th-grade/xe731db3f95b84f06:get-ready-for-fractions

4th Grade: Add and Subtract Fractions. See Figure 7.28.
https://www.khanacademy.org/math/cc-fourth-grade-math/imp-fractions-2

5th Grade: Multiply Fractions, Divide Fractions, Multiply Decimals. See Figure 7.29.
https://www.khanacademy.org/math/cc-fifth-grade-math/imp-fractions-3

6th Grade: Ratios, Rational Numbers and Rates. See Figure 7.30.
https://www.khanacademy.org/math/cc-sixth-grade-math

Chapter 8

Continental and Oceanic Landforms

Introduction

The first line of a well-known nursery rhyme, "Jack and Jill went up the hill to fetch a pail of water" describes at least two elements of landforms, one above water and one that holds water below the ground. Through the five STEAM Unit Plans, the formation of landforms due to tectonic plate movement and the location of landforms are addressed in science. In technology, students increase their knowledge on searches and the presentation of information. Information in engineering is exciting because students learn about bridge building. Most, if not all, of the students have made little bridges of their own and traveled over bridges. Students will learn to classify materials and processes of bridge design to make sure bridges are safely built. Through the arts, sculpture and drawing enable students to learn features of the landforms they represent. Through mathematics, students will gain hands-on experiences with one-, two-, and three-dimensional shapes. The Unit Plans have nine steps: Become an Expert; Essential Questions; Objectives; Vocabulary; Materials and Resources; Set, Procedures, and Closure; Formative and Summative Assessment; Extend Learning; and a Sensory Checklist. Online References at the of each unit plan contain QR codes that can be optically used to access websites.

Science Unit Plan > Geology

Adapt learning for your grade level and the needs of your students and break it down for multiple daily lessons.

Become an Expert

Learn more than you will ever teach about the formation of tectonic plates and their effect on land and underwater sea formations.

Essential Questions

Determine one to two essential questions for daily lessons to provide a framework for learning, such as:

What new landform changes may currently be forming under the Earth's crust and mantle? How do forces taking place within the Earth create continental and underwater and land formations?

DOI: 10.4324/9781003290889-11

Objectives

Select or adapt one to three objectives for your daily lesson plans.
Students will learn to:

Label and describe the two outer layers of the Earth, the crust and mantle, and the two parts deep inside the Earth, the outer and inner core.
Analyze the composition of the Earth's crust.
Determine how the extreme heat of molten rock in the Earth's core caused the formation of tectonic plates within the lithosphere and the outer crust.
Describe how push, pull, slip, and slide grinding movements caused by heat and gravity within the lithosphere cracked the hard rocky compositions into several tectonic plates.
Design a method to demonstrate the movement of tectonic plates.
Create a model of tectonic plates to show how they comprise about 95% of the Earth's crust and upper mantle.
Describe how the friction between two plate boundaries creates magma that rises through the fractures in the plates, erupts as lava through a volcano, and creates a continental and oceanic hill or mountain from molten and gaseous lava and ash.
Investigate natural formations on land and under the oceans that have been created or changed by tectonic plate movements.
Explain how tectonic plates are responsible for the building and destruction of mountains and trenches on land and under the ocean.
Create a 3-D relief map showing where famous natural landforms and bodies of water were built or changed through the movement of tectonic plates around the world.
Develop arguments for a debate on the constructive and destructive effects tectonic plates have on land and sea formations.

Vocabulary

Choose two to three words to teach in daily lessons. See Chapter 3 for ways to teach vocabulary.

lithosphere	lava
continental crust	tectonic plate
oceanic crust	fault
mantle	rock folding
outer core	subduction boundaries
inner core	convergent boundaries
molten rock	divergent boundaries
magma	transform boundaries
volcano	

Materials and Resources

Use the HELP Hierarchy in Chapter 4 for lists of multisensory materials.

Real-World Experiences

Trowels or small shovels
Outside areas of dirt
Bags to collect dirt specimens
Playdough
Self-hardening clay
Shaving cream
Newspaper strips
Water
Glue
Paint
Acrylic or tempera paint
Food coloring
Cardboard
Glue

Real-World Artifacts

Rocks
Volcanic lava rock (nurseries and online)
Samples of dirt from the crust

Representations

Wood or Lincoln Logs
Tinkertoys
Apples (thick horizontal slice or ½ per student)

Visuals

See Online References at the end of the unit plan.
Printed world maps of tectonic plates and fault lines
Printed world maps that show landforms and bodies of water
Pictures of landforms and water features
Cut-away pictures of the Earth

Written

See Online References at the end of the unit plan.
Chart paper
Pencils
Markers
Kids Guide to Types of Landforms by Baby Professor, all ages
Earth's Landforms and Bodies of Water by Natalie Hyde, ages 6–8
Why do Tectonic Plates Crash and Slip? by Baby Professor, ages 8–12
Earthquakes-An Earthshaking Book on the Science of Plate Tectonics by Prodigy Wizard, all ages

Set, Procedures, Closure

Read Chapter 2 for multiple ways to plan sets and closures.

Sample Set

Ask students whether they have ever experienced an earthquake or read about one. Show a video clip of an earthquake. Tell students they will learn about the forces under their feet that are strong enough to shake the Earth, move continents, and build mountains.

Procedures

Plan a variety of instructional strategies that include direct teaching, modeling, guided and independent practice, and inquiry. Include critical thinking, questioning, and investigation.

Match procedures to daily objectives.

Take students outside to an area of dirt and show them the crust of the Earth that is at least 9 miles, 14.4 km deep. Give students trowels or shovels to dig up parts of the crust. Tell them if they could dig deep enough the temperature would increase and become extremely hot at the inner core located 3,977 miles, 6.4 km deep in the center of the Earth. Have them shovel some of the crust into bags to study the features and composition.

Cover tables with newspaper and have students dump out the contents of the bags and study the color, texture, and types of particles within the Earth's top layer of crust.

Have students research information on the Earth's crust through print and online sources and share what they learned.

Show students how to draw a diagram of the four major layers that constitute the Earth. Discuss each layer using the terms crust, mantle, outer core, and inner core.

Liken the four layers of the Earth to an apple. Give students a thick apple slice or half apple cut horizontally. Ask them to look at the cut side and view it as a model of the Earth's layers. Have them find the thinnest layer of the Earth, the crust, represented by the skin of the apple. Next, have them identify the thickest layer, the mantle, the juicy editable part attached to the skin. Have students identify parts of the apple core that represent the smaller outer and inner core. The Earth's liquid outer core and solid inner core contain nickel and iron that lies just beyond the mantle where the apple seeds are found. Throughout this activity, encourage students to use vocabulary related to the Earth's layers during their questions and discussions. Provide books, pictures, or online information for students to compare and contrast the parts of the apple to the four layers of the Earth. See Figure 8.1.

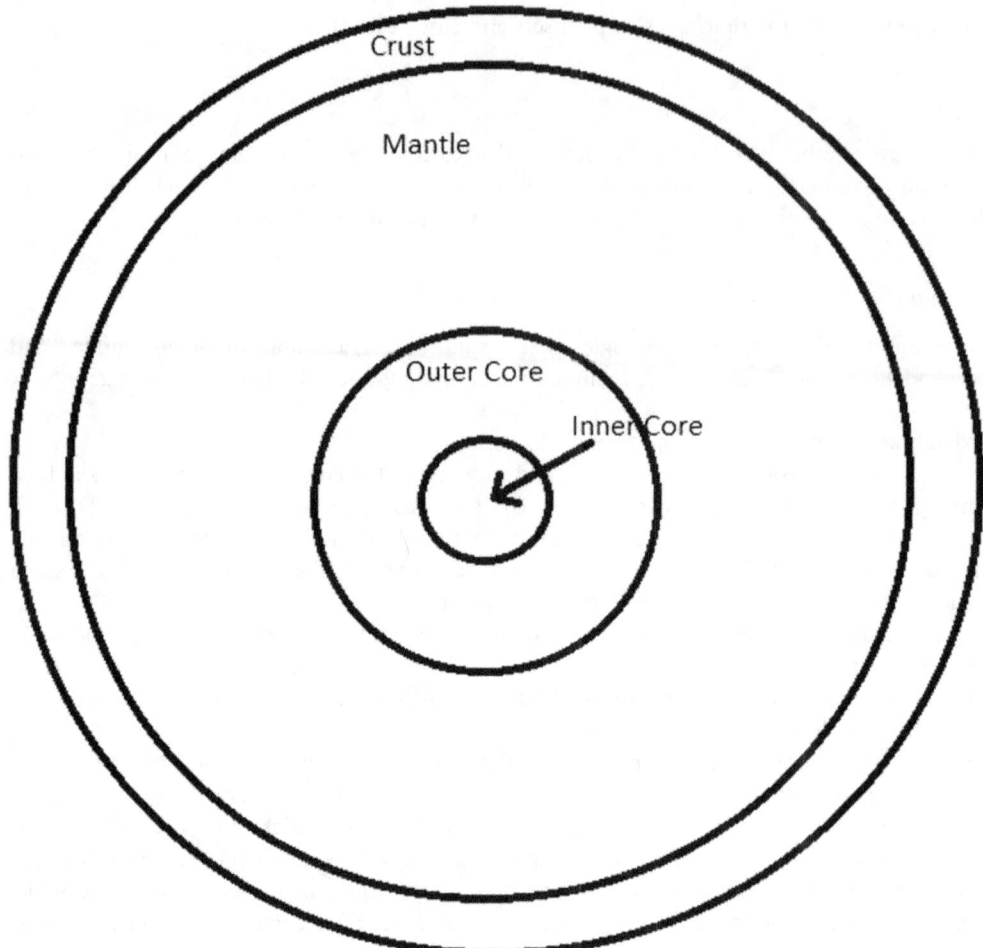

Figure 8.1 Four Layers of the Earth.

    Hang four charts, each labeled with one of the four layers of the Earth's composition: crust: mantle, outer core, and inner core. Ask students to investigate the characteristics of the four layers online or through printed information. Have them write the most important fact they learned about each layer on each of the charts.

    Introduce tectonic plates and how they are formed from the Earth's crust and upper part of the mantle. Explain there are at least seven major rocky plates plus several smaller plates around the world. Show a world map with a picture of the placement of the plates and have students count them. See Figure 8.2.

Continental and Oceanic Landforms 181

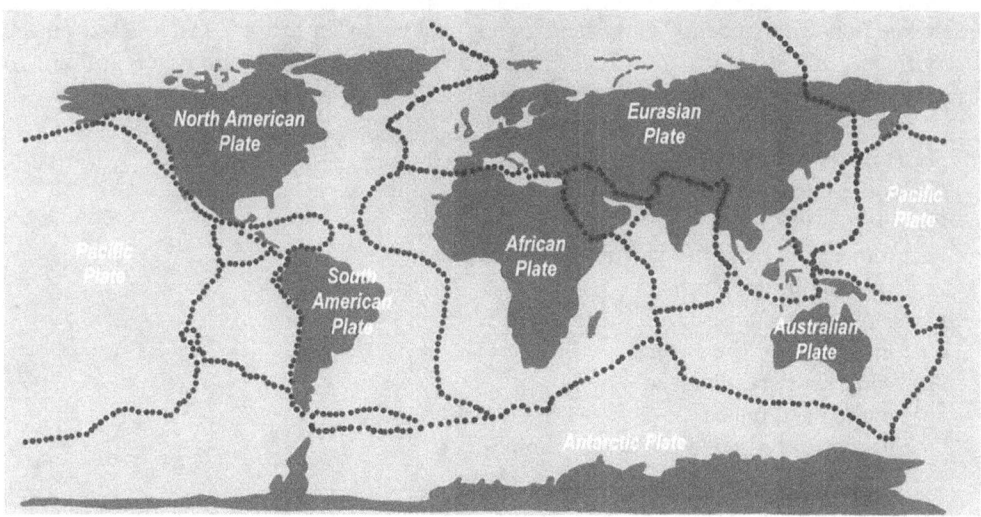

Figure 8.2 Worldwide Tectonic Plates.

Pass out a copy of a world map that shows the continents and boundaries of the tectonic plates to students along with a piece of cardboard to use as backing. Have them glue the map to the cardboard and cut out each of the tectonic plates and fit the pieces together like a jigsaw puzzle. Then have students move the plates so they converge, diverge, or transform boundaries by sliding past each other. Have students notice that plate action occurs on land and under oceans.

Relate the formations of mountains and valleys formed on land to those formed beneath the oceans due to tectonic plate movement. Compare characteristics of each.

Have students illustrate the process of volcano building that begins deep underground through the creation of magma that erupts through fractures in the tectonic plates, cools, and begins to build a volcanic hill and mountain, sometimes in a circle or arc as found in the Pacific Ring of Fire in Japan.

Have students draw an illustration of the transfer of energy from the Earth's inner core to the crust and explain how this energy impacts land and sea formations.

Ask students to write one or two questions about tectonic plates and earthquakes and seek answers through reading and discussions with other students.

Have students research the location of continental and oceanic landforms nearest to them, or in a worldwide area of their choice. Tell them they will be drawing a map that shows the tectonic plate boundaries and locations of the landforms created by tectonic plate movement. To emphasize their appearance, suggest that students draw landforms on their maps. Have students share and explain the location and features of their maps.

182 Planning Sensory-Rich STEAM Unit Plans

Sample Closure

Review key facts with students. Give them a copy of a poem on tectonic plates based on the nursery rhyme, *The House that Jack Built*. Encourage students to work with others at home to create a rhyme about their lesson to read to the class. The following is our example:

> *The Plate that Earth Built*
> This is the silicon all hot and molten
> That created the rock,
> That formed the crust and part of the mantle
> That lay deep in the Earth
> This is the plate
> That moved under the ground
> That converged and diverged
> That pushed and pulled
> That jiggled and wiggled the people upon it.

Formative and Summative Assessment

Formative Examples

LET STUDENTS SHOW OFF THEIR LEARNING

Assemble their tectonic plates puzzles and explain ways they move and how they affect the formation of continental and oceanic land forms.

IF-ONLY STATEMENTS

If only I could wear a fireproof suit, I would _____.

I-CAN STATEMENTS

_____I can explain how tectonic plates are formed.

Summative Examples

Projects, oral and written tests

Extend Learning

Compare the number and size of mountain formations on land to ones under water. Research past and current theories about the formation of the continents.

Sensory Checklist

Check the senses students use during your daily lesson.
See Sensory Chart for Unit Plans, Table 4.4 and downloadable online

Online References

Layers of the Earth. See Figure 8.3.
https://byjus.com/physics/layers-of-the-earth/

Images for World Map of Tectonic Plates and Fault Lines. See Figure 8.4.
https://duckduckgo.com/?q=world+map+of+tectonic+plates+and+fault+lines&ia=web

Plate Tectonics Map—Plate Boundary Map. See Figure 8.5.
https://geology.com/plate-tectonics.shtml

7 Major Tectonic Plates: The World's Largest Plate Tectonics. See Figure 8.6.
https://earthhow.com/7-major-tectonic-plates/

How Many Tectonic Plates Are There? See Figure 8.7.
https://www.worldatlas.com/articles/major-tectonic-plates-on-earth.html

Earth Science for Kids: Plate Tectonics. See Figure 8.8.
https://www.ducksters.com/science/earth_science/plate_tectonics.php

Images of Rock Folding. See Figure 8.9.
https://duckduckgo.com/?q=rock+folding&iax=images&ia=images

Images for Pacific Ring of Fire in Japan. See Figure 8.10.
https://duckduckgo.com/?q=Pacific+Ring+of+fire+in+Japan&ia=web

Caution: Select videos carefully. Some may show images disturbing to students.

Earthquakes and Tsunamis for Kids (5:05). See Figure 8.11.
https://www.youtube.com/watch?v=Q-v-G1iL67w

Earthquakes for Kids/Classroom Learning Videos (6:40). See Figure 8.12.
https://www.youtube.com/watch?v=21q83H7X4uM

Earthquakes 101 National Geographic (2:56). See Figure 8.13.
https://www.youtube.com/watch?v=e7ho6z32yyo

Earthquake Destruction (0:47). See Figure 8.14.
https://www.youtube.com/watch?v=Va5uIvY8qlM

Technology Unit Plan > Search, Keywords, PowerPoint, Book, and Puzzle Making

Adapt learning for your grade level and the needs of your students and break it down for multiple daily lessons.

Become an Expert

Learn more than you will ever teach about keyword searches, presentation tools, and puzzle makers.

Essential Questions

Determine one to two essential questions for daily lessons to provide a framework for learning, such as:

What keywords would you use to search for tutorials on making puzzles?
How would you develop a printable mini-book that contains information and multiple facts about landforms?

Objectives

Use or adapt one to three objectives in your daily lesson plans.
Students will learn to:

Explore different ways to conduct a search on continental and oceanic landforms.
Locate information on continental and oceanic landforms.
Compare sources to find and verify information on landforms.
Select information to represent on a PowerPoint presentation on landforms.
Experiment with different features of a PowerPoint presentation.
Distinguish steps to follow when making a PowerPoint presentation.
Practice steps for using a PowerPoint presentation.
Review information on landforms to include in a presentation for relevance and accuracy.
Select a genre to use for a book on landforms.
Explore ways to use PowerPoint or other presentation tools to make a book.
Experiment with different layouts for a book.
Design a book that includes a mix of images and text.
Create an interactive text with facts about landforms.
Select one or more pictures of a continental or oceanic landform to use on a puzzle.
Explore different websites that have free online puzzle makers.
Experiment with different ways to make a puzzle including crossword puzzles.

Vocabulary

Choose two to three words to teach in daily lessons. See Chapter 3 for ways to teach vocabulary.

continental landform	Microsoft PowerPoint
oceanic landform	print
mountain	slides
hill	insert

valley	folder
plains	task ribbon
plateau	tutorial
canyon	hardware
coast	slash "/"
volcano	clue
caldera	create
glacier	enter key
trench	answer
image orientation	intersect
landscape	title
portrait	subtitle
horizontal	edit
vertical	crossword puzzle
bullets	word search
presentation	

Materials and Resources

Use the HELP hierarchy in Chapter 4 for lists of multisensory materials.

Real-World Experiences

Computer (desktop and/or laptop and iPad)
Printer and printer paper
Stapler and staples
Scissors
Whiteboard

Real-World Artifacts

Online and paper maps of continental and oceanic landforms
Examples of crossword puzzles

Visuals

See Online References at the end of this unit plan.
Online and printed pictures of continental and oceanic landforms

Written

See Online References at the end of this unit plan.
Kid's Guide to Types of Landforms–Children's Science and Nature by Baby Professor, ages 5–18
Mother Earth's Beauty: Types of Landforms Around Us by Baby Professor, ages 5–12
Earth's Landforms by Lisa Schnell, ages 4–7
Landforms: Earth Science for Kids by Sandra Kent, ages 5–8
Land and Water: Landforms and Bodies of Water by Eve Heidi Bine-Stock, ages 4–8
Water Land: Land and Water Forms Around the World by Christy Hale, ages 3–6

188 Planning Sensory-Rich STEAM Unit Plans

Set, Procedures, and Closure

Read Chapter 2 for ways to plan sets and closures.

Sample Set

Show a PowerPoint hidden picture activity on a whiteboard and call on students to name a color block and click on it (see Online References). The block will disappear and a part of the landform picture will appear. Continue the process until someone guesses the landform. The landform image can be changed. Tell students they will learn to make a landform hidden picture on PowerPoint.

Procedures

Plan a variety of instructional strategies that include direct teaching, modeling, guided and independent practice, and inquiry. Include critical thinking, questioning, and investigation.

Match procedures to daily objectives.

Talk with the students about Internet safety, copyright issues, plagiarism, and proper conduct online. Find appropriate websites and bookmark them for use with younger students. Check with your school district's policies for using and downloading information from the Internet.

Tell students they will make a Microsoft PowerPoint hidden picture activity on landforms.

Ask students to find information and pictures of continental landforms by researching the Internet using keywords. Have students repeatedly use vocabulary for landforms as they name keywords, search for, and list information.

Challenge students to find pictures of oceanic landforms under the ocean and compare them to pictures of continental landforms.

Ask students to research how the oceanic and continental landforms were formed. See Figure 8.15.

Figure 8.15 Continental and Oceanic Landforms.

Have students search for continental and oceanic landforms on a map.

Have students research famous landforms around the world.

Show students how to save images they find in a folder that includes their name and a title page.

Brainstorm facts that can be written to describe images. Show them how to use bullets to emphasize separate categories of information.

Ask students to create five PowerPoint slides, one for each of their favorite landforms. Suggest that they place continental and oceanic landforms side by side to show similarities and differences.

Show students examples of an online mini-book and give directions on how to make one. Adjust ways students work with slides by their age level.

Students should experiment with the rotation of landscape and portrait image orientations and select the one that works best for their images and pictures. Have them save and print six slides.

Using scissors, have students cutout each of the first five slides. Leave the last one with the paper between the fifth and sixth slide intact.

Fold the intact space up over the stacked slides with the title page on top and staple along the left edge to make a landforms mini-book. This project can be done individually or in groups. If groups are used, print multiple copies so each group member has a mini-book.

Allow time for the students to share their completed mini-books with their classmates before taking them home to share with their families. Make copies to set up a mini-book library in the classroom.

The following directions for making a mini-book using PowerPoint can be followed by the students or they can follow information from tutorials found on websites.

Directions for Making a Mini-Book Using PowerPoint

Open PowerPoint and select Blank Presentation.

Click on "add title" and type "Landforms." Then click on "Add subtitle" and type "By" and your name. Your first slide is complete.

On the home task ribbon, click on the down arrow beside new slide and select picture with caption. Repeat four more times on new slides. You now have 6 total slides, 1 title slide and 5 picture and caption slides.

Go back to your second slide click on the center of the icon to add picture, then click on the landform pictures folder, and choose one of your favorite landforms and click insert. In the left box, click on the add title and type the name of the landform picture. Now click "add text box" and type a fact about the landform. Highlight the fact and click on bullets. Click once and hit enter. A new bullet is there for you to add another fact. Add 3–5 facts for each landform. Continue this process for the other slides adding a new landform and facts for each.

When finished, on the ribbon, click "File" and choose "Print." Now click on the "Full-Page Slides" down arrow and choose six slides, horizontal, and then click "Print."

Using scissors and a stapler, cut out each of the first five slides, leaving the paper space before the sixth slide intact. Fold up this paper space from the bottom to connect the stacked slides, and then staple the left side to make a mini-book.

To teach students to make puzzles, go to an online puzzle maker website and create a word search using landform words and save. Place the word search on the whiteboard and have the students take turns following the step-by-step directions to use the tools to find and circle a recognized landform word. See Pinterest, www.Pinterest.com for more websites and puzzle ideas. See Figure 8.16 for QR code.

Have students make a crossword puzzle on the theme of landforms using an online puzzle maker (see Online References).

Introduce students to grade-level crossword puzzles and have them work a few.

Ask students to examine the format of the crossword puzzles and ways the clues for words are written. Discuss the format of crossword puzzles and point out how the words intersect with one another. Have students discuss the features and ways they can create a crossword puzzle of their own.

Individually or in a group, have students research class materials, resources, and online information for landform terminology and make a list of these words. Have them read a definition for the words and simplify it to a minimum number of words used in crossword puzzle clues.

Print two copies of students' crossword puzzles. Have students complete one copy to use as an answer key; the other is for students to work.

Have students swap the landforms crossword puzzles with another student to check for clarity and accuracy of the written clues with their classmates.

Sample Closure

Ask the students how technology helped them learn information about landforms. Ask them to tell you how they can use what they learned about technology for finding information and making puzzles and books. Review how to use keywords to locate information on the Internet. Briefly review key vocabulary and steps for using technology.

Formative and Summative Assessment

Formative Examples

LET STUDENTS SHOW OFF THEIR LEARNING

Have students show off their mini-book or crossword puzzle using newly learned vocabulary to describe what they learned about technology and landforms.

IF-ONLY STATEMENTS

If only I could make other landform puzzles to share with my classmates, I would _____.

Continental and Oceanic Landforms 191

I-CAN STATEMENTS

___I can use PowerPoint to make a mini-book about any topic.

Summative Examples

Projects, presentations, oral and written tests

Extend Learning

Create foldable books for students of different ages.
Develop crossword puzzles using related vocabulary from other STEAM content areas.

Sensory Checklist

Check the senses students use during your lesson.
See Sensory Chart for Unit Plans, Table 4.4 and downloadable online

Online References

Puzzle Ideas. See Figure 8.16.
www.Pinterest.com

Example of a PowerPoint Presentation on Landforms. See Figure 8.17.
https://www.worldofteaching.com/powerpoints/geography/Landforms.ppt

Free Projects. See Figure 8.18.
https://www.makingbooks.com/freeprojects.shtml

Three Links to "Books to Make." See Figure 8.19.
https://www.internet4classrooms.com/links_grades_kindergarten_12/books_to_make_teacher_tools.htm

Hidden Picture Games. See Figure 8.20.
https://games4esl.com/powerpointgames/hidden-picture-ppt-games/

Make Your Own Crossword Puzzle Here. See Figure 8.21.
https://www.puzzle-maker.com/CW

Puzzlemaker: Create Your Own Puzzles. See Figure 8.22.
https://puzzlemaker.discoveryeducation.com/

Engineering Unit Plan > Civil Engineering

Adapt learning for your grade level and the needs of your students and break it down for multiple daily lessons.

Become an Expert

Learn more than you will ever teach about bridge building including classifications, materials, and the processes to insure the stability of the bridge.

Essential Questions

Determine one to two essential questions for daily lessons to provide a framework for learning, such as:

How are bridges built?
What is the importance in modern commerce of bridges over waterways and canyons?

Objectives

Use or adapt one to three objectives for your daily lesson plans.
Students will learn to:

Recall difficulties and successes they had when building bridges for toy cars to cross a small body of water.
Describe the bridges they crossed over and under when traveling.
Categorize the bridges they crossed based on whether they crossed land, such as an overpass, or water.
Recall different geometric shapes construction workers used to build the bridge.
Identify different types of bridges.
Identify different forces on the movement of bridges.
Analyze different effects on bridges caused by wind.
Identify landforms that require a bridge to move from side one to another.

Determine the purposes for the various types of bridges.
Establish a reason for selecting one type of bridge and draw plans for building a model.
Determine the materials that must be collected prior to starting construction.
Plan for testing the model after construction with opportunities for feedback.

Use both metric and English measurements in calculation and be able to convert between them.

Vocabulary

Choose two to three words to teach in daily lessons. See Chapter 3 for ways to teach vocabulary.

civil engineer	compression force
load	tension
beam	tension force
arch	pile
truss	abutment
suspension	pier
compression	

Materials and Resources

Use the HELP hierarchy in Chapter 4 for lists of multisensory materials.

Real-World Experiences

Visit nearby bridges over roads and water to see examples of various types of bridges.

Representations

Decks of playing cards
Scotch tape
Light objects (ruler or pencil)

Visuals

Pictures of types of bridges (beam, arch, truss, suspension)
See Online References at the end of this unit plan.

Written

See Online References at the end of this unit plan.
How to Build a Bridge by Square Root of Squid Publishing, all ages
13 Bridges Children Should Know by Brad Finger, ages 8–12
How do Bridges Not Fall Down by Jennifer Shand and Srimalie Bassani, ages 7–10

Set, Procedures, Closure

Read Chapter 2 for ways to plan sets and closures.

Sample Set

Ask students how we get from one side of a river to the other. One answer has to be "Go across the bridge to the other side." But suppose there is no bridge. How would we build one? Today we will try to answer that question. In this unit plan for landforms, bridges are very important because they enable us to move large objects and vehicles (including people) from one side of a waterway or highway to another with safety.

Procedures

Use a variety of instructional strategies that support daily objectives that include direct teaching, modeling, guided practice, independent practice, and inquiry. Include critical thinking, questioning, and investigation.

Match procedures to daily objectives.

Tell the students that perhaps the first bridge was found in prehistoric times when a large log fell across a stream enabling our ancestors to walk across the stream via the log. It may have given the early humans the idea that they could do more than just depend on a random fallen log. Why not carry a fallen log to the place where they wanted to cross the stream and lay it across the stream? Of course, they needed lots of people to help carry the log. They were the first bridge-builders.

Ask students to recall their experiences crossing over bridges and describe the landform they were leaving and the one where they were arriving.

Tell students next time they cross over or under a bridge to study it carefully to determine the shapes used to make it strong as well as other types of construction.

Ask the students how many different purposes modern bridges have. List the purposes shared by the students such as to cross rivers, valleys, canyons, streams, and highways. Tell students that even though humans may want a level, straight, and wide roadway, a hilly terrain may require a bridge to cross the obstacles.

Ask students about the really big bridges: the bridges that cross larger rivers such as the Mississippi River and the Hudson River. How are they built?

Ask students what all bridges have in common. One thing they have in common is that they extend from one side to the other of a canyon, river, or other low obstacle. That is, they are typically *not* supported in the middle, but instead, the compression force (gravity) that holds them in place is transferred to the ends of the bridge (to the *abutments*). Of course, some bridges DO have *piers* of support in the middle, and those bridges tend to be longer and heavier.

Ask the students what the simplest possible bridge is. It's analogous to the fallen log bridge. It is called a *beam* bridge. Ask the students to find information on *beam* bridges. A *beam* bridge simply implies a board laid from one side to the other of depressed terrain, perhaps a waterway.

Ask the students to consider some of the parameters of bridge design such as weight of the bridge itself, weight of its expected load (people, cars, trains, and so forth), length of the bridge, the various materials that could be used. Create a list of uses, materials, lengths, and loads that the bridge should have.

Take a bundle of popsicle sticks or tongue depressors. The bundle will be about 3–4 inches in length. How much weight can it carry? Is it possible to bundle enough sticks so that the bundle could handle a 1-pound weight? A 10-pound weight? Affix the bundle to each *abutment* and then test by placing ever-increasing weights on the sticks. Note the weight at which the bridge fails and collapses.

The *beam* bridge is only used for short bridges. The second kind of bridge that was used frequently in the Middle Ages was the arch bridge. See Figure 8.23.

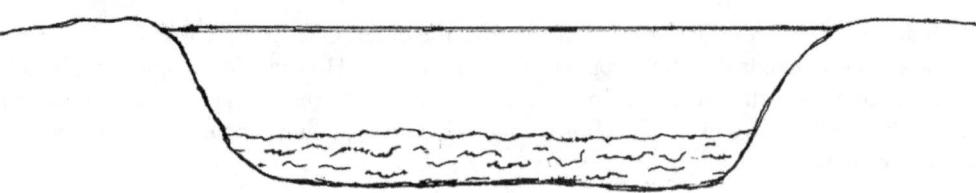

Figure 8.23 Beam Bridge.

Ask the students to find information on *arch* bridges. The information on *arch* bridges is sure to include the fact that the *arch* bridge relies overwhelmingly on compressive forces for its stability. This introduces two terms that bridge builders need: *tension* forces and *compression* forces. Ask the students to differentiate between the two. Have students draw an *arch* bridge. See Figure 8.24.

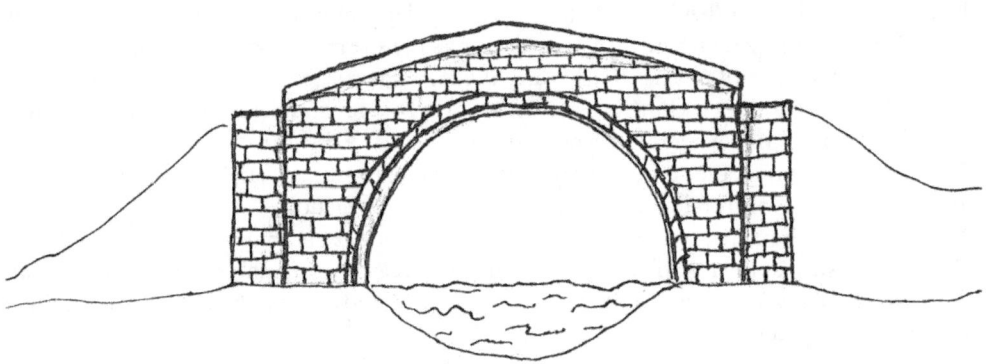

Figure 8.24 Arch Bridge.

Review information on the *beam* and *arch* bridges noting that they are good only for short distances. Modern technology has enabled civil engineers to build longer and stronger bridges. Ask the students to look up *truss* bridges. See Figure 8.25.

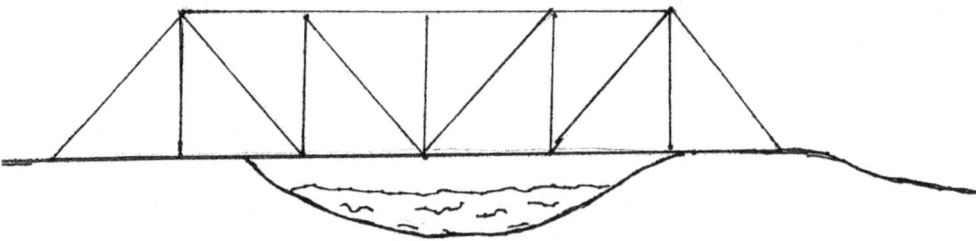

Figure 8.25 Truss Bridge.

Truss bridges can extend the length of the shorter bridges. How are the compression and tension forces balanced in a *truss* bridge, and how long can *truss* bridges be? Have the students draw a *truss* bridge. A *truss* bridge is recognizable immediately because of a row of triangular formations in its construction. The students can duplicate this powerful bridge with nothing more than a deck of playing cards and a small amount of Scotch tape. Take two cards and put about a ½ inch piece of normal Scotch tape on the tops of two cards. Press the cards together. Now pry them apart and set each card next to immovable objects. The two cards will be held together at the top by the tape and will spread into the shape of a triangle against the immovable objects. (Actually, the immovable objects can be as flimsy as two other cards lying face down on the table.) Now do the same with two different cards. Apply the tape and spread the bottoms out so they won't slip. Put the two triangles about 4 inches apart and lay a light object (ruler, pencil, even a pair of glasses) atop both triangles. Does the set of triangles hold up? See Figure 8.26.

Figure 8.26 Truss Bridge Made of Playing Cards.

Triangles resist lateral movement as well as vertical movement. Try to collapse the "bridge" by pushing laterally on it. It won't move. Try to collapse the "bridge" by pushing down on the object that lies across the two triangles. Although every structure will fail when pushed beyond its breaking point, the two triangles hold up well ... much better than if the cards were vertical. The students can see this by attempting to create a bridge with vertical members connected to the same ruler or pencil. First, it is difficult to do; second, the structure will collapse given only a slight nudge laterally.

Truss bridges are strong bridges.

The last bridge to study is the *suspension* bridge. Ask the students to find information on real *suspension* bridges. *Suspension* bridges are used when exceptionally long bridges are necessary. These bridges get their name from the large suspension cables connected to the towers that hold the payload (highway, rail, even footpath).

A bridge must support itself (its own weight) and the added weight of its payload which may be as large as thousands of vehicles or even rail locomotives. What happens when some bridges cannot meet their specifications? Ask the students to research the failure of the Mississippi River I-35W bridge in Minneapolis, Minnesota, USA that collapsed in 2007. Another interesting bridge disaster was the collapse of the Tacoma Narrows Bridge in Washington State in 1940 just four months after it was opened to the public as the third-largest suspension bridge in the world. See Online References for actual film footage of the bridge as it twisted, contorted, and finally collapsed in a strong wind.

Sample Closure

Bridges enable us to go from one side of a river to the other without getting wet. Bridges reduce congestion by providing alternate routes from one place to another. Tell students when they are crossing a bridge, they are duplicating feats that man has done as long as he has walked upon the Earth. Building bridges is a fun, profitable, and challenging civil engineering career. Tell students to look for shapes used on the bridges they cross.

Formative and Summative Assessment

Formative Examples

LET STUDENTS SHOW OFF THEIR LEARNING

Ask students to explain the purposes of bridges and how the different types of bridges are used. Show and explain the plan they made for building a bridge.

IF-ONLY STATEMENTS

If only I could build the longest and strongest bridge in the world, I would_____.

I-CAN STATEMENTS

___ I can name the four principal types of bridges.
___ I can explain how the four principal types of bridges are used.
___ I can describe some of the bridge disasters that have occurred.

Summative Examples

Projects, oral and written tests

Extend Learning

Students can look at local bridges and classify them as to type. Of special note are truss or suspension bridges.
Some bridges are hybrids. That is, they are built with a combination of two or more of the four types. Ask students to identify those hybrids.

Sensory Checklist

Check the senses students use during this lesson.
See Sensory Chart for Unit Plans, Table 4.4 and downloadable online

Online References

Caution: Choose YouTube videos carefully. Some might not be suitable for young children.

Bridges. See Figure 8.27.
https://www.explainthatstuff.com/bridges.html

Let's Make Bridges. See Figure 8.28.
https://instructables.com/howto/bridges/

How Are Bridges Built? A Visual Guide. See Figure 8.29.
https://bigrentz.com/blog/how-are-bridges-built

Why Did the Bridge Collapse, Stawicki, E. See Figure 8.30.
https://www.mprnews.org/story/2007/08/02/inspection

Why the Tacoma Narrows Bridge Collapsed (8:47). See Figure 8.31.
https://www.youtube.com/watch?v=mXTSnZgrfxM

The Tacoma Narrows Bridge Collapse (5:06). See Figure 8.32.
https://study.com/academy/lesson/physics-of-resonance-tacoma-narrows-bridge-collapse.html?src=ppc_adwords_nonbrand&rcntxt=aws&crt=502113368357&kwd=&kwid=dsa-1189880304941&agid=119312276547&&mt-&device=c&network=s&_campaign=SeoPPC

Art Unit Plan > Visual Arts

Adapt learning for your grade level and the needs of your students and break it down for multiple daily lessons.

Become an Expert

Learn more than you will ever teach about the visual arts of drawing and sculpture and ways they enhance knowledge of landforms.

Essential Questions

Determine one to two essential questions for daily lessons to provide a framework, such as:
What elements of art patterns and fillers can be distinguished in landform drawings?
How can art, a distinct form of communication, enrich the understanding of landforms?

Objectives

Use or adapt one to three objectives for your daily lesson plans.
Students will learn to:

Connect scientific knowledge and artistic practices to drawing landforms.
Observe detailed features of landforms to create accurate landform drawings.
Analyze elements of art patterns and fillers in a variety of landform drawings.
Recognize different ways to draw landforms and use elements of art to add details.
Experiment with color, shapes, lines, and patterns to create landform artwork.
Use the elements of art to distinguish individual components of landforms.
Demonstrate differences among foreground, midground, and background in their drawing.
Analyze how lines and patterns are used to illustrate details and texture in drawings.
Demonstrate different ways to show where the sky starts and the land ends.
Connect scientific knowledge to artistic practice when planning and making sculptures of landforms.
Understand ways different materials, including upcycled materials can be used to represent landforms.
Explore various materials that can be used to make landform sculptures.
Analyze ways to use a range of materials to design and make a landform sculpture.
Recognize that sculptures of landforms communicate meaning through images.
Use observation and investigation in preparation for designing and making sculptures.
Examine and discuss sculpture components.
Develop a model of a landform that represents boundaries between land and bodies of water.
Explore how the elements of art (color, form, value, shape, space, and texture) and the principles of art (proportion, orientation, scale, articulation, and balance) are used in sculptures.
Create a model of a landform sculpture.

Vocabulary

Choose two to three words to teach in daily lessons. See Chapter 3 for ways to teach vocabulary.

landform	foreground
mountain	background
hill	midground
valley	doodle
plain	sketch
plateau	color
basin	shading
coastline	value
canyon	horizon line
gulf	space
strait	artistic style
archipelago	free-form
island	pattern
isthmus	zentangle
glacier	cartoon
cave	realistic
arch	angle
cliff	shape
delta	curve
volcano	texture

desert	balance
peninsula	freeform
terrain	realistic
bay	creative
river	collage
lake	3-dimensional
pond	recycle
canal	upcycle
beach	additive
marsh	subtractive
swamp	topographical sculpture
waterfall	

Materials and Resources

Use the HELP hierarchy in Chapter 4 for lists of multisensory materials.

Real-World Experiences

Coloring book with simple pictures
Drawing paper and pencils
Ultra-fine markers
Colored markers

Visuals

See Online References at the end of this unit plan.
Pictures of Romero Britto's work found online and in books

Written

See Online References at the end of this unit plan.
Kid's Guide to Types of Landforms—Children's Science and Nature by Baby Professor, ages 5–18
Mother Earth's Beauty: Types of Landforms Around Us by Baby Professor, ages 5–12
Landforms: Earth Science for Kids by Sandra Kent, ages 5–8
Land and Water: Landforms and Bodies of Water by Eve Heidi Bine-Stock, ages 4–8
123 I Can Collage! by Irene Luxbacher, ages 4–7
3-D Art Lab for Kids by Susan Schwake, ages 7–10
Clay Lab for Kids: 52 Projects to Make, Model, and Mold with Air-Dry Clay, Polymer, and Homemade Clay by Cassie Stephens, ages 4–10
Upcycle It! Crafts for Kids by Jennifer Perkins, ages 8–12

Set, Procedures, Closure

Read Chapter 2 for multiple ways to plan multisensory sets and closures.

Sample Set

Show pictures and sculptures painted by Romero Britto found online. Ask students to discuss Britto's use of lines, color, and shapes within the figures. Tell them they will draw pictures and create landform sculptures using his techniques to color and paint them.

Procedures

Use a variety of instructional strategies that include direct teaching and modeling, guided practice, independent practice, and inquiry. Include critical thinking, questioning, and investigation.

Match procedures to daily objectives.

Find a coloring book with simple pictures and provide each student one page. Tell students to fill in different parts of the picture with different colors, lines, and patterns. Have them refer to the pictures of Romero Britto's work (Online References). Ask students to share the lines and patterns they used in particular parts, why they chose to fill them with a particular element, and whether it enhanced the picture in any way.

Have students review websites, books with images, descriptions, features, facts, and videos to gain basic information to form a picture of each landform in their minds. These facts along with class lessons and discussions will help students with details and accuracy as they draw.

Have students draw simple landscape outlines and fill in with line and patterns, doodles, or zentangles. Within this process, they will understand foreground, midground, and background. See Figure 8.33.

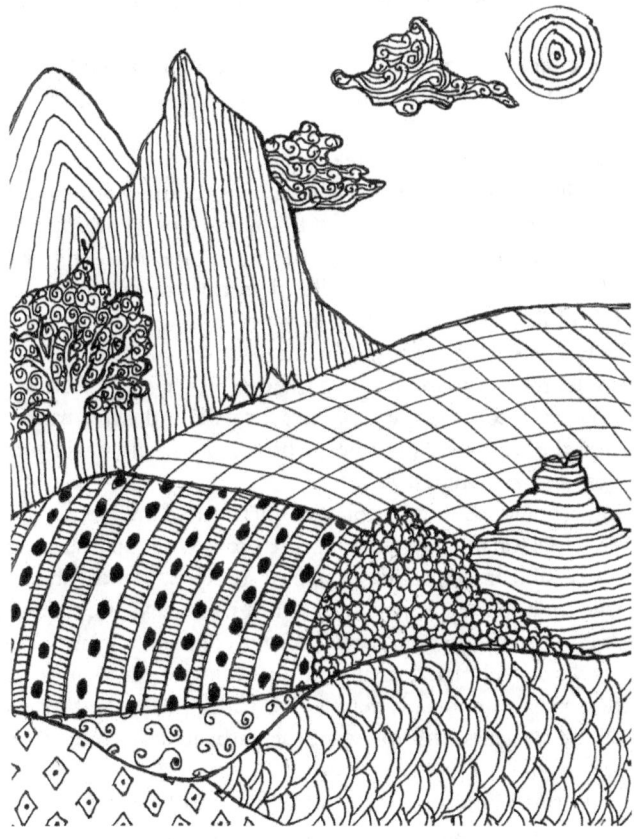

Figure 8.33 Doodles and Zentangles.

Many websites show step-by-step directions for how to draw a landform, depending on the age of the students. Younger students may need more hands-on guidance and assistance. Looking at simple images found on the websites will make it easier for them.

With young students, or even older students, draw on the board as they follow your step-by-step instructions on their drawing paper with a pencil. We have found when working with young children it is easier to draw a box on the board, so they understand it is your piece of paper. This helps them spatially understand the size and position of features you are drawing. Be sure to talk about what and how you are drawing and why.

Allow time for students to share their artwork and discuss it with classmates before they take it home to share with their families. Encourage them to talk about why they used the colors, lines, and patterns for the landform features.

Have students create a project that includes patterns, lines, and shapes of landforms and water features through drawing and coloring. The following directions will help you guide your students through this project.

Have students turn their paper horizontally and use a pencil to sketch a horizon line to show where sky meets land across the paper, a little above center all the way across.

Have them drop down a few inches and add another horizontal line making it random and not a straight line. Then, drop down a few more inches (not the same amount) and add another random horizontal line. Students now have three or four horizontal lines across their papers.

Tell students to draw two or three mountain peaks on the top line, the first line they drew. This would be the background. Talk about how mountains look like triangles or upside-down cones.

The next section will be land. Maybe add grass with trees.

The next section can have water, like a pond or stream that catches runoff. Another section below that could be more land with grass, trees, bushes, and flowers. Now, talk to students about foreground, midground, and background and what that might mean for the size of things. For example, trees in the background would be smaller than trees in the foreground.

Students can add trees, bushes, and flowers in the area they want.

Now let students use colored ultra-thin markers to fill in the features with lines, patterns, doodles, and zentangles. For example, they may use a blue marker to fill the water feature with wavy blue horizontal lines, a brown marker for small vertical lines for bark of the tree trunk, and a green marker for using circles for the leaves on the trees. The websites below will provide examples of lines, patterns, doodles, and zentangles.

Explain characteristics of sculptures and show examples or pictures of different types of sculptures. Ask students to bring in items for an upcycled sculpture project. Set up a large empty box in a special place that is easily accessible in your classroom. Tell students, friends, and family that you are collecting clean garbage for a special project for the next two weeks. Remind them, please no chemical containers, glass, or sharp metal edges. Takeout containers, plastic bottles and tubs, caps off of spray cans or soft drink bottles, small cardboard boxes, plastic jugs, cereal boxes, plastic straws, squirt bottles, plastic spoons, different size paper plates, and plastic or paper cups are needed. Do not tell the students why you want the garbage, but do tell them to make sure the items they bring are clean.

Provide pictures of different landforms found in books and online and have students study features of one of the landforms. Before designing and creating their sculpture, have them consider the types of materials they want to use.

Place a variety of upcycled and recycled materials in an area that is easily accessible for the students along with clay and other art supplies. Have plenty of paper towels, towels, wet wipes, and clean-up supplies available.

Instruct students to choose a landform. Have students use a combination of air-dry clay, polymer clay, or homemade clay along with upcycled and natural materials and acrylic paint to design and construct their landform sculptures. See Figure 8.34.

Figure 8.34 Landform Sculpture with Natural Materials.

Discuss the different techniques they can use with multiple thicknesses of paper. Show they how they can roll pieces of paper to add extra dimension to the sculpture. Give students the choice of using colored pencils, chalks, and markers to add to the dimension.

When landform sculptures are finished, allow each student to share their sculpture and talk about the features of the landform, different materials used to make it, why they were used, and what they would do differently next time. You may want to video this so it can be viewed again or emailed to families.

Sample Closure

Tell students they will turn their classroom into an art museum, a place where they can show off their work. Ask them to share three important things they would tell visitors about their drawing and their landform. Brainstorm ideas and record them on chart paper or the board. From this list, review key concepts about landforms and techniques for drawing and sculpting they might want to share. Tell them that during the next lesson, they will start planning for their art show.

Formative and Summative Assessment

Formative Examples

LET STUDENTS SHOW OFF THEIR LEARNING

Take students outside and ask them to list or draw the shapes they see at the horizon or from natural and man-made landscape forms.

IF-ONLY STATEMENTS

If only I could use color, shapes, lines, and patterns, to design a landform, I would _____ _____.

I-CAN STATEMENTS

___ I can transform upcycled and natural materials into a landform statue.

Summative Examples

Projects, presentations, oral and written tests

Extend Learning

Explore techniques of other artists' styles such as Wassily Kandinsky's concentric circles, Jackson Pollock's spatter style, Piet Mondrian's geometric abstracts, or Georges Seurat's pointillism dots.
Relate angles, curves, lines, and shapes used by various artists to mathematics.

Sensory Checklist

Check the senses students use during your lesson.
See Sensory Chart for Unit Plans, Table 4.4 and downloadable online

Online References

How to Draw an Easy Landscape. See Figure 8.35.
https://artprojectsforkids.org/how-to-draw-an-easy-landscape

80 Easy, Simple & Cool Patterns to Draw for Beginners. See Figure 8.36.
https://www.thebeginningartist.com/how-to-draw-patterns

Doodle Art 1. See Figure 8.37.
https://www.pinterest.com/pin/7740630600260322/sent/?invite_code=e9a0ec1c0180490bbd9b946881060d8d&sender=1885180071810392664&sfo=1

Inspired By Zentangle: Patterns and Starter Pages of 2022 by Joanne Gonzales. See Figure 8.38.
https://craftwhack.com/zentangle-patterns-starter-sheets/

Romero Britto for Kids. See Figure 8.39.
https://duckduckgo.com/?q=romero+britto+for+kids&t=chromentp&iax=images&ia=images

Deep Space Sparkle: How to Teach Line and Pattern. See Figure 8.40.
https://www.deepspacesparkle.com/teach-line-pattern

Beverly Taylor Sorenson Arts Learning Program. See Figure 8.41.
https://btsalp.com/wp-content/uploads/2020/05/Landforms-Lesson-plan.pdf

Easy How to Draw Mountains Tutorial by Kathy Barbro. See Figure 8.42.
https://artprojectsforkids.org/how-to-draw-mountains

National Geographic: Mapping Landforms. See Figure 8.43.
https://www.nationalgeographic.org/activity/mapping-landforms

Mathematics Unit Plan > Geometry

Adapt learning for your grade level and the needs of your students and break it down for multiple daily lessons.

Become an Expert

Learn more than you will ever teach about one-, two-, and three-dimensional shapes, and the classification of these shapes by numbers of sides and angles.

Essential Questions

Determine one to two essential questions for daily lessons to provide a framework for learning, such as:

How does geometry affect our daily lives?
How does the appreciation of dimensionality help us to understand the shapes around us?

Objectives

Select or adapt one to three objectives for your daily lesson plans.
Students will learn to:

Use dimensional analysis to describe the shape of objects.
Learn how objects on the surface of the earth and underwater are measured depending on dimensionality.
Relate objects on the surface of the earth to common one-dimensional shapes such as straight and curved lines.
Define the length of a one-dimensional object.
Relate shapes on the surface of the earth to common two-dimensional shapes such as circles, triangles, rectangles, or irregular polygons.
Recognize attributes of shapes such as the number and length of sides and degrees of angles in everyday objects outside, in the home, and in the classroom.
Experiment with combining shapes with straight lines into new shapes such as two squares become a rectangle, two triangles become a rhombus, and three triangles can become a trapezoid.
Describe objects using names, orientation, and size of shapes.
Recognize shapes in two-dimensional pictures of continental and oceanic landforms such as line segments, peaks, valleys, triangles, rhombuses, and rectangles.
Define the area of a two-dimensional object.
Locate features on the surface of the earth that are essentially one-dimensional, two-dimensional, and three-dimensional.
Distinguish between man-made features (i.e., political boundaries) and natural features (i.e., mountain ranges).
Relate shapes on the surface of the earth and underwater to common three-dimensional shapes such as a cube, sphere, or irregular polyhedron.
Use both metric and English units to measure length, area, and volume.

Vocabulary

Choose two to three words to teach in daily lessons. See Chapter 3 for ways to teach vocabulary.

continental landform	hemisphere
oceanic landform	line
ascending	line segment
descending	side
square inches or square meters	angle
dimension	length
triangle	area
circle	volume
polygon	regular polygon
square	irregular polygon
rectangle	polyhedron
sphere	

Materials and Resources

Use the HELP hierarchy in Chapter 4 for lists of multisensory materials.

Real-World Experiences

Measuring stick or tape
Notebook for observations of objects and their dimensionality
Writing instrument
Rectangular pan or bowl
Water
Rock
Tree
Parallel lines around the building
Perpendicular lines around the building
Two- and three-dimensional shapes in the environment
Geometric blocks

Visuals

See Online References at the end of this unit plan.
World maps showing man-made boundaries of regions
World maps showing natural features of regions of the earth

Written

See Online References at the end of this unit plan.
Must Know High School Geometry by Allan Ma and Amber Kuang, ages 12–up
Geometry for Dummies by Matt Ryan, all ages
Sacred Geometry for Kids, Shapes in Nature by Maria Lute and Dale Lute, ages 8–10
Janice VanCleave's Geometry for Every Kid: Easy Activities that Make Learning Geometry Fun by Janice VanCleave, ages 8–12

Set, Procedures, Closure

Read Chapter 2 for ways to plan sets and closures.

Sample Set

Ask students what is the difference between a string, a piece of paper, and a book. The critical difference among those objects is one of dimensionality. A string is a physical object whose most critical dimension is length. We can agree that the string has some finite (that is, nonzero) width, but we describe string typically by its length. A piece of paper is described by its size; a common size of ordinary paper is 8.5 inches by 11 inches. We don't usually care about the thickness, but somehow "length" of paper doesn't seem to make much sense. Accordingly, a piece of paper is a two-dimensional object, requiring both length and width to describe it accurately. Finally, a three-dimensional object, such as a book, needs three dimensions to describe it. It might be 8 inches tall, 5 inches wide, and 1.5 inches thick. Three dimensions.

Procedures

Plan a variety of instructional strategies that support daily objectives that include direct teaching, modeling, guided and independent practice, and inquiry. Include critical thinking, questioning, and investigation.

Match procedures to daily objectives.

Take students on a tour of the school and point out geometric features, especially one-, two-, and three-dimensional objects. For instance, doors are 3-D, because they have length, width, and thickness, but a doorway is just 2-D because it has no thickness. Observe the intersection of the wall and ceiling. The intersection creates a line, a 1-D feature, that has only has length.

Ask students to describe the attributes of the shapes they see. Attributes include length, area, and volume. For 2-D shapes, important characteristics are number and length of the sides, straight and curved lines, and angles created by two intersecting lines.

Have students combine different 2-D shapes into different shapes such as a rectangle, rhombus, and trapezoid, using straight lines.

Show students pictures of landforms and have them partition segments of the landforms that come the closest to resembling two-dimensional shapes. Tell students that this is what a painter does: he/she accurately transforms a 3-D object into a realistic-looking 2-D painting. On the other hand, a sculptor creates a 3-D likeness from a real 3-D object.

Cut 10 pieces of string into different lengths and ask the students to put them in ascending (or descending) order of length. Have students measure the string lengths and record the lengths in a notebook.

Cut 10 rectangles from scratch paper. Make sure that they have different lengths and widths from each other. Ask the students to order them in the same way as the strings. Why does this not work?

Introduce the concept of area of 2-D shapes. Area measures the size of a 2-D object. Some 2-D objects have three sides (triangles), some have four (quadrilaterals, including squares, rectangles, rhombuses, and trapezoids), and some have more. See Figures 8.44 and 8.45.

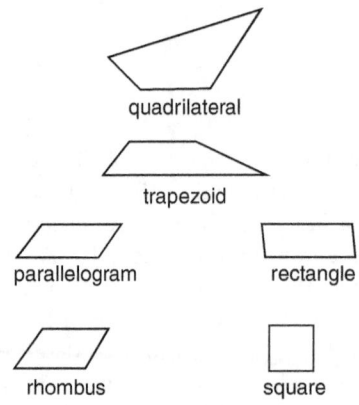

Figure 8.44 Quadrilaterals.

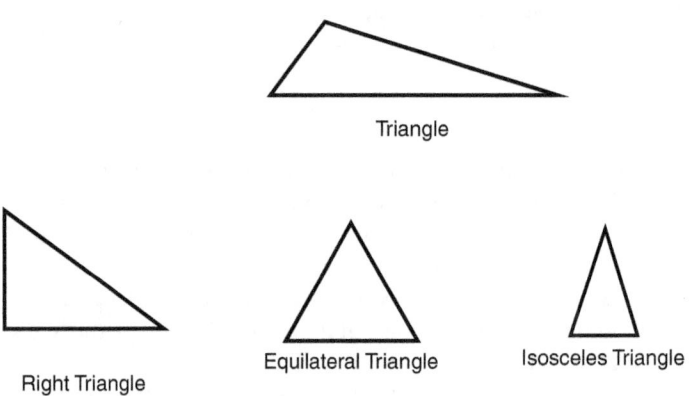

Figure 8.45 Triangles vice Quadrilaterals.

How can area be measured so that the shapes can be ordered as to size? Introduce the idea of "square inches" or "square meters."

Cut an 8.5" by 11" sheet of paper into narrow strips of 1 inch in width so that 8 strips are 11 inches long and 1 inch wide and one strip is ½ inch in width and 11 inches long. Have students observe that 8 of them are equal with the remaining strip being ½ inch narrower. Obviously, the narrower strip has less area. How much less? Use the convention that area equals length times width. Then the 8 strips that are identical have $11 \times 1 = 11$ square inches, and the remaining strip has an area of $½ \times 11 = 5.5$ square inches.

Ask students what the area of the original sheet of paper was. We can get the answer in two ways: one way is to multiply $11 \times 8.5 = 93.5$ square inches; the other is to add up the areas of the 8 strips $(8 \times 11) = 88$ square inches and then to add to that total the area of the narrower strip (5.5 square inches) to get 93.5 square inches.

Ask the students to perform each of the two previous procedures using metric measurements (centimeters). Two ways to do this are available: (1) Convert length and width to centimeters and carry out the procedures (2.54 cm equals 1 inch), or (2) after getting the area in square inches, convert to square centimeters. How many square centimeters are in a square inch? Be careful. Ask students to find the answer (6.45).

The last exercise indicates that area can be calculated by finding the area of smaller regions and adding them together. Ask the students whether we can do that on a large scale. Find a map and look at the Mississippi River. Ask the students to measure the length (one-dimension) of the river. They must use the scale that is shown on the map. One difficulty is that the Mississippi, like most rivers, is NOT a straight line. Can we measure the length by measuring a series of smaller line segments? Yes!

Now look at a map of a continent, country, or state within a country. Ask the students what the area is of the region that they have chosen. Chances are that the region is irregular in shape. That is, it is not a perfect square, rectangle, or other regular shape. Ask the students what to do. Begin by drawing little squares on the map, where each little square is a convenient number of square units (meters, miles, and so forth). Then add them up. When the students get to the edges, that's where the irregularities occur. Tell them to break the region up into smaller and smaller squares and add those contributions to the total area. Keep doing that until exhausted. Find the total area and compare what the students get by looking up the actual area of the region in a reference book.

Volume measures the "size" of a three-dimensional object. In the same way as area is measured in *square* inches or meters, volume is measured in *cubic* inches or meters. But three-dimensional objects are quite irregular and not subject to simple formulas. Ask students how could we measure a simple three-dimensional object's volume. First, find a rectangularly shaped pan or bowl and fill it halfway with water. Now ask, "What's the volume of the water in the pan?" The answer is the length of the pan times the width of the pan times the depth of the water. All three dimensions must be measured in the same units. Now have the students find a large rock that will sink to the bottom of the pan and be completely immersed. Again, measure the water level. Now the students know the volume (length x width x depth) of the water without the rock in it, and the volume of the water *with* the rock in it. What's the volume of the rock?

Ask the students how they could find the volume of a mountain.

Sample Closure

Review key facts with students about length, area, and volume. Ask them to measure their own volume in the bathtub, but be careful to keep their head above water. Have them just estimate the volume of their head.

Formative and Summative Assessment

Formative Examples

LET STUDENTS SHOW OFF THEIR LEARNING

Ask students to share and explain their process for measuring length, area of irregular shapes, and volume of irregular objects.

IF-ONLY STATEMENTS

If only I could move Mount Everest, I would_____

I-CAN STATEMENTS

___ I can show how to measure length.
___ I can explain how to measure area of irregular two-dimensional shapes.
___ I can explain how to measure volume of irregular three-dimensional shapes.

Summative Examples

Oral and written tests and projects

Extend Learning

Calculate the area of regular polygons with any number of sides by dividing the polygon into triangles.
Measure the area of circles.
Measure the volume of spheres.
Calculate the approximate area of Kansas, USA; Uruguay; or Libya.

Sensory Checklist

Check the senses students use during this lesson.
See Sensory Chart for Unit Plans, Table 4.4 and downloadable online

Online References

Geometry of the Earth. See Figure 8.46.
https://www.cs.tufts.edu/comp/50PSS-2013f/handouts/earth.pdf

Identification of the Earth's Features from Maps. See Figure 8.47.
https://www.dbr.sc.gov/geology/pdfs/education/Map%20Identification.pdf

4th Grade Science: Patterns of the Earth's Features. See Figure 8.48.
https://wwwvarsitytutors.com/4th_grade_science-help/earth-and-space-science/patterns-of-earth-s-features

Geometry—Definition with Examples. See Figure 8.49.
https://www.splashlearn.com/math-vocabulary/geometry/geometry

Features That Make Up The Earth—Landforms. See Figure 8.50.
http://kinooze.com/features-that=make-up-the-earth-landforms

Earth's land features. See Figure 8.51.
https://www.slideshare.net/jejones/earths-land-features

Chapter 9

Astronomy and Seasons

Introduction

"Twinkle, Twinkle Little Star" is so popular, we probably all know the words from our childhood. Though this little song refers to the way stars look in the sky, except for the yellow color, they look much different from Earth than our Sun. Though none of us should ever look directly at the Sun, we have caught glimpses of it, especially at sunset. This theme relates directly to students' lives and can be taught through each of the STEAM content areas: Science, Technology, Engineering, Art, and Mathematics. Through science students learn about the rotation of the Earth around the Sun and how the part tilted toward the Sun creates seasons. Through technology students learn to make digital pictures of the Sun. Most recently the James Webb Space Telescope enables students to see pictures of stars and distant galaxies in outer space. Through computer searches, images of outer space and our solar system are just a few keystrokes away. Through engineering, students learn to build a scaled model of the solar system and wire their models with LED lights. Through art, students will dance and move to classical and popular music related to the seasons. Through mathematics, students will gain a deeper understanding of the astronomical distances to the Sun, moon, and other planets using metric and English systems of measurement. Because most very young children begin to count, understand terms "more" or "less," name shapes, and put them together to form different shapes, mathematics has already become an interesting and important part of their lives. Readers will learn ways to extend this early mathematics learning through the integrated unit plans for students in kindergarten through grade 6.

STEAM unit plans follow a nine-step format: Become an Expert; Essential Questions; Objectives; Vocabulary; Materials and Resources; Set, Procedures, and Closure; Formative and Summative Assessment; Extend Learning; and a Sensory Checklist. Many Online References contain QR codes that can be optically used to access the websites at the end of each unit plan.

Science Unit Plan > Physics

Adapt learning for your grade level and the needs of your students and break it down for multiple daily lessons.

Become an Expert

Learn more than you will ever teach about the effects of Earth's tilt and rotation on its axis and revolution around the Sun.

Essential Questions

Determine one to two essential questions for daily lessons to provide a framework for learning, such as:

What would happen if a large meteor hit the Earth and caused the angle of the axis to change? How would you describe the imaginary circles of latitude to an alien?

Objectives

Select or adapt one to three objectives for your daily lesson plans.
Students will learn to:

Identify how the 24-hour daily rotation of the Earth causes darkness and sunlight.
Explain the significance of the Earth's 23-degree tilt on the duration of day and night in different seasons around the world.
Explain the significance of the Earth's 23-degree tilt regarding changes in temperature.
Determine the length of time there would be darkness and sunlight if the Earth's tilt were at 0 or 90 degrees.
Determine the Earth's movement on an orbital plane around the Sun.
Dramatize the Earth's movement as it spins on its axis while at the same time traveling on an orbital plane around the Sun.
Identify seasonal changes around the world due to the Earth's revolution around the Sun.
Locate the circle of zero latitude of the Equator that divides the Northern and Southern Hemispheres.
Identify countries and continents in the Northern and Southern Hemispheres and on the Equator.
Locate countries in the hemisphere where they live.
Determine times the Sun is strongest in the Northern and Southern Hemispheres and at the Equator.
Explain why seasonal weather occurs at different times in different parts of the world.
Define the terms *winter* and *summer solstice*.
Recognize reasons there are two solstices and two equinoxes.
Relate the tilt of the Earth to the summer and winter solstices.
Explain why seasons occur at regular times of the year.
Define the terms *vernal* and *autumnal equinox*.

Vocabulary

Choose two to three words to teach in daily lessons. See Chapter 3 for ways to teach vocabulary.

vernal and autumnal equinox	rotate/rotation
summer solstice	revolve/revolution
winter solstice	seasons
Earth	Sun
sphere	angle
axis	Northern Hemisphere
axial tilt	Southern Hemisphere
ellipse	Equator
orbit	gravity
orbital plane	gravitational force
ecliptic	applied force
latitude	

218 Planning Sensory-Rich STEAM Unit Plans

Materials and Resources

Use the HELP hierarchy in Chapter 4 for lists of multisensory materials.

Real-World Experiences

Sunset and sunrise observations
Log to record observations
Black sharpy markers

Representations

Floor lamp with shade removed labeled "Sun."
Flashlight
Globe of Earth on a stand with a tilted axis
Merry-go-round
Large balloons

Visuals

See Online References at the end of this unit plan.
   Map of Earth's Northern and Southern Hemispheres and the Equator along with the names of the continents and countries

Written

See Online References at the end of this unit plan.
The Reasons for Seasons: New and Updated by Gail Gibbons, ages 4–8
The Reason for the Seasons by Ellie Peterson, ages 6–9
sun Calendar by Una Jacobs, all ages
Space and the Speed of Light: The History of 14 Billion Years for People Short of Time by
   Dr. Becky Smethurst, all ages

Oral and Aural

Hap Palmer, *Spinning on the Same Ball*. For QR code, see Figure 9.1. https://www.youtube.com/watch?v=EypR6IIgTmI

Set, Procedures, Closure

Read Chapter 2 for multiple ways to plan multisensory sets and closures.

Sample Set

Have Hap Palmer's *Spinning on the Same Ball* music playing in the classroom as students enter. Turn out the overhead lights and have a floor lamp in the middle of the classroom with the lamp shade off to expose the lightbulb. This will be the classroom "Sun." Select a student to stand up and face the lamp. Select another student to stand up and face away from the lamp. Relate those positions to "daylight" and "night." Now, have the student turn around slowly and notice the difference between the illumination of the student's face and back as the student turns. Tell them today they will be learning about the causes of day and night and in future lessons, the reasons for the changes in the seasons.

Procedures

Plan a variety of instructional strategies that include direct teaching, modeling, guided and independent practice, and inquiry. Include critical thinking, questioning, and investigation.

Match procedures to daily objectives.

To avoid confusion over the words "rotate" and "revolve" as used by scientists, post a sign that says, "Earth **rotates** on its axis as it **revolves** around the sun."

If you have access to a merry-go-round, take students outside to reinforce the concept of revolution. Determine the number of students who can safely be on the merry-go-round at one time and the number of revolutions you want them to go. Have one or two students push the merry-go-round to start it on its revolution.

Discuss the term "revolution" as well as the friction in the merry-go-round that makes revolution slow and eventually stop.

To simulate revolution about the Sun, have one student stand in one place holding a large poster of the Sun. Have the other students walk slowly around him/her and count the revolutions that they make. Remind the students that every time they make a revolution, they are one year older!

Apply Newton's 2nd law of motion to the rotation of the merry-go-round. Have students note the changes in speed that occur because of the variation of the initial applied force.

Relate these differences in speed to Newton's 1st law of motion. Tell students the Earth is in a constant state of equilibrium as it continues its 24-hour rotation on its axis and its 365-day revolution around the orbital plane. Ask what would happen if the speed of the Earth's rotation on its axis decreased like that of the merry-go-round.

Show a globe of the Earth and how it rotates on its axis. Point out that the axis of the Earth is imaginary, not plastic or wood as used in models. Ask a student to hold a light on the globe of the Earth and have another student slowly rotate the globe to show the changes in darkness and light. Tell students that they would have to be in the classroom for 24 hours and move the Earth on its axis very slowly to re-create the effects of the Earth's rotation on its axis.

Have students start a log where they record the time the Sun rises and sets and determine the duration between sunrise and sunset. Tell students NOT to look directly at the Sun. Ask them to observe dawn early tomorrow morning and notice where the Sun rises. Have them mark the location using a tree, or house as a benchmark. Repeat by observing the sunset in the early evening. Have students make periodic checks on their recorded times to note the differences between sunrise and sunset and determine changes in the location of the Sun at sunrise and sunset. Have students explain why the observations are different.

Introduce or review the names and characteristics of the four seasons, winter, spring, summer, and fall, in the area where you live. Emphasize the importance of solar energy on our lives.

Play the 3-minute video on the Sun: https://www.youtube.com/watch?v=6FB0rDsR_rc. For QR code, see Figure 9.2.

Display or give students a map that clearly shows the Earth's Northern and Southern Hemispheres, the Equator, and continents. Have students name the continents and identify the location where they live. See Figure 9.3.

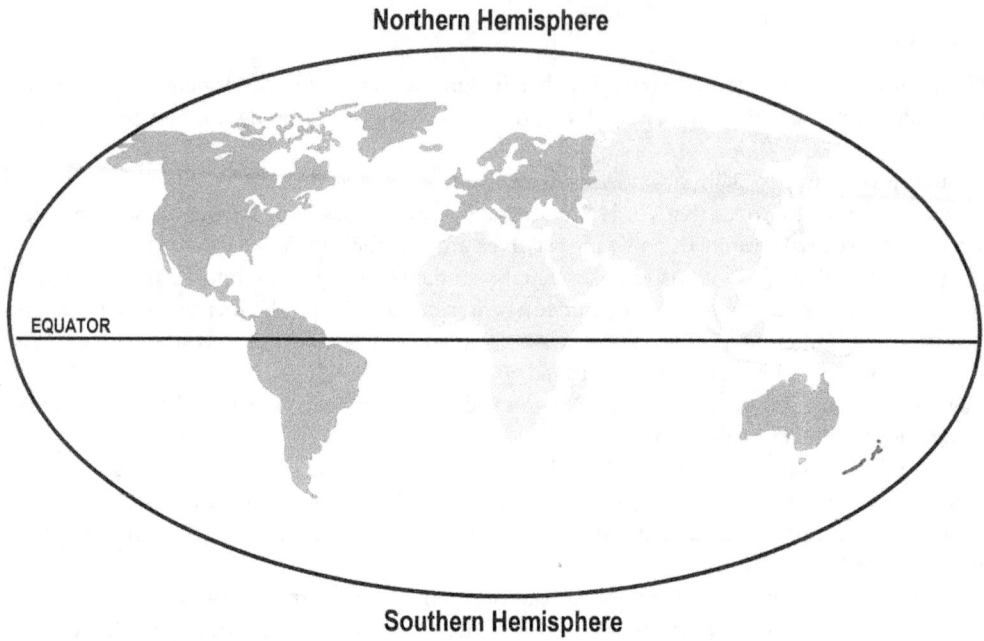

Figure 9.3 Earth's Hemispheres.

Give pairs of students a flashlight and large balloon. Have them draw a sketch of the continents on the Northern and Southern Hemispheres and along the Equator.

Have one student hold the flashlight while another student tilts the balloon 23 degrees and revolves it in an orbit around the "sun." Periodically, ask students to pause the revolution and study the continents that experience the most and least direct sunlight. Have them note that the hemisphere that is pointed toward the Sun receives the most direct sunlight. Ask students to determine the climate in each continent and how it varies from the climate where they live.

Define equinox and solstice. Tell students during the winter solstice, the total daylight time should be substantially less than 12 hours. During the summer solstice, the total daylight time should be substantially more than 12 hours. Have students explain why.

Ask students to determine when the next of the four solar demarcations of the year occurs: summer solstice, winter solstice, vernal equinox, or autumnal equinox. See Figure 9.4.

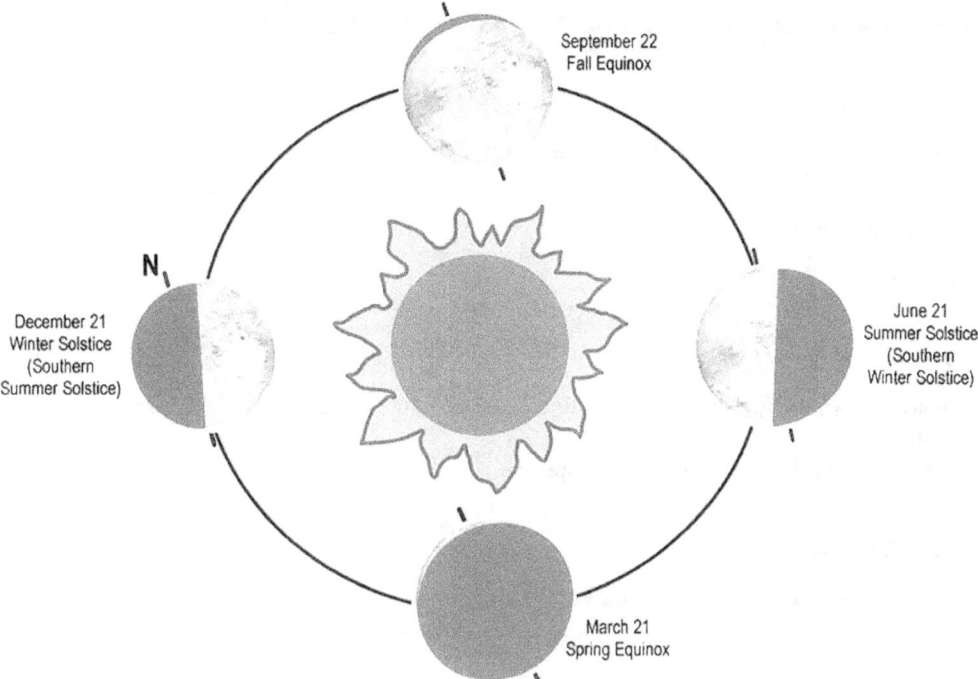

Figure 9.4 Solstices and Equinoxes of the Earth.

On the day of its occurrence, have students record the time of sunrise and sunset. Explain that for both equinoxes, the total time of sunrise to sunset ought to be about 12 hours.

Have students explain differences in day and night and the seasons in the Northern and Southern Hemispheres using relevant vocabulary such as tilt, axis, rotation, and revolution.

Sample Closure

Give students large-size sticky notes and have them write or illustrate one thing they thought was most interesting to learn. Have students remember times they were playing outside and it began to get dark and explain the changes from daylight to night to their family.

Formative and Summative Assessment

Formative Examples

LET STUDENTS SHOW OFF THEIR LEARNING

Ask students to sketch and explain the reasons for day and night and seasonal changes using scientific terms.

222 Planning Sensory-Rich STEAM Unit Plans

IF-ONLY STATEMENTS

If only I could change the tilt of the Earth on its axis, I would_____.

I-CAN STATEMENTS

___I can explain the reason for the changes in the climate between winter and summer.

Summative Examples

Projects, oral and written tests

Extend Learning

Compare the population of people who live in the Northern and Southern Hemispheres and on the Equator.
Research how bodies of water affect temperature.

Sensory Checklist

Check the senses students use during your daily lesson.
See Sensory Chart for Unit Plans, Table 4.4 and downloadable online

Online References

Hap Palmer, *Spinning on the Same Ball*. See Figure 9.1.
https://www.youtube.com/watch?v=EypR6IIgTmI

Here Comes the Sun (3:03). See Figure 9.2.
https://www.youtube.com/watch?v=6FB0rDsR_rc

Astronomy and Seasons 223

Images for picture of the Earth with an imaginary axis. See Figure 9.5.
https://duckduckgo.com/?q=picture+of+the+Earth+with+an+imaginary+axis&ia=web

Map of the World with Equator and Hemispheres. See Figure 9.6.
https://directmaps.blogspot.com/2017/06/map-of-world-with-equator-and.html

Illustrations of Earth's Seasons. See Figure 9.7.
https://duckduckgo.com/?q=illustration+of+whay+Earth+has+seasons&iax=images&ia=images

Images of Newton's First Law of Motion. See Figure 9.8.
https://duckduckgo.com/?q=newton%27s+first+law+of+motion&iax=images&ia=images

Images of Newton's 2nd Law of Motion. See Figure 9.9.
https://www.embibe.com/exams/newtons-second-law-of-motion/

Technology Unit Plan > Keywords, Word Documents, and Digital Pictures

Adapt learning for your grade level and the needs of your students and break it down for multiple daily lessons.

Become an Expert

Learn more than you will ever teach about the roles of the Earth and the Sun on seasonal differences and how they can be represented through word documents and digital pictures.

Essential Questions

Determine one to two essential questions for daily lessons to provide a framework for learning, such as:

How would you search for information to include in a trifold brochure on the seasons?
What are the advantages and disadvantages of using digital pictures in a brochure?

Objectives

Use or adapt one to three objectives from the list below in your daily lesson plans.
Students will learn to:

Create a list of search words to use on the Internet to find information about the causes of the seasons.
Explore different ways to search for information on the Earth's orbit around the Sun and its effect on the seasons in different parts of the world.
Search for information about the timing of the seasonal changes in the area they live.
Experiment with different ways to take quality digital pictures with different devices: cell phone, digital camera, and iPad.
Examine pictures, designs, different fonts, and words used in travel brochures meant to attract interest.

Create and photograph a model of the Earth tilted 23 degrees orbiting the Sun that clarifies the reasons for seasonal differences.

Experiment with background, lighting, and ways to fill the frame entirely with close-up digital pictures of the model.

Identify a digital picture to use in the brochure.

Use the model to show and explain how the Earth's orbit around the Sun causes differences in the seasons in the Northern and Southern Hemispheres.

Design a trifold travel brochure that advertises a specific location in the Northern or Southern Hemispheres.

Create a section of the brochure with factual information on astronomy about the Earth's movement around the Sun and its effect on seasonal differences.

Develop a trifold brochure with photos and fact-based information using varied fonts and colors.

Vocabulary

Choose two to three words to teach in daily lessons. See Chapter 3 for ways to teach vocabulary.

elliptical orbit	print
orbital path	photo
revolution	folder
axial tilt	save
latitude	viewfinder
equator	digital
hemisphere	iPad
poles	tutorial
Winter solstice	trifold brochure
Summer solstice	layout
Vernal equinox	insert
Autumnal equinox	template
computer operations	margins
Microsoft Word	orientation
search engines	landscape
essential words	portrait
accuracy	columns
relevance	tutorials

Materials and Resources

Use the HELP hierarchy in Chapter 4 for lists of multisensory materials.

Real-World Experiences

Hardware and software
Desktop and/or laptop computers
Computer labs
Computer on wheels (COWs)
iPads
Printer and paper
Microsoft Word or Publisher

Visual

See Online References at the end of this unit plan.
Online Tutorials for Trifold Brochures

Written

See Online References at the end of this unit plan
CRAAP Test to Evaluate Sources
The Reasons for Seasons by Gail Gibbons, ages 4–8
Seasons Turn, Tilt and Orbit by Douglas J. Alford, ages 5–11
The Kids Guide to Digital Photography: How to Shoot, Save, Play with & Print Your Digital Photos by Jenni Bidner, ages 10–12
4-H Guide to Digital Photography by Daniel Johnson, ages 11–13
Photography for Kids: A Beginners Book by JP Pullos, ages 9–11
Digital Filmmaking for Kids by Nick Willoughby, ages 10–13

Set, Procedures, Closure

Read Chapter 2 for multiple ways to plan multisensory sets and closures.

Sample Set

Greet students dressed in boots, gloves, and a helmet or hat. Pin or tape a large NASA logo, to the front of your outfit. Tell students they will be scientists learning the same information the astronauts need to know about the Earth's orbit around the sun. Tell them they will use the Internet to explore how the Earth and the Sun work together to create seasons and use this information to make a model of the Earth and the sun. Explain they will design a travel brochure from the information they learned about the Earth's trip around the sun.

Procedures

Plan a variety of instructional strategies that include direct teaching, modeling, guided and independent practice, and inquiry. Include critical thinking, questioning, and investigation.

    Match procedures to daily objectives.
    Check school district policies on using and downloading information from the Internet. Talk to students about Internet safety, copyright issues, plagiarism, and proper conduct online. Bookmark appropriate websites for younger students.
    To help students evaluate Internet sources related to astronomy and the seasons, introduce the elements of the CRAAP worksheet. Explain that CRAAP stands for Currency, Relevance, Authority, Accuracy, and Purpose. Students will probably love the name and think it is cool!
    Provide each student a copy of the CRAAP worksheet and discuss each of its parts. Have them refer to the worksheet as they search for information on the Internet.
    Think of questions or topics specific to differences in the seasons and have students think of key words for their search.
    Pair students. Assign a topic to search related to the differences of the seasons in the Northern and Southern Hemispheres. Engage them in a competition to see which one finds the best source.
    To show why the Earth has seasons, have students create a model of the Earth's orbital path around the Sun for students to photograph.

Provide each student or small groups of students two different-sized plates, 5¼" and 6¼", and a marble. Show students how to invert the small plate on top of the large plate. The small space between the two plates represents the orbital path the Earth takes around the Sun. Have students paint a large yellow Sun in the middle of the circular bottom of the inverted small paper plate. Then have them place the Earth, represented by the marble, on the orbital plane and slowly move it around the Sun. Tell students in real time this would take them a year! See Figure 9.10.

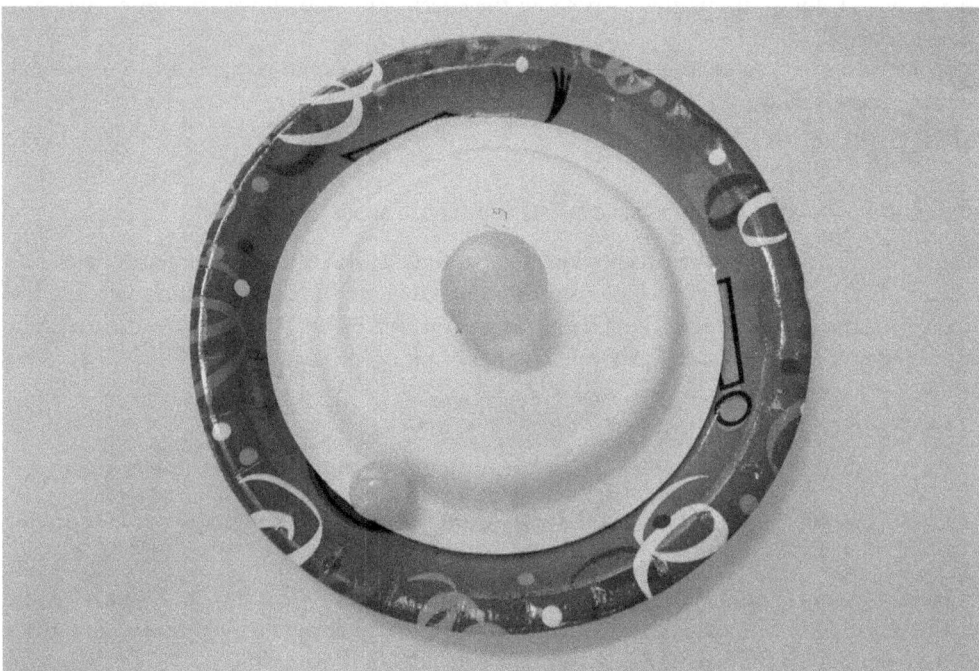

Figure 9.10 Model of the Earth's Revolution Around the Sun.

Have students label each of the parts of their model: Earth, Sun, orbital plane, and orbital path.

Ask students to explain how they built their model and what their model represents using scientific words.

To create a photographic display, ask students to create a background to show off their model. Have them experiment taking digital pictures of their model and evaluate each one based on background, placement, lighting, sharpness, and whether the closeup image of the model fills up the frame.

Have students study their pictures and select the one they want to include in their brochure.

After students have practiced using their models to help them explain how the Earth's revolution around the Sun causes seasonal differences, have them take digital videos of their presentations.

For digital or in-class presentations, print a NASA logo from an online source such as https://www.nasa.gov/audience/forstudents/5-8/features/symbols-of-nasa.html for students to wear on the day of their presentation. For QR code, see Figure 9.11.

Collect travel brochures and place them around the classroom for students to study. Have students list and discuss the features they liked such as photographs, colors, fonts, and wording and point out the features that attracted their attention.

Tell students they are going to make brochures that advertise the seasons common to their geographical location.

Ask students to consult the list of features they liked from the commercial brochures and use them in the brochure they will make.

Have students design and develop a format for a trifold brochure using Microsoft Word or Publisher.

Have students create a science section in their brochure that includes a photo of their Earth and Sun model along with written facts about the effect of the 23-degree axial tilt of the Earth on the seasons.

Encourage students to include digital maps and photos with captions that convey information about the seasons. Have students print a copy to share and use their names to save their work at the end of each session.

DIRECTIONS FOR MAKING A TRIFOLD BROCHURE USING MICROSOFT WORD

Check with your school district technology person for available software programs to make a brochure. Your district may have a site license for one, or money available to purchase one. Most schools probably have Word or Publisher. Search tutorials using Microsoft Word to create a trifold brochure (see Online References). The following is one example.

Open Microsoft Word and select Blank Document.

Click "Layout," and then move the down arrow under Orientation and choose "Landscape."

Click "Layout," and then move the down arrow under Margins and choose the top one, ".05" all around.

Click "Layout," and then move the down arrow under Columns and choose More Columns. This will allow you to check the box that will put lines between your three columns. Adjust the size of the columns or leave the default setting.

Type your information. When it gets to the end of a column, it will automatically wrap to the next page.

To add a picture, click "Insert," and then move the down arrow under pictures and choose from the device or online to add a picture. Choose a picture, click on it, and then insert. The picture will appear where your cursor was. It can be dragged to a different area.

The picture will probably need to be made smaller. To do this, click and hold down the mouse on the top-right corner and you will see a diagonal arrow; drag it toward the center until the picture is the right size.

You will notice the picture interrupted the text. If you want the text to wrap around the picture, click on the picture and click "layout," and then move the down arrow by "wrap text." Choose "square" if you want it to have a box around it and text. There are other wraps available.

Once the students finish their brochure, have them save it by clicking "File, Save as" and click on where to save, such as desktop, and then save.

Next, have them print their brochure by clicking on "File," then "Print," and again, "Print." Allow the students to share their brochures.

Astronomy and Seasons 229

Sample Closure

Review key facts about the tilt of the Earth's axis, the orbital plane around the Sun, and their effects on seasonal differences in the weather. Ask students to share their brochures with their families and friends and describe the most important facts they learned about the seasons.

Formative and Summative Assessment

Formative Examples

LET STUDENTS SHOW OFF THEIR LEARNING

Have students show off the completed brochure and "sell" its strong points.

IF-ONLY STATEMENTS

If only I could teach a younger class to make a brochure about seasons, I would _____.

I-CAN STATEMENTS

____I can use Microsoft Word to make a trifold brochure about any topic.

Summative Examples

Projects, presentations, oral and written quizzes

Extend Learning

Determine other possible technology activities to use to share knowledge about seasons. Write a script for an informational film using the model of the Earth and the Sun.

Sensory Checklist

Check the senses students will use during your lesson.
See Sensory Chart for Unit Plans, Table 4.4 and downloadable online

Online References

NASA logo. See Figure 9.11.
https://www.nasa.gov/audience/forstudents/5-8/features/symbols-of-nasa.html

Online Tutorials for Trifold Brochures. See Figures 9.12–9.14 below.
https://www.officearticles.com/tutorials/create_a_tri_fold_brochure_in_microsoft_word.htm

https://www.vtaide.com/gleanings/BrochureMSWord.htm

https://www.template.net/editable/2520/education-tri-fold-brochure

CRAAP Test to Evaluate Sources. See Figure 9.15.
https://docs.google.com/viewer?a=v&pid=sites&srcid=ZGVmYXVsdGRvbWFpbnw2dGhncmFkZXRlY2hub3xneDo1YTkxNjFhYjY5M2U3MTNl

Engineering Unit Plan > Electrical Engineering

Adapt learning for your grade level and the needs of your students and break it down for multiple daily lessons.

Become an Expert

Learn more than you will ever teach about light-emitting diode technology, electrical voltage and current, the use of scale in preparing an engineering construction project, and the solar system, especially the Sun and the planets.

Essential Questions

Determine one to two essential questions for daily lessons to provide a framework for learning, such as:

How do light-emitting diodes (LEDs) work?
What voltages and currents are normally used in LEDs?
What distance scales are useful in preparing a project on the solar system?

Objectives

Select or adapt one to three objectives for your daily lesson plans.
Students will learn to:

Use addition and subtraction by younger students and the four operations with whole numbers or fractions for older students.
Create a proportional visual of the solar system by cutting and pasting the Sun and the eight planets in a line, beginning with the closest planet and ending with the farthest planet.
Older students can use the proportional visual to create a scaled model of the solar system.
Estimate the size and scale of the project by prior calculations of distances from the Sun to Mercury (the shortest distance) and from the Sun to Neptune (the longest distance).
Determine the materials that must be gathered prior to starting the project.
List the planets in order from Mercury to Neptune and record the sizes of each planet.
Define the astronomical unit of distance (distance from the Sun to the Earth, 93,000,000 miles).
Research the astronomical units for each of the planets from the Sun.
Experiment with the use of light-emitting diodes (LEDs) and understand how they work.
Connect low voltage batteries via wire and alligator clips to light-emitting diodes.

Vocabulary

Choose two to three words to teach in daily lessons. See Chapter 3 for ways to teach vocabulary.

electrical engineer	light-emitting diodes (LEDs)
solar system	outer space
Sun	battery
Mercury	wire
Venus	alligator clips
Earth	volt
Mars	current

Jupiter	ampere
Saturn	milliampere
Uranus	proportional
Neptune	astronomical unit

Materials and Resources

Use the HELP hierarchy in Chapter 4 for lists of multisensory materials.

Real-World Experiences

Wire
2-3 volt battery
LED mini bulbs (colored)
Alligator clips
Logbook for daily entries

Representations

Multiple large posters for descriptions of planets and planet orbits

Visuals

See Online References at the end of this unit plan.

Written

See Online References at the end of this unit plan.
Light Bulb: Eureka! The Biography of an Idea Paperback–Picture Book by Kathleen Weidner Zoehfield and Stephanie Dehennin, ages 4–8
Easy Electronics by Charles Platt, ages 10–12
Space Encyclopedia, 2nd *Edition: A Tour of Our Solar System and Beyond* by David A. Aguilar and Patricia Daniels, ages 8–12
Solar System for Kids: A Junior Scientist's Guide to Planets, Dwarf Planets, and Everything Circling Our Sun by Hilary Statum, ages 6–8

Set, Procedures, Closure

Read Chapter 2 for ways to plan sets and closures.

Sample Set

Ask students how many planets there are. Ask them what color they are. Tell the students that they're going to build a model of the solar system that includes all the planets and facts about each one.

Astronomy and Seasons   233

Procedures

Plan a variety of instructional strategies that include direct teaching, modeling, guided and independent practice, and inquiry. Include critical thinking, questioning, and investigation.

Match procedures to daily objectives.

Ask the students for the steps involved in building a model of a physical structure (such as the solar system). Look for answers along the lines of planning for materials collection, estimation of space involved, estimation of time to complete the project, and estimation of the cost of the project.

One of the first parameters in planning is to estimate the space needed. In the case of the solar system, we must know how big the solar system is so that students can build a model on a smaller scale. Have students list the planets and determine how far they are from the Sun (on average). Find an appropriate website or reference book and have students look up the planets and find the "mean distance from the Sun" for each one. A couple of example values are shown in Table 9.1 below.

Table 9.1 Worksheet for Distances from Planets to the Sun

Planet	Mean Distance from the Sun
Mercury	36,000,000 million miles
Venus	
Earth	
Mars	
Jupiter	
Saturn	
Uranus	
Neptune	2,812,500,000 million miles

Since Mercury is the closest planet to the Sun and Neptune is the farthest, the longest distance in the model will represent 2,815,500,000 miles with the Sun at the center. Notice that the ratio of Neptune's distance to the Sun to Mercury's distance to the Sun is

$2,815,500,000/36,000,000 = 78.1.$

This means that we will need a model big enough to represent distances that differ by a factor of 78.1. That's really big. If we build the model so that the Sun is in the center and one inch represents 36,000,000 miles, then Neptune would be 78.1 inches from the Sun. So, the students need a 7-foot space for the model. And that's for just half the circular orbits for the planets. See Figure 9.16.

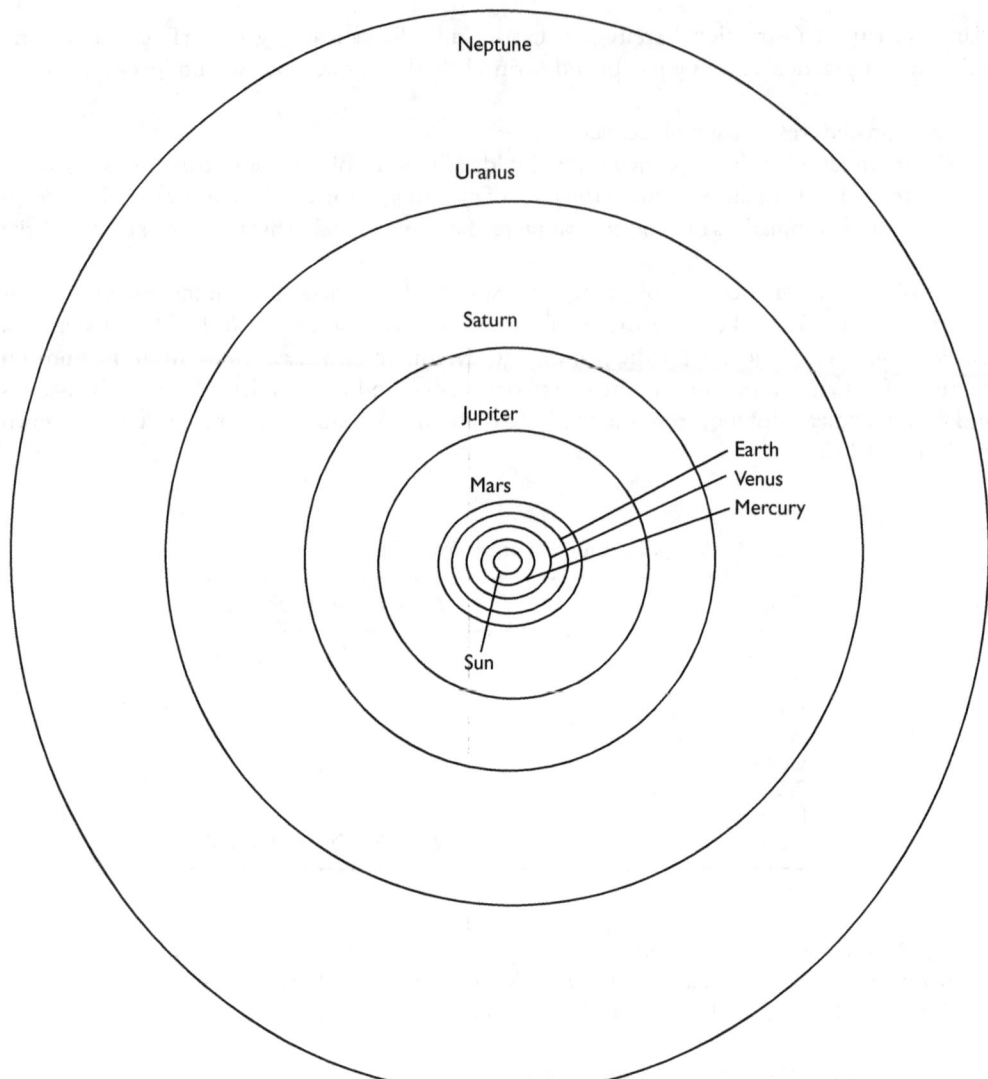

Figure 9.16 Solar System.

Younger students can estimate space needed for a model not drawn to scale.

Tell the students that they are going to represent the Sun and its planets by using light-emitting diodes (LEDs). LED minibulbs are low voltage lamps and tiny in size so that they are not electrical hazards. They *do* require low voltage, however, so that the students need eight lithium batteries for the planets and one battery for the sun. Both the batteries and mini LEDs are easily available and affordable online and can be delivered promptly by the supplier.

Once they know that a 7-foot space is required for just half-orbits, have the students adjust the orbital space requirements so that it fits with the environmental constraints. It is possible that the students will find that a half-inch scale model (1/2 inch = 36,000,000 miles) is better.

The students should make the final determination as to scale. One difficulty is that if the scale is too small, the inner planets (Mercury, Venus, Earth, and Mars) will be very close together. However, that doesn't detract from the accuracy and correctness of their model.

Determine the space where the students will build their project. Options include a stiff cardboard poster, a plastic sheet, and a thin plywood sheet that is at least as big as the largest dimension representing the orbital path of Neptune. Select the option that is right for you. Poke holes in the cardboard or drill little holes in the plastic or plywood to accept the bulb part of the LED. Insert the bulbs into the holes and connect them to the batteries. Use alligator clips for connections. Assist younger students with the holes.

When finished, all the lights will be on. The students should label all the planets and provide details about them. For instance, what color is Earth from space? What color is Mars? Try to match the details to the colors of the mini LEDs. Multicolored LEDs cost no more than transparent (white) ones.

In addition to the astronomy information, students also learn about voltage (2–3 volt batteries) and light-emitting diodes (LEDs), which light when connected to the small batteries, and how to connect the wires from the LED to the battery. The easiest connector for beginners is called an "alligator clip," so called because it resembles the jaws of an alligator. Those clips are also available and inexpensive and they provide an easy assembling and disassembling of the model. Ask students to determine how many lights are required for the project, and how much it will cost. LEDs are also rated for maximum current. Current is the movement of electrons inside a conductor which can be made faster with higher voltage (pressure). Usually, LEDs are rated for milliamperes of current, since more current will overheat the LEDs and cause them to fail.

Sample Closure

Tell the students that they will invite the principal or parents to see their model. Ask them to write an explanation of what they did and what they learned, not only about astronomy, but also about electricity.

Formative and Summative Assessment

Formative Examples

LET STUDENTS SHOW OFF THEIR LEARNING

Have students state the names of the planets, starting from the planet closest to the Sun.

Have students locate the major planets and the describe the relative sizes of the Sun, major planets, and minor planets.

Ask students to tell what the approximate ratio of the diameter of Neptune's orbit to Mercury's orbit is.

IF-ONLY STATEMENTS

If only I could build a model 1/10 the size of the solar system I would_____.

If only I could land on the Sun in a fireproof uniform, I would_____.

I-CAN STATEMENTS

___ I can build a model of the solar system.

Summative Examples

Projects, oral and written tests

Extend Learning

If bigger models of the solar system were built, what different materials could be used? Some students may be interested in building a model of the entire galaxy. Have them calculate the distances involved and establish a scale that would fit on a poster for display in the classroom.

Sensory Checklist

Check the senses students use during your daily lesson.
See Sensory Chart for Unit Plans, Table 4.4 and downloadable online

Online References

Solar System Educational Teaching Poster Chart. See Figure 9.17.
https://products.bestreviews.com/p/solar-system-educational-teaching-poster-chartperfect-for-toddlers-and-kids-expanded-edition-30-x-15?yb=&cid=367741698&aid=1209463238887234&eid=&tid=kwd-75591782457001%3Aloc-190&ul=80408&mt=p&n=s&d=c&dm=&dt=&sn=&adid=&k=solar+system+educational&p=&pc=&ap=&msclkid=8b308099825e136e004be22953859115

NASA Space Place: Solar System. See Figure 9.18.
https://spaceplace.nasa.gov/menu/solar-system/

26 Solar System Project Ideas for Kids That Are Out of This World. See Figures 9.19 and 9.20. https://planetsforkids.org/solar-system.html

https://www.teachingexpertise.com/classroom-ideas/solar-system-project-ideas/

Art Unit Plan > Music and Dance/Movement

Adapt learning for your grade level and the needs of your students and break it down for multiple daily lessons.

Become an Expert

Learn more than you will ever teach about ways the seasons can be represented through music, dance, and movement.

Essential Questions

Determine one to two essential questions for daily lessons to provide a framework for learning, such as:

How does tempo create a mood for different seasons?
What dance movements can you create to represent the seasons?

Objectives

Use or adapt one to three objectives for your daily lesson plans.
Students will learn to:

Describe how seasons are formed through the 23-degree tilt of the Earth's axis from the perpendicular to the orbital plane.
Apply knowledge of the physical image of the Earth's revolution around the Sun to movements that dramatize the meaning of perpendicular and orbital plane.
Differentiate between the themes and words of songs about the seasons in the Northern and Southern Hemispheres.
Connect knowledge of the seasons to musical color tones of instruments such as bright, deep, warm, and muted that are made by various instruments such as a flute, tuba, violin, bass guitar, triangle, and kettle drum.
Compare adjectives for color tones for musical sound to adjectives used in art.
Identify the sounds made by various stringed instruments based on their pitch and the combined ways they coordinate to emphasize melody, tone, rhythm, harmony, and dissonance used to convey images of the seasons.
Observe the force musicians use when playing string, brass, woodwind, and percussion instruments to create the vibrations necessary to change tone and loudness.
Distinguish differences among the sounds of a range of musical instruments and how each one enhances the mood of a particular season.
Recognize differences between the sounds of major and minor keys.
Describe how music played in major and minor keys creates different emotions.
Experiment with dance movements to represent musical passages related to the seasons.
Demonstrate differences in tempo through movement and how they represent the seasons.
Create different movements for music written in major and minor keys.
Explore how movements to specific seasons will differ depending on geographical locations of countries on the Equator and in the Northern and Southern Hemispheres.
Use a variety of movements to communicate meaningful weather events that occur during each season.
Use props to support movements that enhance the meaning of seasonal differences.

Vocabulary

Choose two to three words to teach in daily lessons. See Chapter 3 for ways to teach vocabulary.

orchestra	props
concerto	interpretation
violin	imitation
trumpet	mood
organ	locomotor movement (run, glide, hop)
flute	non-locomotor (sway, wiggle, point)
percussion	accentuate moves
woodwind	flowing moves
brass	dynamic force and energy
string instrument	emotion

harmony	seasons
dissonance	hemispheres
major and minor keys	Equator
tempo	tilt of Earth's axis
melody	revolution
rhythm	orbit
tone	orbital plane
color tone	winter solstice
vibration	equinox
crescendo	vernal equinox
diminuendo	autumnal equinox

Materials and Resources

Use the HELP hierarchy in Chapter 4 for lists of multisensory materials.

Real-World Experiences

Computer
Sound system

Real-World Artifacts

Props

Representations

Globe of the Earth
Light representing the sun
Colorful scarves
Movement props

Visuals

See Online References at the end of this unit plan.
Pictures of seasons around the world.

Written

See Online References at the end of this unit plan.
The Reasons for Seasons by Gail Gibbons, ages 4–8
Seasons Turn, Tilt and Orbit by Douglas J. Alford, ages 5–11 *Classics for Kids*
I Am Earth: An Earth Day Book for Kids by James and Rebecca McDonald, ages 4–7
4 Seasons Make a Year by Anne Rockwell, ages 5–11
Princess Naomi Helps a Unicorn: A Dance-It-Out Creative Movement Story by Ethan Roffler, ages 4–7

Freedom Soup by Tami Charles, ages 6–8
Step on the Beat: Rhythms and Rhymes to Get Kids Moving by Kate Kuper, ages 5–11
Some Stories Have All the Luck: Antonio Vivaldi (Little Stories of Great Composers) by Ana Gerhard, ages 7–9

Oral and Aural

See Online References at the end of this unit plan.
Pictures of seasons around the world

Set, Procedures, Closure

Read Chapter 2 for multiple ways to plan multisensory sets and closures.

Sample Set

Have Vivaldi's music, *The Four Seasons,* playing softly as students enter the classroom. Display pictures of each of the four seasons that occur in the Northern Hemisphere and pictures of spring and summer to represent the Southern Hemisphere. Ask students why the seasons have different weather patterns in different parts of the world. Show them a globe and review how the tilt of the Earth on its axis creates the seasons as it revolves around the Sun.

Procedures

Plan a variety of instructional strategies that include direct teaching, modeling, guided and independent practice, and inquiry. Include critical thinking, questioning, and investigation.

Match procedures to daily objectives.

Show students the location of countries and continents on a map or globe that are located at the Equator and comprise Northern and Southern Hemispheres.

Review seasonal differences between regions in the Northern and Southern Hemispheres and the Equator.

Discuss the causes of weather differences in the seasons and how the differences occur using a globe for the Earth and a light. Remind students that the Earth rotates on its axis at a 23-degree angle.

In small groups, ask students to dramatize the Earth's movement as it rotates on its axis and revolves around the sun. Remind students that the axis of the Earth is tilted 23 degrees from the perpendicular to the orbital plane. This tilt causes differences in the duration of day and night and the Earth's revolution around the Sun causes differences in the seasons around the world. The students can brainstorm other actions to dramatize the effects of hot and cold temperatures as they revolve around the Sun. See Figure 9.21.

Astronomy and Seasons 241

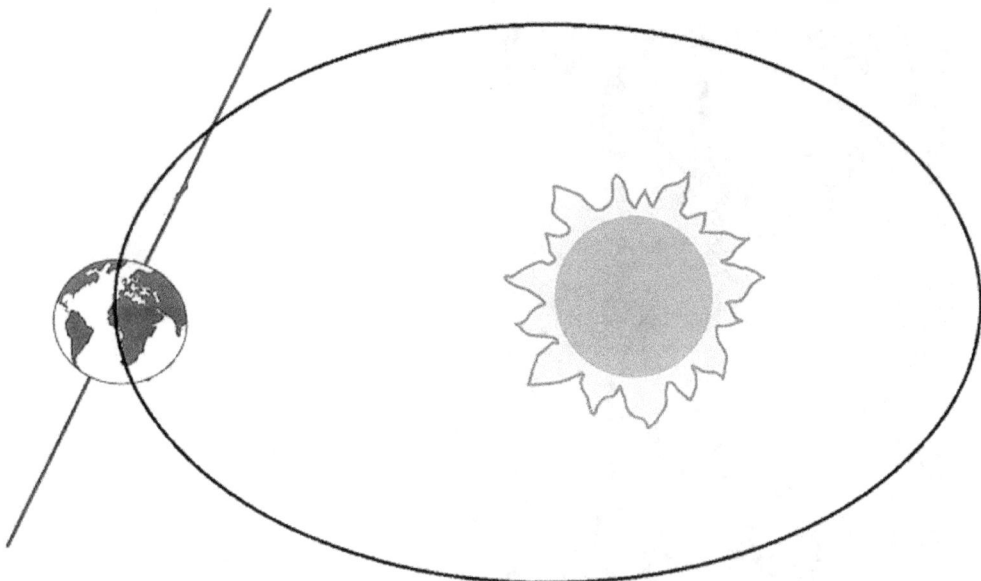

Figure 9.21 Dramatization of the Earth's Movement Around the Sun.

Introduce musical names and terms students can use when discussing music, movement, and dance. Make sure they know the major groups of instruments that comprise an orchestra. Relate the force used by musicians to the tone, loudness of the notes they play. Introduce major and minor keys, musical timing, accent, tempo, and degrees of loudness (crescendo and diminuendo).

Play different types of songs related to the seasons and ask students to tell you the parts of the music they liked and did not like and explain why using at least one of the vocabulary terms.

Boom Chicka Boom Summer Songs

https://www.youtube.com/watch?v=hfZ438DrIs (4:00). For QR code, see Figure 9.22.
   Autumn Leaves by Roger Williams
https://www.youtube.com/watch?v=88Js16yeHl4 (3:05). For QR code, see Figure 9.23.
   Rustle of Spring by Christian Sinding, played on the piano by Amaral Vieira
https://duckduckgo.com/?q=Spring%3A+Rustle+of+Spring+by+Christain+Singding+played+by+Amara+Vieira&iax=videos&ia=videos&iai=https%3A%2F%2Fwww.youtube.com%2Fwatch%3Fv%3DAAX3SZPcvi0 (3:05). For QR code, see Figure 9.24.

Replay one or more of the musical pieces from YouTube, or similar ones of your choice and have students create movements to go with the music.

Make props students can use for movement and dance to music. Attach colorful yarn, ribbon, or crepe paper streamers to a small paper plate or milk jug handle. See Figure 9.25.

Figure 9.25 Upcycled Props for Dance and Movement.

After students receive their props, give them time to explore, create, and practice different movements and effects they can make.

Show students how locomotor movements (running, gliding, hopping) and non-locomotor movements (twisting, bending, swaying) communicate meaning or establish mood.

Ask students to identify props that represent the seasons where they live. Have them make or find some of the props, such as cutout snowflakes, a large painting of the sun, a collection of dead leaves, or branches with no leaves to represent the seasons. To help with the props, hang strips of crepe paper to simulate rain and purchase artificial flowers and plants to represent spring and summer.

Place props around the room and have students select the ones they want to use to communicate the different types of weather that occur during one or more of the seasons through dance and movement.

Have students listen to Antonio Vivaldi's *The Four Seasons* and think about what movements they could use while listening to the *Spring Concerto from The Four Seasons*. Play YouTube videos that show images of the changing seasons as the music plays.

Play Vivaldi's *The Four Seasons* for violin for students to hear the tones and emotions written over 300 years ago that continues to make it famous around the world today. https://www.youtube.com/watch?v=0vRLqLpK-Ko (For QR code, see Figure 9.26.) and Vivaldi's *The Four Seasons, Violin Concerto No. 4 in F Minor,* (Christian Li, child violinist) https://www.youtube.com/watch?v=AG2U_i_6jg4 (For QR code, see Figure 9.27.)).

Play Vivaldi's *The Four Seasons Translated to Another Medium* https://interlude.hk/translated-to-another-medium-vivaldis-spring-concerto (For QR code, see Figure 9.28 to show how his work, written for violins, sounds when played by an organ, trumpet, flute, and brass instruments). Discuss what students hear and how different instruments affect the tone and quality of Vivaldi's work.

Replay *The Four Seasons Translated to Another Medium* and give the students a card with the names of the of the instruments (organ, trumpet, flute, brass) featured in the video. Have them hold up the name of the instrument when featured on the YouTube video. Remind students that Vivaldi wrote the concerto for violins. Replay https://www.youtube.com/watch?v=0vRLqLpK-Ko For QR code, see Figure 9.29.

Discuss with the students why they think Vivaldi's *The Four Seasons* begins with *Spring*.

Ask students to experiment using different movements and props they think go with each of the musical versions of Vivaldi's *The Four Seasons*.

Pair students and provide them with an iPad to record each other moving to Vivaldi's music. Once they have recorded each other, watch the videos and discuss what movements they liked about each other's performance, and why they made the movements they did to particular parts of the music.

Sample Closure

Review the reasons for the seasons around the world. Remind students that weather that feels like winter in the Northern Hemisphere, feels like summer in the Southern Hemisphere, and that people who live at the Equator feel very little difference in temperature. Play one of the songs about the seasons listed above as students leave and have them make two movements that fit with the music as they line up to leave the classroom.

Formative and Summative Assessment

Formative Examples

LET STUDENTS SHOW OFF THEIR LEARNING

Demonstrate movements that can represent each season.

IF-ONLY STATEMENTS

If only I could use a unique movement to show the reasons for the seasons, I would _____.

I-CAN STATEMENTS

____I can identify other songs and music that are about the seasons.

Summative Examples

Projects, presentations, oral and written quizzes.

Extend Learning

Compose one or more themes about the seasons. Write the notes and play it on an instrument. Compare the sounds and style of music by composers who lived in the 17th and 18th centuries to modern composers who have access to electronic instruments.

Sensory Checklist

Check the senses students will use during your lesson.
See Sensory Chart for Unit Plans, Table 4.4 and downloadable online

Online References

Boom Chick a Boom Summer Songs. See Figure 9.22.
https://www.youtube.com/watch?v=hfZ438DrIs (4:00).

Autumn Leaves by Roger Williams. See Figure 9.23.
https://www.youtube.com/watch?v=88Js16yeHl4 (3:05).

Rustle of Spring by Christian Sinding played on the piano by Amaral Vieira. See Figure 9.24.
https://duckduckgo.com/?q=Spring%3A+Rustle+of+Spring+by+Christain+Singding+played+by+Amara+Vieira&iax=videos&ia=videos&iai=https%3A%2F%2Fwww.youtube.com%2Fwatch%3Fv%3DAAX3SZPcvi0 (3:05).

Vivaldi's *The Four Seasons*. See Figure 9.26.
https://www.youtube.com/watch?v=0vRLqLpK-Ko

Vivaldi's *The Four Seasons, Violin Concerto No. 4 in F Minor*, (Christian Li, child violinist). See Figure 9.27.
https://www.youtube.com/watch?v=AG2U_i_6jg4

Vivaldi's *The Four Seasons Translated to Another Medium*. See Figure 9.28.
https://interlude.hk/translated-to-another-medium-vivaldis-spring-concerto

246 Planning Sensory-Rich STEAM Unit Plans

Colorful creative pictures and music of autumn. See Figure 9.29.
https://duckduckgo.com/?q=autumn+leaves+instrumental+You+tube&iax=videos&ia=videos&iai=https%3A%2F%2Fwww.youtube.com%2Fwatch%3Fv%3DApfrGlQOVQ8

Classics for Kids: Rhythm (Beat; Tempo) Moving; Listening; Describing; Creating; Relating by Dr. Kay Edwards. See Figure 9.30.
https://www.classicsforkids.com/downloads/vivaldi/Vivaldi_LessonPlansK-2_part1.pdf

Richard Clayderman *Piano Instrumental Music: Autumn Leaves,* YouTube, 5:24
https://duckduckgo.com/?q=Richard+Clayderman+Piano+Instrumental+Music%3A+Autumn+Leaves%2C+YouTube&iax=videos&ia=videos&iai=https%3A%2F%2Fwww.youtube.com%2Fwatch%3Fv%3DApfrGlQOVQ8
See Figure 9.31.

Mathematics Unit Plan > Rates

Adapt learning for your grade level and the needs of your students and break it down for multiple daily lessons.

Become an Expert

Learn more than you will teach about astronomical distances to the sun, moon, and other planets and the concept of rates, which relate one unit of measure to another, especially the metric and English systems.

Essential Questions

Determine one to two essential questions for daily lessons to provide a framework for learning, such as:

In astronomy, what are the essential units for measuring distance, speed, and time?
How do astronomy and mathematics combine to affect our lives?

Objectives

Select or adapt one to three objectives for your daily lesson plans.
Students will learn to:

Understand that a rate compares to events, such as miles per hour, dollars per pound, or minutes per homework assignment.
Tell how to represent information in hours, half hours, and minutes.
Determine how many hours are in a school day.
Calculate how many minutes are in a day.
Determine the duration of an astronomical earth year and why it is so defined.
Determine the duration of an astronomical earth day and why it is so defined.
Calculate how many earth days are in an earth year.
Summarize numerical data related to minutes and hours in a day, a week, and a year.
Calculate the time it takes for the Sun's rays to travel to Earth.
Calculate rates in both metric and English systems.
Calculate the distance of a light-year in kilometers and miles.
Recall what the speed of light is in kilometers per second and miles per second.

Vocabulary

Choose two to three words to teach in daily lessons. See Chapter 3 for ways to teach vocabulary.

orbit	circumference
average distance	revolution
planet	axis
pi	rate
average speed	constant
sun	astronomical units
light-year	

Materials and Resources

Use the HELP hierarchy in Chapter 4 for lists of multisensory materials.

Real-World Experiences

Measurement of the duration of day and night

Visuals

See Online References at the end of this unit plan.

Written

Best Buys, Ratios, and Rates by Catherine Twomey Fosnot and William Jacob, ages 9–11
Space and the Speed of Light: The History of 14 Billion Years for People Short of Tim by Dr. Becky Smethurst, all ages
The Milky Way (Our Galaxy) by Grace Hansen, ages up to 7
Super Stars: The Biggest, Hottest, Brightest, and Most Explosive Stars in the Milky Way by David A. Aguilar, ages 7–9
The Lives of Star by Ken Croswell, ages 9–12
Universe by Robin Kerrod, ages 8–12

Set, Procedures, Closure

Read Chapter 2 for ways to plan sets and closures.

Sample Set

Tell students that they are going to learn about *rates*. Specifically, what is a *rate*? Give an example of a rate: miles per hour or minutes per class. Ask the students for more examples. In this lesson, you will learn about rates of all kinds. Many, but not all, rates compare occurrences of various events with time.

Procedures

Plan a variety of instructional strategies that include direct teaching, modeling, guided and independent practice, and inquiry. Include critical thinking, questioning, and investigation.

Match procedures to daily objectives.

Tell students that a rate compares a set of two different units. The first unit describes what is being measured, the second unit often, but not always, is a unit of time. Ask students to share their examples from the set and identify the which unit of time is used.

Ask students to find examples in which the second unit is NOT time. Tell the students to draw a picture and give them three crayons each. Three crayons per student is a rate not involving time. At recess, pass out the balls. Provide four balls for the class. If the class size is 20, the rate for balls per student is $4/20 = 1/5$. This is another rate not involving time. Time for lunch is perhaps 30 minutes. Thirty minutes per lunch is another rate, this time involving time as the first unit, the one that is being measured. Once the insight of relating two variables is learned, all kinds of activities can be included. Ask the students how long it takes for the class to line up? Count the minutes next time. The rate will be minutes per line up.

In the next few procedures, "miles" and "kilometers" will be used interchangeably. Ask the students to find the factor which can convert miles to kilometers and vice versa.

Explore the students' examples of rates and demonstrate that a rate is a relationship between two variables and is often characterized by the word "per." Miles per hour is a very common rate of distance per time (speed). Price per pound is another rate that one sees when going to the grocery store. A pump has a maximum gallons per minute, for instance. A tire makes a number of revolutions per minute, depending upon its speed and that same tire has pressure inside it of about 33 pounds per square inch. Emphasize that rates almost always have the word "per" in their name, label, or title.

Remind students that a noun is the name of a person, place, or thing and, in a rate, the words on each side of the "per" are nouns. So, a rate relates two nouns. The first noun, usually plural, tells us how many of such events occur, on average, in the second noun. For example: miles per hour is a rate. "Miles" is the first noun, usually plural, and "hour" is the second noun, normally singular. Another example is people per square mile: "people" is the first noun and "square mile" is the second. The latter example is taken from population density.

Give students time to discuss and write other examples of rates using that same template.

Notice that "per" appears to be a word for division. That is, when the total distance in miles is found and the time duration is also determined, we get the rate in miles per hour by dividing the miles by the hours. An important step when actually doing the calculation is to carry along the names of the units with the numbers on paper. So, write

xxx miles/yyy hours = zzz miles per hour

Have students set up and work division problems using examples of rates.

Ask the students for other commonly used rates and write them on the board. Underline both nouns and their abbreviations, if appropriate.

When a few rates are identified, ask the students to name the appropriate nouns in the rates. Emphasize that every rate must have two nouns.

Ask the students to find the rate of rotation of the Earth about its axis. In order to calculate this, they must know the two nouns that are related. The first, the plural one, is kilometers, that is, how many kilometers does a person on the equator travel. The second noun, the singular one, defines the amount of time we allot for the travel. Ask the students to find the distance around the Earth at the Equator. That will be the value for noun #1. One day is the value for noun #2. But we prefer to have the answer in kilometers per hour, not kilometers per day. So, the value for noun #2 is the number of hours in a day. That is easy. It is 24. So, the rate or speed of the person at the Equator is distance of the circumference of the Earth in kilometers/24 hours = speed in mph. Check yourself: The answer is about 1,678 kilometers (1,042 miles) per hour.

Ask the students about the relative speeds of an outstanding runner who can run a mile in 4 minutes. What is the speed in miles per hour? Which is faster: The person standing on the Equator spinning about the Earth's axis or the track star running a mile in 4 minutes?

Ask the students what is the rate in revolutions per year of the Earth on its path around the Sun?

As we have seen, the Earth makes one revolution per year around the Sun. So, what is the rate of speed in miles per hour?

Remind the students to consider the two nouns that must be related. In this case, the distance around the Sun that the Earth's path takes is one noun and the duration that is necessary for the Earth to return to its starting point is the second noun.

Have students look up the distance that the Earth travels on its orbit around the Sun. That is the first noun and it is almost always plural. The second noun, hours, has to be the number of hours in a year. Calculate the rate in miles per hour for the journey of the Earth around the Sun.

The numbers that the students come up with are extraordinarily large because astronomical distances are large, speeds of planets around the Sun are large, and planets spin very fast. Have older students compare these magnitudes with rates they are familiar with and note the tremendous differences.

Pose the question, "How can we be going so fast and yet we seem as though we're standing still?"

Finally, the Sun is on a trip around the center of the galaxy. Ask older students to look up the approximate distance of its path around the center of the galaxy and determine how long it takes. These are numbers that must be determined by researching websites or reference books. Now determine the rate in kilometers per hour that the Sun (and with it, the Earth) is traveling.

Most calculations associated with such vast distances use a new unit of distance, called the light-year. The light-year is the distance that light travels in one Earth year (365.24 days). Ask the students to determine how many miles or kilometers is equivalent to a light-year.

This is another rate problem. A light-year = distance traveled by light in one year.

The students can find the speed of light in reference books or websites. It is approximately 300,000 kilometers per second. Then the students must apply their knowledge of rates to find out how many kilometers per year light travels. That means they must determine how many seconds are in a year, (answer 31.6 million). Finally, they use their knowledge of rates and work backwards by multiplying the speed of light by the number of seconds in a year to get about 9,467,020,800,000 kilometers.

Ask the student to convert that large number to miles.

Sample Closure

Review information on rates. The basic rule for rates is that they must relate two nouns. In the case of miles or kilometers per hour, the two nouns are distance (miles or kilometers) and time (hour). Rates like this are expressed as a ratio (miles or kilometers /hour = speed), so if we know any two of these variables, we can find the third by arithmetic. Ask students to write one question about the lesson to give to the teacher or leave on a table.

Formative and Summative Assessment

Formative Examples

LET STUDENTS SHOW OFF THEIR LEARNING

Ask students to define what a rate is and what the word "per" means that separates the two nouns.

IF-ONLY STATEMENTS

If only I could change the rate of the Earth's rotation on its axis, I would_____.
If only the Earth revolved around the Sun every 6 months, I would_____.

I-CAN STATEMENTS

___ I can explain what a rate is and how the Earth's motion is characterized by several rates.

Summative Examples

Oral and written tests and projects

Extend Learning

Research the rates of planetary spins for other planets.
Learn about the speeds of other planets in their orbits around the sun.
Calculate the time it takes for light to get from the Sun to the Earth.

Sensory Checklist

Check the senses students use during this lesson.
See Sensory Chart for Unit Plans, Table 4.4 and downloadable online

Online References

The Physics Factbook. An encyclopedia of scientific essays. See Figure 9.32.
https://hypertextbook.com/facts/2002/StacyLeong.shtm (Click on table of contents.)

The Latest News on the Solar System and the Universe, all ages. See Figure 9.33.
https://www.universetoday.com/

StarChild: A Learning Center for Young Astronomers, ages 5–13. See Figure 9.34.
https://starchild.gsfc.nasa.gov/docs/StarChild/StarChild.html

Chapter 10

Problems and Pitfalls Planning Multisensory STEAM Unit Plans

Introduction

In this chapter, the authors take the readers through the decision-making process on ways to plan sensory-rich thematic units. We expose the problems we encountered, the pitfalls we were determined to avoid, and the mistakes we made while writing 25 unit plans. Having just been through the experience, we were acutely aware of things that could go wrong. In the hopes that our problems could be anticipated, rather than unexpected, we share our thoughts on the decisions we made while creating unit plans for each STEAM content area: Science, Technology, Engineering, Art, and Mathematics for each of the five themes, Rabbits and Hares, Water Cycle, Nutrition and Health, Landforms, and Astronomy and Seasons.

Okay, let us get started! Right off the bat, we found choosing a theme was difficult because of all the options available to us. We chose themes that were popular with the students we taught and were used frequently in the classrooms we observed. We then considered the ways they could be addressed in each STEAM unit plan. Because a primary emphasis of this book is on the use of multisensory materials, we first considered real-world materials before moving to less authentic materials. You will find multiple ways we obtained and used sensory materials for our unit plans.

As we wrote the chapters for the unit plans, we frequently consulted each other for ideas and advice. It always helped to have fresh eyes read each other's work to catch errors, difficult to understand sentences or passages, and ask questions. Each comment and question showed us where the problem areas were in our planning. We quickly learned that the STEAM unit plans could not be written in two or three days. They actually took far more time than we expected. Much of the time we spent was to review and learn thoroughly the content we wanted our students to learn. We consulted print and online sources and each other during the time we were becoming the experts our students deserved. Each unit plan we wrote took us down false starts and blind alleys. Armed with content knowledge, we were able to cull away trivial information and activities so that only information for knowledge-rich lessons remained. To ensure we involved students at low and high levels of thinking, we consulted the original and revised versions of Bloom's Taxonomy to help us use a variety of verbs to stimulate thinking at all levels (VALAMIS, 2022).

First Steps

The first thing we did was to determine a format for the unit plan. We made many revisions, but after many trials and errors we arrived at one. Together, we agreed it served us well and became our road map for planning STEAM lessons for Science, Technology, Engineering, Art, and Mathematics for each theme: Rabbits and Hares, Water Cycle, Nutrition and Health, Landforms, Astronomy and Seasons.

The first item on the unit plan is **Become an Expert.** If we want our students to have high-quality knowledge-rich lessons, we had to become experts ourselves in the subjects we planned. It was time consuming, yet very exciting, to revisit and learn facts about each of the five themes. This first step proved to be one of the most enjoyable and beneficial parts of writing the unit plans. We read print, online sources, and consulted each other to expand our knowledge base. Each of us has varied areas of expertise which, when combined, helped us select the concepts and skills we thought were important to emphasize in lessons.

We were determined to avoid the pitfall of planning fun activities with no depth of learning such as how to dress in seasonal weather or on the healthy foods students should eat. After researching information on nutrition and health, we found that our knowledge from popular diets, attempts to cook healthy meals, and growing vegetables in our backyards had not been enough to write rigorous objectives that led to deep learning. So, we had to read and share up-to-date information on nutrients in food content, healthy diets, and the effects of heat on food. We discussed ways to limit a wealth of information on nutrition and health into the five STEAM unit plans.

It was more difficult than we thought to write relevant high-level **Essential Questions** that require students to think about multiple concepts to arrive at an answer. Frequently we fell into the pitfall of writing questions that had a single right answer or worse, ones that could be answered "yes" or "no." We addressed this problem by discarding or reworking them. To keep from lapsing into low level questions, we began each question using the words, "What" and "How."

Because **Objectives** are explicit learning goals that require different levels of thinking, we listed them third. We debated whether to move objectives to the number two slot and essential questions to the third slot. We finally felt like we were toying with the "Which came first, the chicken or the egg?" quandary so we left it as number three. To select action verbs to ensure that we planned for students to engage in low and high levels of thinking, we consulted the original and revised Bloom's Taxonomies (VAlAMIS, 2022) along with goals and recommended practices from national standards, listed in Chapter 4. Using a taxonomy of thinking levels helped us consider a variety of action verbs to use in our planning. We kept copies of these sources handy and consulted them frequently to make sure we aligned our objectives and procedures with them. Each time we viewed an online video, read a book, and talked to others, we found even more information we wanted to include. To avoid the pitfall of writing a hodge-podge of objectives that do not connect or build on each other, we rechecked the K–6 standards for each STEAM content area and sought goals that could be altered for young children and extended throughout the grades.

We think so highly of the role of **Vocabulary** in learning that we wrote an entire chapter on it, Chapter 3. During our quest to consult and become experts on each of the themes, we learned and listed all sorts of terminology students should know for the five themes. Making an ongoing vocabulary list made it much easier to choose the words we wanted students to learn. We experienced a problem trying to determine how technical the words should be and which ones would most benefit the students. Words that represent concrete objects and actions were obviously the easiest for us to connect to multiple sensory experiences. From our lists, we selected words we thought students must know and use for each theme and content area. We noticed that many of the words could be applied to each content area. We immediately considered this to be a good thing! This way, students were able to have multiple exposures to the words. Eliminating words from the unit plans was a difficult problem because deep in our hearts, we wanted students to learn them all! You will notice that the word lists for each STEAM content area are still long, which will give you many choices and perhaps ideas for other words you want to teach.

It was fun, yet often a challenge, to come up with **Materials and Resources!** We sought to include a variety of materials in the unit plans based on the materials hierarchy, HELP, described in Chapter 4. We considered materials teachers could make, find, collect, and borrow. We admittedly had the most problems thinking of materials for taste and smell that would be important to the lesson. We were worried about a possible pitfall by suggesting materials that may not be available to all teachers. For example, not all teachers have access to technology, yet we chose to include it because it is available to many teachers today. Problems associated with using websites and YouTube videos concerned us about the amount of time it took to review them. A promising website that sounded as though it would be exactly what we wanted, contained little or no pertinent information. Some YouTube videos may show things teachers deem inappropriate for their students. We placed online resources along with the QR code for easy access. You will find these resources at the end of each unit plan in a section, "Online Resources."

Teachers may not have access to live animals called for in unit plans on Rabbits and Hares. We had to think of other ways teachers could teach about rabbits and hares through pictures, videos, and artifacts. For lessons on the water cycle, we thought of using hot pans and boiling water to demonstrate condensation. After trying the activities, we eliminated them due to the extreme danger it would pose to students.

Oh, the things we could do for lessons on landforms, if only they could be seen outside every student's classroom window! Furthermore, what could we do to provide sensory learning experiences for oceanic landforms? After much thought, we found realistic online pictures of land and underwater landforms online and in books. Acting as civil engineers, students could build models of bridges that connected landforms, as artists they could represent continental and oceanic landforms using different media, and through geometry and measurement, students could further their learning of shapes and sizes of landforms.

With the problems and pitfalls in mind, we "reached for the stars," keeping our expectations for sensory materials high. Our goal was to provide as many multisensory materials-based activities as possible to teach, reinforce, and extend learning.

It was exciting to learn ideas for **Sets** that set the tone for lessons. We sought information for the most successful ways to get and keep students' attention from other teachers and professional lecturers. We worked to plan eye-catching displays to hook students on learning as soon as they walk into the classroom. We considered ways to turn the entire room environment into an exciting learning place through lights, sounds, and displays. We all had personal memories of teachers who went out of their way to get and keep our attention when they were animated, jumped up and down, and moved quickly from place to place in the room. They had our full attention when they assumed different attitudes or used different voices often supported by the goofy hats, accessories, or simple costumes they wore. A possible problem is that teachers may think they could never look, act, or be corny without feeling ridiculous. However, from our experiences, the cornier the better to attract students' attention and set them up for learning! If necessary, start small, and dream big!

We kept the objectives in mind as we planned the **Procedures** to engage students in multisensory activities. To do this, we copied the list of objectives and kept it handy for easy reference. We found that some activities, though fun, did not further learning in a robust way. So, we replaced them. Then the quandary arose whether we wanted students to learn information directly followed by hands-on exploration and inquiry, or have students explore and discover information that was reinforced and extended through direct teaching. We sought to include both types of instructional methods in our procedures.

We found from our classroom experiences that students frequently did not use their senses of touch and movement, smell, and taste. Most teachers used visual and auditory materials for their lessons. The problem was finding ways to integrate the lesser used senses as often as possible.

As it turned out, we imagined far more procedures for experiments and activities than what we thought teachers could actually implement. Our problem was selecting the activities to discard. The first, to go were the ones devoid of much learning and not worth the class time. We rejected the following idea, shown in italics, that we thought had a lot of promise, but when tested on students, was simply too hard to keep their attention on the subject matter while also concentrating on technology:

Without a live rabbit or hare, we used a video as a visual source where students could use rulers to measure the size of rabbits' and hares' bodies, legs, feet, and the distances they hopped. By now you probably see something we failed to see. We packed too much into one activity and it fell apart. When we had fourth and sixth grade students stand at the screen, we had to keep the video running so they could measure the distance the rabbits and hares hopped, then quickly pause it so they could measure the rabbit's and hare's legs and feet. The students became frustrated and lost interest. For simplification, we substituted paper figures of rabbits and hares for the activity and then let them watch the video of the rabbits and hares hopping to get a sense of their leg movement.

Closures are a brief time at the end of the lesson to review key information and help students organize this information into a meaningful context. We had some problems trying to select key vocabulary and concepts for review. To avoid the pitfall of overwhelming students with a barrage of facts and newly learned words, we selected a few for our sample closures that we felt were most important. We all agreed that this task felt like trying to stuff 5 lbs./2.27 kg of flour into a 1 lb./0.454 kg bag.

We also had problems coming up with ways to write a multisensory closure that helped students recall, discuss, and organize key facts and skills in a relatively small amount of time. A pitfall we frequently saw during classroom observations and our own experiences as teachers was not leaving enough time at the end of the lesson to engage students in a meaningful closure. When we taught "to the bell," it was almost impossible to keep students' attention and interest on the lesson. This is a shame, because closure is a prime time for learning. One of the primary goals of our closure is to have students outside the classroom think about and discuss what they learned inside the classroom. We focused on ways to motivate students to think about what they learned as they left the classroom and were surrounded by real-world encounters with such topics as cloud formations, landforms, puddles, energy, forces, food, and nutrition. We sought to plan for this school-to-world connection for each STEAM content area within many of the closures.

Formative and Summative Assessments. To make sure our planning had an effect on student learning, we included a sample of different formative assessments. The problem was determining effective, yet fast ways to assess the students during the lesson. A pitfall was trying to assess all students through questions and discussions during the closure. Asking questions and listening to answers often occurred with just a few students, the ones whose hands were always in the air. Our goal was to give all students opportunities to discuss or show what they know thus putting them in a positive position. If you have students show you the work they were most proud of, or have them demonstrate a skill they had learned or were learning, you would receive vital information upon which to build and correct misconceptions.

We had a problem writing specific summative assessments because it is up to the teacher to customize them to the lessons they teach. Therefore, we did not provide examples of summative assessments, but did indicate forms of assessments to use to measure long-term achievement. Oral and written tests can require students to label, illustrate, and explain reasons for their answers in addition to the more traditional forms of multiple-choice and short-answer questions.

We wanted to provide meaningful topics that would **Extend Learning** for advanced and interested students, the ones who were eager to ask and answer questions, and relate the topic to experiences they have had. The students in our mind's eye were clearly excited about learning and wanted to learn more! Because we had done our due diligence to become experts, we had few problems coming up with interesting facts to include in our suggestions on ways students could extend their learning while keeping their interest high. A *pitfall* we tried to avoid was to include content too advanced for some students, or not advanced enough for others. We wanted to challenge students, not frustrate the eager learner or bore the advanced one. We chose to err on the side of challenging the students, thinking that the interested and high-ability students would both benefit under the skillful facilitation of teachers.

The last part of the unit plan, the **Sensory Chart for Lesson Plans,** is a simple way to keep track of senses students would use during lessons. See Table 4.4 in Chapter 4, page 55. We frequently consulted the HELP Hierarchy in Chapter 4, Table 4.3, page 43 when writing the unit plans to remind us of ways to add multisensory materials in our lessons. We hope this checklistart serves as a reminder to include multisensory materials in your lessons as often as possible. Our biggest problem was to determine whether the less used multisensory materials provided students enough relevant information to warrant preparation and class time before we suggested teachers use them.

Online Reference

Valamis (2022). Instructional Design: Bloom's Taxonomy. See Figure 10.1. https://www.valamis.com/hub/blooms-taxonomy

Index

abutment 194–195
academic achievement 53
acceleration 72
act out 36, 38
Action Fractions 16
algorithm 169
Anansi The Trickster Spider 17, 19
Archimedes 47
Arctic Hares 67, 71
Armstrong, Louis 26
artifact 36, 81, 88, 96, 104, 112, 120, 127, 178, 187
art 47–48
assessment 54; art 92, 131, 167, 206; engineering 84, 123, 158, 198, 235; mathematics 99, 138, 173, 213, 250; science 69–70, 108, 145–146, 182, 221; technology 78, 115, 151–2, 190, 229
astronomy 3, 216, 225–6, 235, 247, 252
atmosphere 103
atom 103, 106–7, 155–6
attention 14, 22–4, 26, 38
attributes of words 36
autism 7, 13, 19
auditory sense 8–9, 12, 31; description 7; experiences 34; learning 15–16
avatar 141, 147–9, 151
average 95, 98
axes, horizontal and vertical 73–4, 77
axon 11, 19

background 201, 203–4; knowledge 13
Bartlett, Frederick Sir 7, 13, 19
Baylor College of Medicine 7
become an expert 50; art 87, 125, 160, 200, 237; engineering 80, 118, 154, 193, 231; mathematics 94, 134, 169, 209, 247; science 63, 102, 141, 176, 216; technology 73, 111, 147, 186, 224
biology 141
block centers 53
Bloom's Taxonomy 253
boxes and bags 24

Braille 8
bridge 193–5; arch 195–6; beam 194–6; building 193, 195; suspension 194, 197–8; truss 194, 196–8
brain 1; basic workings 9; development 7, 12; growth 1, 8, 19; hemispheres 9; plasticity 8; sensory learning 1
Bruner, Jerome 42, 56
Bucharest Early Intervention Project 7

calorie 142, 145, 148, 172
carbohydrate 142, 143, 145, 147–8, 174
cartoon 91
cause and effect 107–8
Ceausescu 8
Celsius 155–6
cerebellum 10
Cézanne, Paul 162, 164–8
chemistry 102; process 141–2, 154, 157
civil engineering 118, 193
circle 171–2
classroom environment 24, 53
clay 161
climate 139
closure 22, 26, 52–4; art sample 90, 131, 166, 205, 243; engineering sample 84, 123, 158, 198, 235; mathematics sample 99, 138, 173, 213, 250; science sample 69, 108, 145, 213, 250; technology sample 78, 115, 151, 190, 229
code 33; written 33
cognates 39
collage 161, 163, 166
collection 102–3, 105–7, 112, 119, 129, 134, 137, 139
column, clustered 78
compression 194–6
concrete operations 42
condensation 103, 105, 107, 112, 126–30, 135
consumption 135
core 177; inner 177, 179–80, 182; outer 177, 179–80
cortex 8; cerebral 9–11, 19

CRAAP 226, 230
crust 176
cubic 213
cues 32

dairy 142–4, 150, 160–1
Dale, Edgar 7, 19
dam 118–25
decimal 169–70, 175
dendrites 11, 19
denominator 169–73
diets, healthy 141–2
Diamond, Marian 7, 19; human brain experiment 8
dimension 160, 205, 209–10; one- 176, 209, 213; three- 176, 202, 209–11, 213–14; two- 176, 209–11, 214
dinosaur 105, 110
Discovery Learning Model 43
doodle 201, 203–4, 207
drama 125–6
drought 103
Dry Bones 16
DV 170, 172–4

Earth 103, 105–7, 120, 122, 131, 138, 176–84, 187, 198, 202, 209–10, 214–18, 224, 226–7, 231, 233, 235, 239–40, 247; axis 219, 223, 229, 238, 240, 249; color 235; day 247; equinoxes and solstices 221; hemispheres 220; movement 225, 240, 250; orbit 224–7, 250; revolution 227, 238, 240, 250; seasons 223, 226; tilt 222, 224, 228, 240; year 247
earthquake 178–79, 181, 185; Four layers 179–80
Ebbinghaus, Hermann 22–3, 28
echolocation 8–9
ecliptic 217
electrical engineering 231
emotions 22
equinox 217, 221, 239; autumnal 217, 220, 225, 239; vernal 217, 220, 225, 239
Esquith, Rafe 18, 19
essential questions 51; art 87, 125, 160, 200, 237; engineering 80, 118, 154, 193, 231; mathematics 94, 134, 169, 209, 247; science 63, 102, 141, 176, 216; technology 73, 111, 147, 186, 224
estimate 94
evaporation 103, 105–6, 109, 112, 126, 128–9, 134–5, 137–8
experiences, multisensory 18
extend learning 5; art 92, 131, 166–7, 206, 243; engineering 85, 124, 159, 198, 236; mathematics 100, 138, 174, 214, 251; science 63, 70, 109, 146, 182, 222; technology 79, 115, 152, 191, 229

Fahrenheit 155–6
Faraday, Michael 119, 121
fats 142–6
fiber 142–3, 145, 148
five foods groups 142–4, 148–51, 160–1, 163–4, 166
Five Green Speckled Frogs 16
flood 103, 119, 122, 124, 135
force 69, 71–2, 95, 98, 119, 176
foreground 201, 203–4
fractions 169–75; adding 169; definition of 169; divide 169, 174–5; equivalent 169–71; multiply 169, 171, 173–5; subtraction 169
fruit 142–4, 146, 150, 158, 160–2, 164, 167, 170

gas 103, 105, 112, 119, 126, 141, 154–5, 157–8
geology 176
geometry 209–10, 214–15
Gershwin, George 26
glacier 103, 106
grain 142, 144, 150, 161
Grandin, Temple 7, 13–14, 19
gravity, force of 63–4, 68, 112, 126
Gutenberg, Johannes 47

Hare profile 66, 76
hemisphere 217, 220, 223, 225, 238; northern 217–18, 220–2, 225–6, 238, 240, 243; southern 217–18, 220–2, 225–6, 238, 240, 243
Hungarian Rhapsody Number 2, 26
Head, Shoulders, Knees, and Toes 16
heat 154–9; transfer 141, 154–5
HELP: Hierarchy for Effective Lesson Planning 43–4, 64, 103, 178, 187, 218
Holocaust 16
hydroelectric 118–121, 123–5

"I Can Statements" 27, 54; art 92, 131, 166, 206, 243; engineering 85, 124, 166–7, 198, 236; mathematics 100, 138, 174, 214, 250; science 70, 108, 146, 182, 222; technology 79, 115, 152, 182, 222, 108, 115
Ice 106
iconic 43
"If-Only Statements" art 92, 131, 166, 206, 243; engineering 85, 123, 158, 198, 235; mathematics 99, 138, 174, 213, 250; science 70, 108, 145, 182, 222; technology 78, 115, 151, 190, 229
International Society for Technology in Education 47, 57
inertia 68
isosceles 212
The Itsy Bitsy Spider 102

James Webb Space Telescope 216
Jeopardy 111–12, 114–15
journal 26

Keller, Helen 7–8, 19
keyword 111, 186, 188, 190
kinetic energy 63–4, 68–9, 121, 155
Kish, Daniel 7–8

lagomorph 73–4
landform 3, 103, 107, 252
languages 32
LED (light-emitting diode) 216, 231–2, 234–5
Link Ness Monster 15
liquid 103, 105, 108, 112, 126, 134, 136, 141, 154–5, 157–9
Liszt, Franz 26
Little Bunny Foo Foo 25, 63
Little Peter Rabbit 25
lobes of brain 10; frontal 10; occipital 10; parietal 10; temporal 10
Lunch Atop a Skyscraper 14

magma 177, 181
magnetism 119, 121
mantle 176
mass 64, 68, 72
materials and resources 28, 52, 254; art 88, 90, 127–8, 161–2, 202, 229; engineering 81, 119–20, 155, 194, 232; mathematics 95–6, 135, 170, 210, 248; science 64–6, 103–4, 142, 177–8, 217; storage of 28; technology 74–75, 112–13, 149, 187, 225–6; upcycled 160–3, 166, 216, 218, 225, 232, 239, 242; use of 28
mathematics 48; standards 48–50
mean 95, 98
midground 201, 203–4
mini-book 186, 189–91
mixed numbers 174
model 80, 82–84, 88, 90, 106, 119, 235–6
molecule 103, 106–7, 155
momentum 64
movement 17, 19, 36, 92
Mozart, Wolfgang Amadeus 47
multisensory experiences 18; approaches 42; materials 22; sights and sounds 23
music 25–6, 133, 237–8, 240–3, 245–6

National Reading Panel 32, 39
Neptune 231–5
neural networks 8; forests 12
neurons 9, 11
Next Generation Science Newsletter 44, 60
Next Generation Science Standards 44–6, 59–60
Newton, Isaac 63–4, 219; first law 63–4, 67, 219, 223; second law 219, 224

nine-step thematic unit plans for STEAM learning 50
nucleus of brain 11
numerator 169–73
nut 143
nutrient 142–3, 145, 146, 148, 152, 161, 170–2, 174
nutrition 3, 252

objectives 51–2, 253; art 87, 126, 160, 201, 238; engineering 80, 119, 154, 193–4, 231–2; mathematics 95, 134–5, 169, 209, 247; science 64, 111, 148, 177, 217; technology 73, 111, 148, 186, 224–5
ocean 103, 106
oil 142–3, 147
Old McDonald 34
onomatopoeia 34–5
organizer, graphic 14–15
orphanage 8
ounce, fluid 135–7

Palmer, Hap 16, 19, 218
Paper Clips Project 16, 19, 21
parallelogram 212
pastel 141, 160–2, 164–6
pendulum 68
per 247–250
percent 169–173
Peter and the Wolf 90, 94
physics 102
Piaget, Jean 7, 13, 21, 42, 54, 60
pictures: still life 160, 165–6, 168; thinking in 14
pie chart 172
pier 194–5
Pierson, Martha 7, 21
plane, orbital 217, 219, 227, 229, 238, 240
planet 216, 231–5, 237, 247, 250
plateau 187, 201
plates, tectonic 176–8, 180–4
Poe, Edgar Allen 25, 30
polyunsaturated fats 146, 148
potential energy 63–4, 68–9, 121
Potter, Beatrix 87, 91
PowerPoint 186, 188–9, 191–2
precipitation 103, 105–6, 112, 126, 128–9, 131, 135, 140
prefix 33
pre-operative stage 42
primacy-recency effect 22
procedures 52–3, 254; art 90–2, 129–31, 162–6, 203–5, 240–3; engineering 82–84, 120–3, 156–8, 195–7, 233–5; mathematics 96–9, 136–7, 170–1, 211–13, 248–50; science 67–9, 105–8, 143–5, 179–81, 218–21; technology 76–8, 113–15, 149–51, 188–90, 226–8

Prokofiev, Sergei 90, 94
propositional formal operations 42
prosody 35
protein 142, 144, 148, 150, 161
puppet 125–6, 128–31
puzzle 182, 186, 189–93; crossword 187, 190–2; jigsaw 181

quadrilateral 211–12
quotient 170, 174
QR 102, 111–15, 117–18, 127–8, 131

rabbits and hares 2, 63, 66, 68–74, 77, 90, 92, 94, 101, 252; anatomy 64, 86–7, 95; environment 96; femur 64, 81–2, 88, 97; fibula 64, 81, 88; hind leg 82–4; images 65, 71, 79, 101; leg and foot structure 64, 87, 91, 95, 98; physical characteristics 86; physiological differences 80; picture 91, 93 profile 76, 89; replica 88; skeletons 79, 81–3, 85, 97, 100–1; tendons 64; tibia 64, 81, 83–4, 88, 97; toes 82–3; videos 93
Ranger Rick 27
rat experiment 7–8
rate 175, 247
ratio 80–1, 83, 92, 93, 95, 98
RDA 170, 172, 174
real-world experiences 64, 127; artifacts 65, 104, 127
rectangle 170
representations 65, 74, 81, 88, 96, 104, 178, 194, 232
Rhapsody in Blue 26
rhombus 209, 211–12

saturated fats 142–6, 148
schema theory 7, 12–13
science 44; practices of 45–6, 59
sculpture 141, 160–4, 166, 168
search 186–9
senses, learning through 2
sensorimotor stage 42
sensory checklist 55, 256; art 93, 132, 167, 206, 244; engineering 85, 124, 159, 198, 236; mathematics 100, 109, 146, 182, 222, 251; science 70, 109, 146, 182, 222; technology 79, 115, 152, 192, 229
serial position effect 2
sets 22, 52, 254; art 90, 128, 162, 202, 240; engineering 81, 120, 155, 195, 240; examples of 23; mathematics 96, 136, 170, 211, 240; science 66, 104, 143, 179, 217; technology 75, 113, 149, 188, 226
shadow 36
skull 9
slinky 68

smell sense 8–9, 12, 31, 44; description 7, 37; experiences 37–8; for survival 18; walk 37
solar system 216, 231–7, 251
solid 103, 105, 112, 123, 126, 141–2, 154–5, 157–8
solstice 217, 221; summer 217, 220, 225; winter 217, 220, 225, 239
Sound of Music 42
sounds 25, 34; of musical instruments 35
Sousa, D. 23, 29
Sousa, John Philip 25
species 73
speech 35; pitch, stress, speed, rhythm 35
square (geometric figure) 209–13
standards 44; National and State 44
STEAM 16, 31, 42, 48, 53, 55, 63, 102, 141, 191, 216, 252
steam 106
subduction 177
suffix 33
Sun 102–3, 105, 107, 126, 134, 137, 216–20, 222–4, 228, 231–5, 238–40, 247, 249–250; calendar 218; seasons 216, 224, 226; sunrise 218–19, 221; sunset 218–19, 221
sunscreen 159
summative examples 70
symbolic 43
synapse 11

tactile/kinesthetic 8–9, 12, 31, 44, 55; description 7; experiences 35–6; learning 16
Tacoma Narrows Bridge 197, 200
Take Me Out to the Ball Game 16
The Tale of Peter Rabbit 87, 91
tape, painters' 16
taste sense 8–9, 12, 18, 31, 44; description 7; experiences 38
technology 47; standards of ISTE 47
The Tell-Tale Heart 25
temperature, ambient 155
template 102, 111–12, 114–15
tempo 237–8, 241, 246
tension 194, 196
theme selection 42
Thorell, Sammie 24, 27, 30
token 77
tongue twisters 35; use of 38
touch 17, 19; explore by 36
trajectory 95
trans fat 148
trapezoid 209, 211–12
triangle 197, 204, 209–12, 214
trifold brochure 224–6, 228–30
Two Cool Cows 27

unit plans 42, 50, 176, 216, 218, 224, 252; art 87, 125, 160, 200, 237; engineering 80, 118, 154, 193, 231; mathematics 94, 134, 169, 209, 247; science 63, 102, 141, 176, 216; technology 73, 111, 147, 186, 224

valley 181, 187, 195, 201, 209
vegetable 142–4, 146, 150, 160–1, 167, 170, 172
The Velveteen Rabbit: How Toys Become Real 91
Vivaldi, Antonio 240, 242, 243, 245, 246
visual sense 8–9, 12, 31, 64, 74; description 7; images 14
vocabulary 2, 52, 253; art 87–8, 126, 160–1, 201–2, 238–9; building 31; engineering 80–1, 119, 154–5, 194, 231–2; formal 32; informal 32; instruction 31; mathematics 95, 135, 169–70, 209–10; science 64, 103, 142, 177, 217; teaching 142, 148, 151, 154, 160, 169, 177, 186, 194, 201, 209, 217, 225, 231, 238–9, 247; technology 74, 111–112, 148, 186–7, 225; through senses 33

volcano 107, 109, 177, 181, 187, 201
von Restorff 22–3, 30

War of the Ghosts 13
water 102, 158; cycle 3, 252; disruptions 110; molecule 107; pail of 176; stages 103, 107; states 103–4, 157–8; vapor 103, 107, 112, 126, 135, 157
What a Wonderful World 26
white boards 26
Whitwell, Tennessee 16
The Wide Mouth Frog 27
Word 31–2; basketball 36; build a word 33–4; category 34; compound 34; knowledge of 38; listen 34; meanings 40; root 33; use of 38; Word Activity 34; wall 37
Wormeli, Rick 21, 24, 30

YouTube 16

zentangle 201, 203–4, 207

For Product Safety Concerns and Information please contact our EU representative GPSR@taylorandfrancis.com
Taylor & Francis Verlag GmbH, Kaufingerstraße 24, 80331 München, Germany

www.ingramcontent.com/pod-product-compliance
Lightning Source LLC
Chambersburg PA
CBHW080935300426
44115CB00017B/2828